UNDERSTANDING THE NEW AGE

UNDERSTANDING THE NEW AGE

Revised—Updated—The Most Powerful
and Revealing Analysis of the New Age
Now with Discussion Guide

RUSSELL CHANDLER

ZondervanPublishingHouse
Grand Rapids, Michigan

A Division of HarperCollins*Publishers*

128733

Understanding the New Age
The Most Powerful and Revealing Analysis of the New Age
Now with Discussion Guide
Copyright © 1991, 1993 by Russell Chandler

Requests for information should be addressed to:
Zondervan Publishing House
Grand Rapids, Michigan 49530

Library of Congress Cataloging-in-Publication Data

Chandler, Russell.
Understanding the New Age / Russell Chandler.
p. cm.
Originally published: Dallas : Word Pub., 1991.
Includes bibliographical references and index.
ISBN 0-310-38561-X (paper)
1. New Age movement. 2. United States—Religion—1960—
I. Title.
BP605.N48C52 1993
299′.93—dc20   93–19903
                                            CIP

Cover designed by Cheryl Van Andel
Cover photo by © Mark Tomalty/Masterfile

Printed in the United States of America

93 94 95 96 97 / DH / 5 4 3 2 1

This edition is printed on acid-free paper and meets the American National Standards Institute Z39.48 standard.

To my mother, Mary Beth Chandler,
. . . with affection and gratitude

Contents

Preface and Acknowledgments

As a religion writer for the *Los Angeles Times* newspaper for eighteen years, I saw a plethora of religious organizations firsthand. Their gurus and teachers have usually been anxious—although not always—to explain their groups' spiritual underpinnings.

Whenever I write about these groups, I am often bombarded by letters and phone calls from people who want more behind-the-scenes information. For the most part, these people fall into two groups: those who are curious or searching, and those who are concerned for family members or friends "caught up" in the mystique of some alternate spiritual lifestyle.

In the 1970s—following the "flower children" era of the 1960s—numerous tightly knit religious groups formed around autocratic, self-styled gurus who demanded intense loyalty and devotion. But in the 1980s and 1990s, the style is changing. Many are embracing a more open, yet elusive, movement that is abroad in our land. Collectively, this ideology is known as the New Age.

This introspective movement, which embraces "Higher Consciousness" as the supreme quest of humankind, is shaking loose an avalanche of ideas that question our traditional Western philosophies and our long-held Judeo-Christian ethos. Meanwhile, the media vacillate between scrutinizing and smirking at such New Age tangents as fire walking and channeling off-planet entities.

Some Jewish and Christian groups have rigorously condemned New Age thinking; others have selectively adopted parts of its meditative rituals and teachings. But most onlookers are simply confused by the diffuse tenets of this

9

recycled Eastern worldview. They wonder, for example: Where does yoga exercise end and self-worship begin? Where does an appreciation of New Age music merge with acceptance of a concept of cyclical history spiraling in endless repetition?

I wanted to gather well-researched information and insights about these and many other questions surrounding the New Age. So I requested—and was generously granted—an eight-month leave of absence from my beat at the *Los Angeles Times* to write this book. As a result, I hope you, the reader, will come along as we explore the many strands of this intriguing and often puzzling movement that have drawn—and continue to draw—millions into the web of the New Age.

Part I begins with an overview of the prevalence and premises of the New Age movement, followed by a scrutiny of the human mind and how New Age thought utilizes nonverbal thinking.

Part II presents a roster of major players, groups, and events—and their contributions—within the New Age arena.

In Part III, we consider how New Age theories, therapies, and activities are working their way into America's economic, corporate, cultural, social, academic, political, and religious life.

Part IV aims to give tools for discerning and evaluating the New Age. (For your convenience, there is a short glossary of New Age terms at the end of the book.)

And in Part V, the final section, I present the Judeo-Christian alternative and the theistic worldview.

*   *   *

I wish to express deep gratitude to Word Publishing for the support and help the staff gave me during the writing and publication of the first editions of this book and to Zondervan Publishing House for this revised edition.

Editor par excellence Judith Markham at Blue Water Ink in Grand Rapids, Michigan, smoothed out the rough spots, caught spelling errors, polished the style, and sharpened clarity at key points. Working with Judith on several projects has been a joy and an inspiration!

And the faithful teamwork of my partner and wife, Marjorie

Lee Chandler, made all the difference in meeting the manuscript deadline. This project would never have succeeded without her diligent research at libraries, her telephone interviews seeking and verifying information, and her tireless expediting of a host of business and social needs during my writing "hibernation" time. I also want to thank her for reading the draft version and making many valuable suggestions and contributions to improve and strengthen the book.

Grateful acknowledgment is expressed to all who read selected portions of the manuscript as it was in progress and made helpful comments. Thanks also to those who provided insights about the New Age movement, shared articles, materials, and books—even their private libraries—and granted me interviews, sometimes with minimal advance notice. And I thank my mother, Mary Beth Chandler, for being understanding when I wasn't always available at times that she hoped to spend with her son.

Hopefully, the sum total is a book that will bring significant new understanding about one of the most important social and religious phenomena of our time.

Russell Chandler
November 1992

PART I

THE NEW AGE AND YOU

1

Preview of the New Age

Daunting!

That was the word for the giant jigsaw puzzle chosen one holiday from the jam-packed game cupboard in our Forest Falls mountain cabin. Not only did there seem to be a jillion pieces, but they all looked alike, except the few that formed the border. And they were so *tiny*. We despaired of ever piecing the monstrosity together.

So there it sat. A rough outline of two edges, a couple of clusters of interlocking pieces in the center, and a jumble of unmatching squiggly shapes heaped to the side.

Months passed. The puzzle was carefully transferred onto a large board, moved from the living room to the upstairs back bedroom, and perched atop a fiberboard packing barrel. Now and then, when they were bored, one or another of the kids would wander in and fit in a piece or two. We began to wonder if half the parts had been lost or if someone had mixed in pieces from some other game, for the puzzle seemed to be fighting to preserve its anonymity.

But gradually—piece by piece and over many months— the jigsaw finally made "sense." A coherent whole began to take shape.

When, in the summer of 1987, I first contemplated writing a book that would make sense of the amorphous New Age movement, it also seemed a daunting task. So many bits and pieces. Uncertain borders. Shifting spheres of activity. And a revolving cast of characters.

Of all the writing projects I have undertaken during my twenty-five-plus years as a journalist covering religion, this subject has been one of the most formidable—and the most fascinating. Many of the organizations and individuals I have followed through the years seemed to reemerge. Some of the history of philosophy and patterns of thought I had studied long before in theological schools in Edinburgh and Princeton took on new perspective. Yet much of my research, particularly on the human mind and quantum mechanics, covered territory I had seldom charted before.

Eventually, a profile of the New Age began to emerge, like the recalcitrant jigsaw puzzle. "There *is* a picture here, even with some detail and color," I kept saying to myself.

Indeed, I soon discovered that much had already been written on the subject, and I have referred to these sources liberally. Also, I met experts whose knowledge of the New Age far exceeded my own. Dozens of them were willing to share information and insights as we talked in person and by telephone.

One conversation particularly stands out: November 24, 1987, in Berkeley, California, with Brooks Alexander. This gray-bearded, owlish-eyed, cap-wearing, researcher-author is an articulate spokesman for the Spiritual Counterfeits Project, an organization that thoroughly examines and critiques America's new religious and spiritual groups and their leaders. He is also a consummate authority on the New Age.

"You can do one of two things," Brooks cautioned me when he learned the scope of my project. "You can either keep up with the New Age movement, or you can write about it—but not both."

I soon learned how right he was. New Age in the late 1980s was on the move. In newsbiz we call it "hot."

The media and publishers, responding to interest as well as creating it, have swarmed to print, film, and televise profuse accounts of trance channeling (the new version of spirit mediumship); healing with crystals; reincarnation; out-of-body experiences; altered states of consciousness; meditation techniques; UFO abductions; and the intuitive powers of the brain's right hemisphere.

Meanwhile, Shirley MacLaine, the bubbly dancer-actress-author turned New Age gourmet, became the number one news magnet for mysticism's latest incarnation. Her best-selling books and television miniseries (*Out on a Limb*) turned the movement into a fad.

For all its faddishness, however, the New Age is hard to define; its boundaries are fuzzy. It's a shifting kaleidoscope of "beliefs, fads and rituals," as *TIME* magazine duly noted in its December 7, 1987, cover story, "New Age Harmonies."

New Age is a hybrid mix of spiritual, social, and political forces, and it encompasses sociology, theology, the physical sciences, medicine, anthropology, history, the human potentials movement, sports, and science fiction.

New Age is not a sect or cult, per se. There is no organization one must join, no creed one must confess. Identifying individuals as "full-blown" New Agers is baffling. Some subscribe to certain portions of New Age, some to others; some dissociate themselves from the movement altogether, though they embrace core aspects of its thinking.

The New Age influence touches virtually every area of life, and thousands of New Age activists seek to transform society through New Age precepts. Millions more have adopted the movement's view of reality, though they may simply think of it as a pragmatic, humanistic philosophy of life.

Although "new" in style and vocabulary, the movement is in many ways as old as the Eastern religions of Hinduism and Buddhism, Western occultism, and the mystical oracles of ancient Greece and Egypt. New Age has simply recast the theory of reincarnation into the language of Western humanistic psychology, science, and technology.

The multiple tracks of the New Age movement also trace to free-based versions of Abraham Maslow's "self-actualization" and the fundamental optimism of the 1960s, while the imprints of Maharishi Mahesh Yogi's Transcendental Meditation and Werner Erhard's "est" are also apparent.

I have taken a journalistic approach to putting the New Age puzzle together and have tried to be fair and balanced throughout. In my opinion, the New Age—insofar as one can corral this moving, many-sided, cultural transformation—is neither the hellish conspiracy that fundamentalist critics charge, nor the utopian bliss its fondest supporters imagine.

Rather, the insidious danger of the New Age is its view of the nature of reality, which admits to no absolutes. History provides evidence that relative standards of morality breed chaos and—ultimately—the downfall of society. However, these are conclusions reached only after a careful look at New Age strengths and weaknesses, stabilities and follies.

Understanding the New Age is my attempt to slice the New Age movement at a point in time, even as events have continued to move ahead.

Remember, "New Age" is an umbrella term. A precise definition is a chimera. But broad lines of commonality form a pattern, and for me, at least, the big New Age picture-puzzle has come together. I hope it will for you.

By the way, we never did complete that jigsaw puzzle at our mountain home. But then, there really was no mystery about what the finished product would look like. The picture was printed on the outside of the box.

Besides, there was little incentive to complete the game. The puzzle depicted the front page of the *New York Times*. For a *Los Angeles Times* writer to give such expression to a chief rival would have seemed an act of treason.

2

Prevalence of the New Age

The New Age has touched you.

You've heard its ideas, listened to its music, viewed its artwork, watched its superstars, read its literature, and bought its products. You may even have participated in its therapies, shared in its rituals, and embraced its philosophies—all without knowing them as New Age.

The New Age spirit is an ineluctable and elusive movement. Its broad umbrella shadows a diverse and shifting culture that is now in the midst of a change that New Agers believe is potentially as sweeping as the Renaissance or the Protestant Reformation. They believe the world is on the verge of a profound breakthrough. The limited, finite, Old Order will give way to a glorious, unlimited New Order of peace, prosperity, and perfection. This radical "paradigm shift" is to occur as more and more people question traditional assumptions about life, the nature of reality, and the future of the planet.

The New Age consciousness is multifaceted and multifocused.

"It's from the grassroots up . . . a transformation going on everywhere," said Roland Mick, director of development for the Association of Wholistic Practitioners, a New Age health organization based in Pittsburgh. "This is unique in our recorded history." As we chatted at the Celebration of Innovation, a New Age exposition in San Francisco, Mick compared the movement to a "rough gem" that's been discovered by many groups of people. And each group is busy "polishing a particular facet" of the gem.[1]

New Age influence has indeed touched every facet of contemporary life. Its popularizers and their beliefs are often visible on your television set, at the movies, in printed horoscopes, or at your local health-food store. Even sports and exercise programs, motivational training, psychological counseling, and religious classes are frequent pipelines for New Age thinking.

Purveyors of New Age thought have found a receptive audience.

Thirty-four million Americans are concerned with inner growth, including mysticism, according to SRI International, an opinion research organization in Menlo Park, California.[2] Nearly half of American adults (42%) now believe they have been in contact with someone who has died—up from 27% in a previous national survey eleven years earlier.

Sociologist-priest Andrew Greeley found that still higher percentages of Americans reported having had psychic experiences such as extrasensory perception (ESP)—67% of all adult Americans, or some seventy million. By comparison, 58% said in 1973 that they had experienced ESP.

Roughly 30 million Americans—about one in four—now believe in reincarnation, a key tenet of the New Age, and 14% endorse the work of spirit mediums, or what New Agers often call "trance channelers."

"What was paranormal is now normal," Greeley declared. "It's even happening to elite scientists and physicians who insist that such things cannot possibly happen." The priest-professor added that persons who have paranormal experiences "are anything but religious nuts or psychiatric cases."[3]

National surveys by the Gallup organization corroborate Greeley's findings: Paranormal experiences and belief in New Age suppositions are on the rise, making New Age "the fastest-growing alternative belief system in the country," according to new religions researchers Bob and Gretchen Passantino.[4]

A 1978 Gallup Poll indicated that 10 million Americans were engaged in some aspect of Eastern mysticism and 9 million in spiritual healing.[5] And the same polling organization found that between 1978 and 1984 belief in astrology had risen from 40% to 59% among schoolchildren.[6]

According to the results of a 1987 survey conducted by Northern Illinois University, 67% of American adults read astrology reports, while 36% believe that the reports are scientific.[7]

In May 1988 the media was abuzz with reports—based on revelations in a book by former White House chief of staff Donald T. Regan—that President and Mrs. Reagan frequently read astrology forecasts and that Nancy Reagan consulted astrologers to help schedule her husband's activities and travel.

The Northern Illinois University survey also reported that more than half of Americans think extraterrestrial beings have visited Earth, a belief held in many New Age circles.

Credence in such New Age articles of faith have been bolstered considerably by entities like NBC-TV's *ALF*, a puppet "alien" whose ratings have sometimes hit the Nielsen Top Ten. Spinning the saga of his journey from Melmac to Earth, ALF—for Alien Life Form—climbed to the top three ratings for Saturday-morning TV cartoon shows. No harm in introducing a little magic and fantasy into children's lives— or ours—especially if toy makers and *schlockmeisters* can peddle 250 ALF items with sales rocketing above $200 million.[8]

Shades of *E.T.*!

There's no business like show business to introduce New Age suppositions and make them appear credible to a general audience. Take science fiction cinema, for instance.

George Lucas's *Star Wars* epics, in which the Force is "an energy field generated by living things," easily pass muster as a New Age definition of God.

Characters in the *Charlie's Angels* TV program talk about the energy fields of the *chakras* of the human body, "subtly injecting change and acceptance into public consciousness in just 10 years," New Age aerospace engineer Jack Houck observed approvingly.[9]

Tal Brooke, author of *The Cosmic Circuit*, considers the "Hollywood connection" a chief channel for "vigorously injecting Eastern mysticism" into the national culture. Such films as *Clockwork Orange, Rosemary's Baby, the Exorcist,*

2001, Dr. Strangelove, Cocoon, and *Angel Heart* convey New Age themes and occultism, Brooke said over a spicy Indian dinner in Redwood City, California.[10]

The Last Temptation of Christ touched off what *TIME* magazine called "the angriest religious debate in years"[11] over the nature of God and the person of Jesus Christ. The movie, based on Nikos Kazantzakis's 1955 novel, injects pantheistic and mystic thinking into a startling rendition of a fictionalized Jesus who doubts his messiahship and struggles with lustful temptations.

"Everything's a part of God," declares the tormented Christ.[12] Small wonder. On the introduction page of the script is this quotation from Kazantzakis: "It is not God who will save us—it is we who will save God, by battling, by creating and transmuting matter into spirit."[13] In the prologue to his novel, Kazantzakis speaks of the "yearning . . . of man to attain God, or more exactly, to return to God and identify himself with him." The supreme purpose of the struggle between the flesh and the spirit in the book and the movie is "union with God," a very Eastern concept of the pathway to godhead and release from the cycle of birth and death into bliss.[14]

"The culture is being permeated with New Age. The media started out with jokes about channeling, but recently there have been actual attempts to contact the dead on television," says Gordon Lewis, a specialist in cultural apologetics at Denver Seminary.[15] Celebrities like Shirley MacLaine publicly endorse their spirit guides. Linda Evans of *Dynasty* and Joyce DeWitt, formerly of *Three's Company*, follow guidance from a discarnate entity named Mafu. Other celebrity subscribers who have publicly affirmed their New Age connections include chocolate-chip-cookie king Wally (Famous) Amos, actress Marsha Mason, singers Helen Reddy and Tina Turner, musician Paul Horn, and entertainer Lisa Bonet.[16]

Until 1986, asserts University of Denver humanities professor Carl A. Raschke, "the New Age was a subculture, a counterculture; but it didn't have the bucks to go public." Somehow, says Raschke, they got the bucks. And they're putting them into "celebrities, advertising and testimonies. . . . It got glossy and glitzy overnight. . . . That gets the media interested, and that gets public attention."[17]

Testimonies like the one by CNN mogul Ted Turner also project New Age before the public. Turner was quoted in the *Denver Post* as saying that America needs to elect a New Age president if it is to survive through the Year 2000.[18] San Francisco physician Raphael Ornstein was quick to oblige: He announced his candidacy for the presidency under the banner of the Human Ecology Party on April 22, 1988.

Meanwhile, Ornstein's Global Peace Foundation has a vision to convert Alcatraz into a New Age holistic health spa and peace center. Some $60 million to $100 million is all that is needed to crystallize this "international showcase."[19] The project, even on the drawing board, lavished mega-attention—if not megabucks—on New Age agendas.

New Age theories have also been polished up for the military brass. Marilyn Ferguson, the leading New Age theoretician, has lectured at the U.S. Army War College. And the Army's Organizational Effectiveness School has used New Age-oriented curriculums in some of its programs.

Major corporations have hired New Age consultants to help increase employee productivity. New Age ideas have percolated into political action groups, consciousness-raising groups, think tanks, and holistic health associations as well as creative imagination workshops, "superlearning" programs, and management training seminars. (To be consistent, however, we note that programs and curriculums devised by adherents of Judeo-Christian faith may also contain elements of their belief systems.)

Although Yoga, a popular therapy for high-stress professionals, is touted as a form of exercise and relaxation—not a religion—it is based on assumptions shared with the New Age worldview. Whatever its posture, Yoga is thriving: The *Yoga Journal* had jumped to a circulation of about 50,000 by 1988, an increase of 40% in less than four years.[20]

As the public has grown more tolerant of psychic phenomena, the nation's courts have increasingly called on psychics to use their reputed powers to weed out lying witnesses, pinpoint suspects, and locate missing bodies.[21]

New Age publishing is a billion-dollar phenomenon unto itself. Nearly everyone's bookshelf contains self-improvement psychology books that incorporate New Age ideas. The movement is also well reflected in literature that sell heavily in bookstore religion sections: from Scott Peck's *Road Less Traveled*, to the ponderous 2,097-page *Urantia Book*, allegedly dictated, or "channeled," from an extraterrestrial source, to *A Course in Miracles*, one of the most widely read New Age "spiritual" books. Talk show superstar Oprah Winfrey said that the "Course" was her favorite spiritual reading during the summer of 1988.

Waldenbooks sought to capture both the Christian and New Age markets by promoting seer Jeane Dixon's *Yesterday, Today and Forever* with the pitch: "Live a more meaningful life by linking astrology with Christianity."[22]

New Age has likely touched you through its myriad products and gadgets. Consider just a few: crystals, singing Tibetan bowls, pyramids, statues, incense, greeting cards, tarot cards, charms, pendants, talismans, fortune-telling devices and astrology charts, computer software, herbal medicines, esoteric vitamins, "bonkers" massage tools, "rebirthing" tanks, and colonic cleansers. And that's just the beginning.

Maybe you've found New Age music soothing in freeway traffic. Need a companion? Try a New Age dating service waiting to make "synchronicity" happen for you and your "soulmate." And, as *Wall Street Journal* reporter Meg Sullivan lists, there are New Age travel agencies, New Age accountants, and even New Age attorneys.[23]

The prevalence of the New Age is assured for the foreseeable future; in fact, as the year 2000 approaches, New Age millennial expectations will likely crescendo to fever pitch. The movement's major drawing power, according to Berkeley sociologist Robert Bellah, an author of the acclaimed *Habits of the Heart*, comes from those in the younger ranks of the well-educated middle class who are discontent with "vague spiritual orientations."[24]

Across the bay in San Francisco, philosophy professor Jacob Needleman, an expert on new religious movements, commented, "A whole new set of categories has taken root which express the search for new ways of relating to other people and to the events of one's life. Their prevalence is a clear sign of the great shift in the consciousness of the West."[25]

For many attracted to the New Age, "the dominant

Christian view has broken down, or the church as they have known it has disappointed them."[26] They are yearning for a source of meaning and value—something they can believe in, says New Age author Marilyn Ferguson.[27]

The movement's "promise of omnipotence and indestructibility" lures converts, according to humanistic psychologist Maxine Negri. All human goals appear possible, "even the elimination of death—not through Jesus Christ or Mohammed or other 'divine' messengers but through one's own human, independently earned spiritual enlightenment."[28]

From the evangelical Christian perspective, writer Robert Burrows sees the New Age movement as "real and pervasive" and not about to go away. "As its beliefs and practices continue to be assimilated into the general culture, mingle with compatible currents, and tug at the natural inclinations of the fallen human heart, it can do nothing but grow."[29]

In its current expressions, the most durable legacy of the New Age may well be its influence on the way you and I— and those around us—think. To understand that, let's take a closer look at the movement's assumptions and premises.

3

Premises of the New Age

When the American Atheists held their national convention in Denver in 1987, Madalyn Murray O'Hair said *there is no God*. Soon after, Shirley MacLaine toured Denver and told her listeners that *she and everyone else is God*. Then Billy Graham came to town and declared at a crusade that *Jesus is the only God*.[1]

It all depends on your *worldview*, which is the cherished premises or assumptions you hold about ultimate reality, human beings, and the relationship between the two.

Worldviews—and the implications drawn from them—differ from group to group within the diverse and eclectic New Age ranks. In fact, New Age doesn't refer to a particular group or collection of groups, nor to a specific period in history. New Age *movements* is a more apt description. The New Age has no overarching superstructure. Its beliefs and practices vary as widely as those within the Christian and Jewish traditions.

"No one speaks for the entire New Age community," said Jeremy P. Tarcher, spokesman for a Los Angeles firm that publishes New Age books. "Within the movement, there is no unanimity as to how to define it or even that it is significantly cohesive to be called a movement."[2]

Tarcher, like other New Age leaders, does agree, however, that the movement is based on salient premises. And more than anything else, the New Age movement is distinguished

26

by a common vision, a shared worldview about the nature of existence and the purpose of life in the cosmos.

Members of the New Age Society—subscribers to the *New Age Journal*—were asked, "What does 'New Age' mean to you?"

"It is the beginning of a spiritual reawakening for many people of Earth," one member replied.

"Ideally, it represents nonhierarchical, global consciousness, respect for our bodies and who we are," said another.

Suzanne Robinson of Sugar Hill, Georgia, defined New Age as "moving into an era that emphasizes self-discovery, spiritual growth, and enlightenment. It is an exciting time of reaching past our limitations."

And Carolyn D. Ladner of Rancho Cordova, California, called New Age "a global and individual change in perception that promotes a shift in thoughts and actions toward a more cooperative way of being, instead of our current separating, competitive way of existence."[3]

The New Age, says new-religions expert J. Gordon Melton, "is ultimately a vision of a world transformed, a heaven on Earth, a society in which the problems of today are overcome and a new existence emerges."[4]

Underlying this radical vision are the following New Age premises regarding ultimate reality, humanity, God and religion, humanity's problems, solutions to the present crisis, and an agenda for the planet's transformation.

Ultimate Reality

The New Age bottom line can be stated in three words: "All is One." The cosmos is pure, undifferentiated, universal energy—a consciousness or "life force." Everything is one vast, interconnected process.

"The mystical experience of wholeness encompasses all separation," says Marilyn Ferguson.[5]

This premise is known as *monism*, where distinctions of apparent opposites disappear, as does the line between material creation and the force or energy that creates it. Consciousness is not confined to human beings, but applies to all reality. It is best described in impersonal terms such as Principle, Mind, Power, Unity, and, especially, Energy. This reduction of all reality to energy derives from metaphysical speculations extrapolated from quantum physics theories of matter and light.

In the ultimate state of consciousness, says New Age physicist and philosopher Fritjof Capra, "all boundaries and dualisms have been transcended and all individuality dissolves into universal, undifferentiated oneness."[6] (This idea will be analyzed more fully in a later chapter.)

Humanity

Flowing from the premise that All is One is the twin assumption that, therefore, humanity is All One. In the New Age worldview, this is more than a figurative assertion.

Humans are nothing but "congealed energy," the seeming solidification of thought. Hence the oft-quoted New Age slogan: "You create your own reality."

"YOU are the only thing that is real," insists New Age editor Jack Underhill, publisher of the fast-growing *Life Times* magazine. "Everything else is your imagination, movie stuff you've brought into your screenplay to help you see who you really are. Nudge that around for awhile. . . . There are no victims in this life or any other. No mistakes. No wrong paths. No winners. No losers. Accept that and then take responsibility for making your life what you want it to be."[7]

In the New Age context, humans, like everything else, are an extension of the Oneness, which is all the divinity there is. In other words, the only "miracles" are natural "processes" of impersonal energy.

The unity of all things, the subjective revelation most common in mystical experience, is usually called *pantheism*. There are not many selves but one Self, the One. This New Age version of the secular humanist position, which places great faith in human potential, has been dubbed "Cosmic Humanism."

"Man," comments New Age critic Douglas Groothuis in his book, *Unmasking the New Age*, "is not only [seen as] the measure of all things, he is the metaphysical master; we are one with the One and thus have access to unlimited potential."[8]

God and Religion

Humans have a "suppressed, or hidden, Higher Self that reflects, or is connected to, the divine element of the universe," according to Tarcher, publisher of Marilyn Ferguson's *Aquarian Conspiracy*.[9] Ferguson goes further, saying that the "separate self is an illusion"; reality consists of an "even larger Self."[10] This is the New Age "God," sometimes referred to as "Infinite Intelligence."

So, we can expand the bottom line of the New Age premise: <u>All is One. We are All One.</u> All is God. And we are God.

"I am God," shouts Shirley MacLaine on the Malibu beach.

"You are God. Honest," swears Jack Underhill in his magazine. "I know your driver's license says differently, but what does the DMV know?"[11]

But then, the God of New Age is nobody special. He—or, rather, it—is *everything*. There is nothing that *isn't* God. Human beings are a mode, or an expression of, the God who is a principle, a consciousness, a life force. The God of pantheism, remarked Christian theologian Vernon Grounds, is "merely a convenient designation for the all-embracing process which has been grinding on through the ages."[12]

This premise doesn't nullify appreciation for the man Jesus. But most New Agers regard him as one of many enlightened masters. To use popular New Age phrases: We, too, may share the "Christ consciousness" or "the cosmic Christ Spirit." Or, as Ferguson declared in an interview with the *Yoga Journal*: "The myth of the savior 'out there' is being replaced with the myth of the hero 'in here.' Its ultimate expression is the discovery of the divinity within us. . . . [I]n a very real sense, *we* are each other."[13]

The New Age movement considers Christianity just one of many inner spiritual paths, all leading to the same goal of cosmic unity. <u>All religions are essentially one.</u> Jesus, Krishna, Buddha, Lao-tse, and other founders of major religions all taught the same thing: how to become one with the One. This is called *syncretism*.

Rounding out this "universal religion" is the common belief in reincarnation, the theory that the soul progresses through many life cycles according to the working out of one's *karma*—the rule by which the universe returns rewards and punishments."[14] The final goal is to merge with the cosmos, or God, and end the repetitious and painful birth-death-rebirth process.

Humanity's Problem

What's wrong with the human race? Why can't we achieve instant God-consciousness or godhood? The problem, according to the New Age worldview, is our essential blindness. "Metaphysical amnesia" has caused us to forget our true identity.[15]

"The New Age movement says we have forgotten we are one with God and we ... have infinite potential at our fingertips if we allow it to flow," summarized Dean Halverson, a researcher-critic of new religious movements.[16]

According to the New Age mind-set, much of the blame lies with the numbing influences of Western culture, which has caused most people to accept the fragmented vision of self-limitations and "failures" rather than to know they can be "like God." But New Agers believe a "New Order" is about to break out of the "old" epoch of rationalism: The Age of Aquarius, with its mystic way of "knowing," is dawning.

Solution to the Crisis

Just when the darkness seems blackest, the despair seems deepest, there is a way out of the contemporary crisis. Spiritual evolution often comes through an intuitive leap that brings enlightenment. New Agers buoyantly refer to this opportunity for change as a "paradigm shift": a distinct new way of thinking about old problems.

Here's how Marilyn Ferguson describes it: "New perspectives give birth to new historic ages. Humankind has had many dramatic revolutions of understanding—great leaps, sudden liberation from old limits. We discovered the uses of fire and the wheel, language and writing. We found that the Earth only *seems* flat, the sun only *seems* to circle the Earth, matter only *seems* solid. We learned to communicate, fly, explore."[17]

Each of these discoveries, Ferguson says, were paradigm shifts.

How does humanity embark upon a paradigm shift? Through an "awakening experience" that changes the way people think and live and communicate and perceive "reality," by taking part in "conscious evolution." And in adopting a new worldview that sees "holistically" rather than "dualistically." The old paradigm that divides and separates and analyzes must be sloughed off—even abruptly snuffed out—to make room for the new assumed unity between reality and the divine. All is One; God is All, and All is God. Humanity is deified, death is denied, and ignorance—not evil—is the enemy.

The New Age premise is that knowledge, or *gnosis*, is the key to being awakened from our ignorance of divinity. The slumbering "Higher Self" can be roused. Creation and humanity are simply "elevated" to divine status through personal transformation.

Each individual may "actualize" his or her divine nature and achieve union with the Ultimate Unifying Principle by applying a plethora of consciousness-changing techniques, or "psychotechnologies," to body, mind, and spirit.

Some examples of what Ferguson calls "intentional triggers of transformative experiences"[18] are: meditation, Yoga, chanting, mood-altering music, mind-expanding drugs, esoteric systems of religious mysticism and knowledge, guided imagery, balancing and aligning "energies," hypnosis, body disciplines, fasting, martial arts, mechanical devices that measure and alter bodily processes, and mental programs ranging from contemporary psychotherapies to radical seminars designed to obliterate former values and inculcate the New Age mind-set.

Mastery of "spiritual tech" and mystical experience leads the New Ager to psycho-spiritual power and enlightenment. And power-filled, self-realized individuals stand poised to enact "a benign conspiracy for a new human agenda" on a larger scale.[19]

The New Age Agenda

The sequel to expanded personal awareness is planetary transformation, characterized by mass enlightenment and social evolution. Although New Agers selectively endorse programs and causes, the New Age agenda shares major planks with liberal American politics and with the concerns of many Americans who are in no way connected with the movement.

The movement's broad agenda advances ecology (nature and God are merged); androgyny (because all are One, male-female distinctions are irrelevant); world peace and nuclear disarmament (including rapprochement and possible political unification between the United States and the Soviet Union); and natural foods and healing processes. Other goals are to overcome world hunger; humanize technology; dismantle much of corporate America and replace it with "alternative" economic units such as small industrial and agricultural collectives; foster cooperative living styles; and organize global politics.

All is One also applies to nations. National boundaries are obsolete, according to the New Age worldview. Thus, the New Age agenda calls for an emerging global civilization and one-world government, including "planetary taxation" and the United Nations as the sole central governing agency. It would also create an eclectic "world religion" that closely resembles Eastern religious systems rather than Western monotheistic faiths.

Undergirding the New Age worldview is this crucial premise: Humans have access to a source of "transcendent knowing, a domain not limited to time and space."[20]

The "Source" of New Age transcendence, which animates the cosmos, is said to be tapped intuitively by the brain's right hemisphere via the various psychotechnologies.

To attain godhood, New Age style, writes psychologist Maxine Negri in a critique of the movement, "one has only to rid oneself of the limitations imposed by the human brain's left hemisphere's reasoning which Western culture, by way of its technological advances, holds in such high esteem. The pathway to godhood lies not in the left-hemisphere logic but in the right hemisphere's intuitive 'knowing' and creativeness."[21]

To understand the New Age, therefore, we need more information about that marvelous "three-pound universe" we call the brain.

4

The Mind of the New Age

This is a cerebral chapter. It's about the brain, the mind, intuition, and consciousness.

In many ways, the human mind is the heart of the New Age. Within the movement there is a near fixation with exercising the underdeveloped right hemisphere of the brain to generate new ideas and attain spiritual power.

"Step by step, we have been ferreting out a transcendent panacea, to get some right-brain or intuitive control over this left-brained mess of things," rhapsodized New Age advocate-author Kathleen Vande Kieft.[1]

But what is the mind? Is it the same as the brain? Is it more? The most mysterious and least-known human frontier is not in some outer galaxy; it is between the ears. It is a three-and-a-half-pound object about the size of a grapefruit, pinkish-gray in color, with the appearance of a giant fissured walnut and the consistency of Jell-O.

Your brain is you, the master control behind all you do and say, the central panel for thought and consciousness. And the agent for transcendence.

In recent years, neuroscientists have made Promethean strides toward unlocking many of the brain's secrets. Thus far, however, the brain has stubbornly refused to yield up its deepest mysteries; its powers and limits remain beyond our powers and limits. Scientists seek to understand exactly how the brain records memories, how it learns, and how it is aware of itself. As biology writer Lyall Watson said of the catch-22 of brain research: "If the brain were so simple we could understand it, *we* would be so simple we couldn't" understand it.[2]

What *does* human intelligence know about human intelligence?

For starters, there are as many as 100 billion nerve cells in your brain. Each one connects to between 5000 and 50,000 others. For math buffs, that's at least 100 *trillion* connections under your dome. And for trivia pursuers, a computer with the same number of bytes would be 100 stories tall and cover the state of Texas![3] These nerve cells—called neurons (the "gray matter")—"talk" to each other by means of pulsating electricity and chemicals—called neurotransmitters—that flow between neurons.

But perhaps the most fascinating aspect of the human brain is its process of perceiving, processing, storing, and recalling information.

Researchers have mapped out different functions for discrete areas of the brain, but not in the old way the phrenologists did—by studying the bumps on your skull. Actually, anatomist Franz Joseph Gall, founder of the pseudoscience of phrenology (in 1810), wasn't far off in his belief that the brain housed particular mental faculties in specialized "zones."

Ever since the 1860s and 1870s, when neurologists Pierre Paul Broca and Karl Wernicke reported that damage to the left cerebral hemisphere produced severe speech disorders but that comparable damage to the right hemisphere did not, "split-brain" researchers have known that the two hemispheres tend to have unique functions.

Each hemisphere influences the other. They are joined through the *corpus callosum*, a kind of telephone trunk line connecting the two halves.

In general, the left hemisphere does the thinking; the right side does the feeling. (These functions are reversed for left-handed individuals.) So there's some truth to the saying, "I'm of two minds about that." Fortunately, the left side prevents (usually) the right side from bursting out with inappropriate emotions.

For a right-handed person, the left hemisphere acts as a sort of "super press agent," says Harvard Medical School

Professor Herbert Benson, who believes meditation techniques can produce dramatic changes in the mind's capabilities. "It tries to make sense out of the huge quantities of new and stored information; it sifts and categorizes data. It makes inferences and predictions based on that information. To facilitate this inference-making function, the left hemisphere relies on vast reservoirs of analytical, logical and verbal skills. The fact that we can put thoughts in language and give precise reasons for why we do things is largely a direct result of this function of the left side of the brain."[4]

Benson, as well as many behavioral scientists, maintains that the right hemisphere has the ability to change ingrained habits and thought patterns. This right side—overshadowed by the linear, analytical, and wordy left side—is the center for many of our intuitive, creative functions. Flashes of insight and images of ideas, seemingly coming out of nowhere, enter our consciousness through neurotransmitter activity originating in the right hemisphere.

Neurological psychologist Michael S. Gazzaniga, author of *The Social Brain: Discovering the Networks of the Mind*, believes the human brain has a modular organization; it is made up of units that function in relatively independent, parallel ways. Based on extensive post-surgical studies of "split-brain" patients, Gazzaniga concluded that each brain module is "capable of action, of carrying out activities that test and retest the beliefs that are maintained by our dominant left brain. . . . If the brain were a monolithic system with all modules in complete internal communication, then our beliefs would never change."[5]

A linear system can't generate new information, agrees Arnold Mandell, an unorthodox brain chemist at the University of California, San Diego. "The brain has this spontaneous, self-organizing activity, like clouds, air, and water. It makes eddies and whorls. As you go from the level of neurons, to electromagnetic fields, to a person, to a family, to a society, you get emergent properties."[6]

But the current mod metaphor of "left brain" versus "right brain" leans on gimmickry borrowed from a quasi-scientific foundation, cautions William H. Calvin, a professor of neurophysiology at the University of Washington. Metaphor has been confused with reality in New Age circles, he says, spreading a number of myths. Chief among them is an exaggerated notion of the dichotomy between the two hemispheres and their characteristics and abilities.

Calvin noted that a percentage (about 7%) of people have *right* brains that are language dominant. Often when one hemisphere is damaged—especially in very young children—tasks processed by that hemisphere can be "taken over," though usually not as well, by the other side.[7]

The excuse that "it's tough being a right-brained person in a left-brained world" may be funny, but it's half-brained and fallacious, concurs Jerre Levy, a biopsychologist at the University of Chicago. That the left hemisphere controls logic and language, and the right controls creativity and intuition is a half-truth, she says. "To the extent that regions are differentiated in the brain, they must integrate their activities. . . . There is no activity in which only one hemisphere is involved or to which only one hemisphere makes a contribution."[8]

Many New Agers do not look at it quite this way. To them, there is a "higher wisdom" in the right hemisphere, a kind of "body-knowing" that attunes one to God. This is the pure consciousness the New Age seeks, the cosmic awareness Eastern mystics and sages have long exalted.

New Age reasoning goes along this line: "If we can still the wordy chatter of our left hemisphere and become aware of the messages from the silent, mystical half, we could be more in touch with the deepest reality."

Explains Shirley MacLaine:

A person who thinks laterally, or with the right hemisphere, is capable of seeing a broader connectedness to events that would be little more than a contradictory puzzle to a left-brained Westerner. . . . Eastern thinkers are more open to intuitive thinking . . . [which] addresses higher dimensions and more realities, which enable us to feel connected to the source of what I call God Energy. It speaks to the language of the soul, the universality of the spirit. . . . [W]hen we "go within" ourselves there will be something there.[9]

God in the synapse. God in the neuron. "Place the thinking mind on hold so these subtle energies can be perceived," says Kathleen Vande Kieft.[10] Short-circuit the rational mind and tune in Mind-at-Large.

"Tacit knowing . . . the silent partner to all our progress," mused Marilyn Ferguson.[11] " 'Overstanding' the mind," she explained later. "But only when you get yourself out of the way. You have to be willing to have experiences and not have words for them."[12]

"All the brain is contained in the mind, but not all the mind is contained in the brain," concludes Ferguson, quoting a Hindu swami. "A tricky thing to talk about. . . . But there is something that acts upon the brain."

Wrote the late Wilder Penfield, the renowned Canadian brain surgeon: "There is no good evidence that the brain alone can carry out the work the mind does."[13]

The mystery of the mind/brain remains. From whence do our brightest ideas, deepest emotions, and grandest dreams arise?

"The workings of an organ capable of creating *Hamlet*, the Bill of Rights, and Hiroshima remain deeply mysterious," wrote neurologist Richard M. Restak in his odyssey *The Brain.* "How is it constructed? How did it develop? If we learn more about the brain, can we learn more about ourselves? Indeed, are we anything *other* than our brain? Some of these questions remain unanswered; others ('Is the brain the mind?') may remain forever unanswerable."[14]

Where is the mind of a person in a coma? Is something you previously thought but no longer believe still a part of your mind?

An essential fact of the human condition, notes science writer Douglas Hofstadter, is that people—no matter how aware they are of their minds—cannot fully take their own complexity into account in attempting to understand themselves.[15]

"Can a three-pound organ the texture of warm porridge account for consciousness?" ask Judith Hooper and Dick Teresi near the conclusion of their epic *Three-Pound Universe.*[16]

Can godhood be unleashed by restructuring the way we think? If so, observes Brooks Alexander, an analyst and critic of the New Age, "this always involves shutting down our rational, critical mind. . . . New Age 'empowerment' comes only to those whose rational, critical filter has been removed or disabled."[17]

Astronomer Carl Sagan, science popularizer and naturalist, also puts it bluntly: "There is no way to tell whether the patterns extracted by the right hemisphere are real or imagined without subjecting them to left hemisphere scrutiny."[18]

The greatest endowment of the human mind is its ability to discriminate between what is true and what is false, and to verify what is real and what is illusion or delusion. But New Age superconsciousness is programmed to ignore those distinctions.

Humans are rational beings, and our correspondence with God is in that rationality. If God, as a transcendent Superior Being, created the finite human mind and placed the capacity for rationality within the human brain, then it's logical to assume we can understand his revelation to us.

As seventeenth-century astronomer Johannes Kepler exclaimed when he studied the universe and Scripture: "O God, I am thinking Thy thoughts after Thee."[19]

PART II

WHO AND WHAT IS
THE NEW AGE

5

Historical Roots

To understand the contemporary New Age movement, we must trace out some of the divergent roots of its origin. By and large, New Age is a modern revival of ancient religious traditions, along with a potpourri of influences: Eastern mysticism, modern philosophy and psychology, science and science fiction, and the counterculture of the '50s and '60s. But underlying all these influences is the New Age understanding of the human mind.

The Zen Buddhist view of reality, for example, is that higher consciousness, or the true self, is none other than the Buddha-Mind. For the Zen practitioner, distinctions are meaningless. There is no "internal" or "external." Nothing exists outside the true self. Things that appear to be external are only stirrings within the Buddha-Mind.

In other words, the mind includes everything. Buddha-Mind is not a *thing*, but paradoxically, nothing has existence apart from it.[1]

This is an ancient concept, arising from the life and teachings of a monk named Siddhartha Gautama who wandered India 2,500 years ago and came to be known as the Buddha, "the Enlightened One." Today, the way of the Buddha has more than 500 million followers worldwide; most are concentrated in Asia, but significant numbers also inhabit Europe and North America.[2]

Buddhism, like other major world religions, is not one

monolithic system of belief and practice; neither, of course, is the New Age philosophy. But Buddhism's influence on New Age thinking is indisputable. So is that of Buddhism's parent religion, Hinduism, which predates Buddhism by at least a thousand years. Both traditions stress reincarnation and *karma* (we will consider these in detail in a separate chapter).

Hinduism and Buddhism teach that the inevitable birth-death-rebirth cycle can only be broken by accumulating enough good karma, which frees one from the illusions of the material world and makes liberation possible. In Buddhism that state is called *nirvana*, the cessation of suffering and the enjoyment of perpetual bliss. Belief in evolution of spirits through additional lifetimes is also a tenet of Native American religions; this, too, is incorporated into New Age thought.

Zen (a Japanese word meaning meditation) has also directly shaped New Age thought, and bears the marks of the traditional Chinese religion of Taoism. Fundamental to Taoism is the belief that "in and behind the phenomenal world lies the Tao, the eternal unchanging principle. The Tao is the original source of everything in the universe; it spontaneously produces everything through harmonious interplay of two forces, *yin* (the principle of passive receptivity) and *yang* (the principle of activity)."[3]

Gnostic influence on New Age thought is also unmistakable, as New Age leaders freely acknowledge. Gnosticism, which was branded a heresy by the early Christian church, maintains that humans are destined for reunion with the divine essence from which they sprang. Those "in the know" (the literal meaning of *gnosis*) "understand that man is divine, that his divine origin and destiny set him apart from the rest of creation and that there is no limit to his powers. Death itself is an illusion," explains noted historian Christopher Lasch.[4]

Carl A. Raschke has described traditional Gnosticism as a myth of secret illumination "built upon the motif of esoteric wisdom accessible only to the privileged or initiated few. This wisdom, or *gnosis*, entails an antagonistic struggle with the ruling powers of the material world, a journey into forbidden territory in order to snatch away the elixir of eternal life. . . . The method of salvation for Gnosticism . . . demands an immediate glimpse of the inner workings of the cosmos, a decisive clue that deciphers the riddles of heaven and earth."[5]

Gnosticism emanated from Pythagorean metaphysics, Neoplatonism, and various occult or mystery schools. Modern Gnostic historian Robert Anson Wilson traces "higher intelligence" back through the Rosicrucians, the Renaissance magic societies, "medieval witchcraft, the Knights Templar, European Sufis, etc., to Gnosticism and thence back to the Eleusinian mysteries and Egyptian cults."[6]

New Age also owes much to the "cosmopolitan paganism used by the ancient Hellenistic rulers and Roman Caesars to weld together a lush diversity of religions and cultures"[7] as well as American movements from the last century, when Eastern mysticism first took root on New England shores.

The Transcendental movement (1836–60) was shaped by philosopher-authors like Henry David Thoreau and Ralph Waldo Emerson, who were deeply influenced by the wisdom of the East. Emerson's development of the "Over-Soul" expressed a pantheistic worldview, and Thoreau "relaxed with a copy of the *Bhagavad Gita*" at Walden Pond, observed Jerry Yamamoto.[8] The Transcendentalists eclectically borrowed from the Eastern scriptures, molding them to fit American standards of autonomy and individual determination and set the stage for New Age luminaries to take the spotlight 130 years later. (We'll take a closer look at some of the key actors of Transcendentalism and New Thought in chapter 22.)

Transcendentalism was the first major religious movement in this country with a substantial Asian component, points out J. Gordon Melton, director of Santa Barbara's Institute for the Study of American Religion. That migration continues, Melton said in an interview, with several hundred thousand Asians "dumping into the United States annually, including tremendous numbers of Hindus and Buddhists."[9]

Spiritualism was another strand of nineteenth-century American religious consciousness.

The way for Spiritualism had been paved by an Austrian physician named Franz Anton Mesmer (1734–1815), whose disciples brought the "new mental healing movement" to America. Mesmer taught "mesmeric sleep" techniques based on "animal magnetism." Psychic healer Phineas Parkhurst

Quimby, a New England clockmaker, took notice, and soon he—and one of his pupils, Mary Baker Patterson Eddy—were spreading the teaching that disease was caused by false beliefs and not physical disorders. Out of this came Christian Science, Divine Science, Science of Mind, Religious Science, and the Unity School of Christianity.

Hypnosis "taught people that there are many phenomena people could do in trance they could not do in normal consciousness," noted Martin Katchen, a student of mind-control and hypnosis. "This opened the door to the belief they could do many other things such as clairvoyance and prophecy."[10]

Rappings allegedly heard by two young sisters in a Hydesville, New York, house in 1848 caught the attention of an entranced population—and set off a movement. The Fox sisters said the knockings, which spelled out messages, were from the spirit of a murdered peddler whose body lay interred in the basement of their home. Whether or not the whole phenomenon was made up (one of the sisters later confessed to causing the noises by cracking her knee joints), a Spiritualist explosion began.

Recounts psychic researcher Colin Wilson: "People discovered that all they had to do was sit in a darkened room, preferably with a 'medium' present—someone who had already established a communication with the spirits—and the manifestation would usually follow immediately. No apparatus was required, except possibly a few musical instruments. In the Rochester [New York] area, more than 100 'mediums' appeared in the year 1850."[11]

Spiritualism was also the cradle for Theosophy, the creation of Madame Helena Petrovna Blavatsky (1831–91), an eccentric Russian mystic who lived a life of scandal and died amid accusations that she was a fraud. She and her close companion, Colonel Henry S. Olcott (1832–1907), returned to America in 1879 after an extended visit to India. Their imported brand of Hinduism became a part of the Theosophical Society, an occult organization they had formed in 1875.

Nina Easton, writing in the *Los Angeles Times* magazine, said Blavatsky might well be called "a godmother of the New Age movement" because, in the words of Blavatsky's biographer, Marion Meade, she "paved the way for contemporary

Transcendental Meditation, Zen, Hare Krishnas; yoga and vegetarianism; karma and reincarnation; swamis, yogis and gurus."[12]

Blavatsky's successors—Annie Besant (1847–1933), Guy Ballard (1878–1939) of the "I AM" Activity, and Alice Bailey (1880–1949)—continued Theosophy's messianic vision of a coming new world religious teacher, inspired by channeled prophecies from a hierarchy of "ascended masters."

Bailey seems to have coined the phrase, "New Age," which recurs throughout her writings. But the wide popularity of the expression settled in only after "New Age" became associated with the "Age of Aquarius," the title song in the 1960s musical, *Hair*.[13]

"Aquarius," remarked New Age pacesetter Marilyn Ferguson, is "the waterbearer in the ancient zodiac, symbolizing flow and the quenching of an ancient thirst. [It] is an appropriate symbol . . . the time of 'the mind's true liberation.'"[14]

While some seekers went to the East to find wisdom, Eastern purveyors of mysticism were migrating to the West. In 1893, the first Parliament on World Religions was held in connection with the World's Fair in Chicago. Spiritual masters, swamis, and gurus washed onto American shores en masse for the first time, making Eastern mysticism accessible—and acceptable—to thousands of Americans.

After wowing the crowds at the world religions expo, Indian Swami Vivekananda (1862–1902) remained in this country to form the Vedanta Society. Paramahansa Yogananda arrived in 1920 and later established the Self-Realization Fellowship. And "the silent, self-avowed avatar" Meher Baba came to the United States in the early 1930s to found the Islamic-oriented Friends of Meher Baba group.[15]

In later chapters we'll consider the roles of psychoanalysts Sigmund Freud and Carl Jung, as well as Albert Einstein and quantum mechanics scientists, for they, too, helped roll out the red carpet for the present New Age movement. Native American religions, neopaganism, and the influence of the feminist "Goddess" movement are also worthy of special attention in subsequent chapters.

Contemporary roots of the New Age can be found in the counterculture movement of recent decades. The beatniks of the 1950s were fascinated with Zen; a decade later came the hippies "with their acid dreams and Eastern gurus, their flower power and utopian radicalism," wrote Brooks Alexander. "Next in line was the 'human potential movement' of the 1970s, spearheaded by 'humanistic' therapists of various mystical inclinations. Esalen was the touchy-feely Mecca for the upscale, post-hippie seeker. In the 1980s, all these strands and more came together, mingling in new, fanciful ways."[16]

Gordon Melton pinpoints 1971 as the galvanization date for the movement in America. It was the year that the national periodical, *East-West Journal*, was first published, as well as the first representative book, *Be Here Now*, written by Baba Ram Dass, the Jewish-born Richard Alpert. A former psychology professor, he and colleague Timothy Leary—both were fired from Harvard—extolled "psychedelic mysticism" produced by using LSD and other hallucinogenic drugs.

Alpert, finding his personal guru in India, reemerged as Ram Dass and "preached a new, hybrid message of spiritual ecstasy and 'nowness,' which he committed to print as a crazy pastiche of bold-face words strewn all over the pages in scissors-and-paste fashion," described Raschke.[17]

Meanwhile, Carlos Castaneda's books about his Mexico desert adventures with a bizarre Yaqui Indian sorcerer, Don Juan, "sold millions of copies and . . . attracted many who followed his path of initiation through the experience of hallucinogenic mushrooms."[18]

Other prime New Age influences of the 1970s and early 1980s include: Swami Muktananda with his peacock-feather wand and siddha Yoga; Maharishi Mahesh Yogi, onetime hero of the Beatles and father of Transcendental Meditation; and cherubic teenage guru Maharaj Ji, "Lord of the Universe" and overseer of the Divine Light Mission. Each skillfully filtered his own peculiar brand of Eastern mysticism through the American psyche and experience, Robert Ellwood, a scholar of Oriental religions at the University of Southern California, has pointed out.[19] And then there were the American gurus: novelist Jack Kerouac, a master of California's "beat Zen" generation; poet Allen Ginsberg, a fellow traveler with Kerouac and a character in *Dharma Bums*; and, perhaps most supremely, showman Alan Watts, the erstwhile Episcopal priest and chaplain at Northwestern University.

Watts, who died in 1973, wrote twenty-four books on Eastern thought, including the influential *Way of Zen*.

The New Age movement has been "fed by many tributaries, but cannot be reduced to any single one," Robert J. Burrows wrote in *The New Age Rage*. "The strands of the ancient wisdom . . . are now all aswirl, one virtually indistinguishable from the next, and all drawing on one another."[20]

But Martin Katchen, an Orthodox Jew and keen analyst of historical currents, sees haunting parallels between the contemporary New Age movement and the social landscape as it existed in America 150 years ago.

"The New Age today," he said, gesturing toward a mountain of books he had brought along to an interview to support his premise, "is a logical continuation of trends existent in American liberalism since the 1830s. The same ideas seem to be in proximity: channelers, Eastern spirituality, political liberalism pointing towards socialism, liberal Christianity, and New Thought.

"The way it was is the way it is."

6

Headliners and Honchos

The expression "New Age" swept into vogue in the 1970s and 1980s, helped along by circulation of the *New Age Journal* and a book by Mark Satin called *New Age Politics*. Marilyn Ferguson's best-selling *Aquarian Conspiracy*, a compendium of the New Age social agenda and philosophical vision, attained status as the unofficial scripture of the movement.

But if Ferguson wrote the New Age bible, Shirley MacLaine became its high priestess.

"I'm just a human being trying to find some answers about what we're doing here, where we came from and where we're going," the bubbly actress demurred in an interview with *TIME* magazine. Nonetheless, the newsweekly called her "the New Age's reigning whirling dervish."[1]

In her earlier professional incarnations as a Broadway singer and dancer and a Hollywood actress, she is perhaps best known for her roles in *Sweet Charity* and *The Apartment*, as well as her Oscar-winning performance in *Terms of Endearment*. Yet the copper-haired MacLaine was obviously having the time of her lives, as *People's Weekly* put it, starring as the celebrity evangelist of New Age metaphysics.[2]

In *Out on a Limb*, she chronicles her reluctant conversion to New Age belief. Her travels and studies—which included science fiction-like dimensions of out-of-body travel, contact with extraterrestrial beings, and "trance channeling" (seances)—provide a "guided tour" of the unseen world.

"Perhaps," she writes, "as philosophers and even some scientists have claimed, reality is only what one perceives it to be."[3]

Science writer Martin Gardner, however, called MacLaine's writing "kindergarten metaphysics" in his column in the *Skeptical Inquirer*, a quarterly devoted to debunking fringe science.[4]

MacLaine's second book about her spiritual saga, *Dancing in the Light*, is a farther reach into the realms of yoga, reincarnation, crystal power, Hindu mantras, and past-life recall experiences mediated through acupuncture. Her spirit guides inform her that each individual is God, and she passes along the wisdom to a friend: "You are unlimited. You just don't *realize* it."[5]

In the five-hour ABC-TV movie, "Out on a Limb," aired in January 1987, a radiant MacLaine dramatically played herself to the hilt and affirmed her belief that "her pals in the spirit world" had selected her to "channel" the word of new-old enlightenment to a skeptical age.[6]

Primed by voluminous reading and much conversation with mystics, MacLaine's "moment of naked truth" comes in a hot sulfur pool in the Andes where she feels her conscious self drift from her body and soar high into the Peruvian sky. In her luminous description, her "spirit, or mind, or soul, whatever it was" flowed out of her body—though the two were connected by a "thin silver cord." She rose so high, she said, she could see the Earth's curvature.

"I was just flowing, somehow flowing. I didn't want to return, which made me question whether I'd gone too far, and that was enough to take me back.... Then, well, I just became 130 pounds again."[7]

This bizarre miniseries was greeted with gasps and guffaws. "Shirley You Jest," headlined the *Rivendell Times*, a Colorado newsletter that critiques social trends.[8] "The Far Side" cartoon portrayed a desert scene and two large Gila monsters, with one saying to the other: "There it is again . . . a feeling that in a past life I was someone named Shirley MacLaine."[9] Martin Gardner called the film "pervasive, paranormal poppycock . . . its dialogue unbearably banal."[10]

It's All in the Playing, MacLaine's third metaphysical book, records the ghostly events surrounding the making of the TV miniseries. This includes beyond-the-grave assistance from the late Alfred Hitchcock and changing the weather via visualization techniques. The book was ridiculed in the *New Age Journal* as "a plodding affair, rife with cliché-ridden characterizations, Day-Glo landscapes, and fortune-cookie wisdom." Ripped reviewer Dennis Livingstone: "What Mac-Laine needs is less from the spirit guides, and more from a ghost writer."[11]

Still, MacLaine's unabashed New Age advocacy—including two-day, one-woman "Connecting With the Higher Self" seminars held across the country in 1987—struck a responsive chord in millions of Americans.

MacLaine "made it semi-chic to talk about our mystical encounters," declared Terry Clifford in *American Health* magazine.[12]

"You and I might laugh at this person," ex-White House counsel Charles Colson agreed as we conversed over the roar of jets at Los Angeles International Airport. "But the world takes her very seriously. People think, if someone as famous as she believes it, then there must be something to it."[13]

Once a "confirmed atheist," MacLaine in childhood attended a Baptist Sunday school in Virginia with her brother, actor Warren Beatty. She now believes the Bible is "extremely metaphysical." It's full of descriptions of UFOs, angels emerging from spaceships, channeling, and spirit voices, she said on the "Phil Donahue Show." And, she added, she was doing "mind traveling" into the future, assisted by entities and "helpers" from the other side.[14]

One channeler Shirley relied on to put her in touch is Kevin Ryerson, a former sign painter turned medium who played a prominent role in *Out on a Limb*. She has called the highly acclaimed, highly articulate, and highly priced Ryerson "one of the telephones in my life."[15]

MacLaine has also flipped to the channel of Ramtha, the alleged 35,000-year-old ascended master from the lost continent of Atlantis. "The Ram" speaks through former housewife J. Z. Knight of Yelm, Washington.

Knight, who has been dubbed the Tammy Faye Bakker of the New Age movement, has profited considerably by having a direct channel to the stars. Besides MacLaine, her clientele reportedly has included Burt Reynolds, Clint Eastwood, Richard Chamberlain, the late Joan Hackett, Shelley Fabares, and Mike Farrell of the television series *M*A*S*H*.[16] And she counts actress Linda Evans, who bought a home near Knight's in order to be in touch with Ramtha, among her good friends.[17]

Hundreds of Knight's followers have packed up and moved to the rural Northwest to survive the destruction that Ramtha has predicted will precede the millennium. Meanwhile, J. Z. waits it out in luxury. Supporters' bucks have helped build her a lavish mansion and outfitted her Messiah Arabian Stud, Inc. Stables with chandeliers and wall-to-wall carpeting.

"How strange," remarked an interviewer on a Los Angeles talk show, "that Ramtha, a 35,000-year-old warrior, is telling people to buy your Arabian horses."

Rousing to the joust, the white tunic-wearing Knight rejoined: "You know ... we have a wonderful energy working around some of the horses that people are involved in. We're involved more than anyone; we've put everything we have into it."[18]

The honey-blonde Knight, who relaxes after a channeling session by smoking a cigarette and downing a Cherry Coke, adds that The Ram first appeared to her in 1977 when she was experimenting with paper pyramids in her kitchen. But she can't channel the warrior just any old time: "He doesn't have a contract with me."[19]

The ancient entity, however, has issued his own book of stylized, channelized prophecies. *I am Ramtha* is illustrated by photographs of Knight going into a trance on the "Merv Griffin Show." The phenomenon caused New Age critic Robert Burrows to gibe that this was "proof that even if you perish, you can still publish."[20]

Taking responsibility for your own life is the heart of Ramtha's message. "Every destiny changes every moment; we can change our mind and thus our future every moment. . . . Collective will manifests the shadows of tomorrow. . . . God is within."

J. Z. Knight grew up as Judy Hampton in Artesia, New Mexico. Her alcoholic father deserted the family, and she was raised by her fundamentalist Christian mother. Popular as a teenager, J. Z. was voted the prettiest girl in her high school class. A devout believer in God, J. Z. once suddenly began speaking in a strange male voice during a prayer meeting, according to one of Knight's former high school classmates, Sandy Fallis. The voice identified himself as a demon named Demias, said Fallis on a segment of ABC's *20/20*.

"She was holding her neck and saying, 'I can't breathe!' At that point the male voice broke out and again and said, 'You want this body and you can't have it!' "[21] (Knight says the incident never happened.)

Whether or not another personality comes out that she cannot entirely control, Knight seems to have her destiny well in command; she and her staff continue to channel Ramtha's energies into seminars, books, tapes, and an adept form of psychological and spiritual counseling. Although not a few New Age followers have grown disillusioned with J. Z.'s Ramtha seminars, others still consider them helpful enough to shell out $400 per lecture.

In a different way, Marilyn Ferguson has spread the New Age word on a global basis. One of the movement's intelligentsia, Ferguson kindled fire in kindred hearts when she wrote about "an evolution of consciousness," a transformation "anticipated by older prophecies in all the traditions of direct knowing—the death of one world and the birth of a new, an apocalypse . . . the awakening of increasing numbers of human beings to their godlike potential."[22]

Within weeks of publication of *The Aquarian Conspiracy*, in 1980, leaders of the Solidarity movement in Poland had ordered ten copies. The book became a text in college courses, and was published in eight countries and translated into ten languages. By early 1988 it had sold more than 500,000 copies in North America alone. Discussion groups sprang up in prisons, churches, government agencies, and even in a South African village.

Ferguson, who finished only two years of college, soon found herself speaking to such diverse groups as the U.S. Army War College, health educators, nuclear physicists, Canadian farm wives, members of Congress, data processing managers, hotel executives, state administrators, medical librarians, college presidents, and international gatherings of youth and business leaders.

The Aquarian Conspiracy was as much a social phenome-non as a book. "Books like this," wrote Robert Ellwood, a University of Southern California historian of religion, "have a way of not only describing what they are about but also becoming part of it—even of helping to make it happen."[23]

Initially, Ferguson seems an unlikely chief apostle for the New Age. She talks rapidly, her ideas often outrunning her ability to articulate them. She starts on one track and, after a few words, backtracks. Nevertheless, she is a lucid writer, a clever thinker, and a creative organizer. But there seem to be loose circuits in her stream-of-consciousness logic. The light at the end of the wires doesn't always come on as she says it will when you throw the switch. There are flickers of greatness and flashes of insight, but the maze of connections isn't firmly plugged into the power line.

That was my impression, at least, as we talked in her Mount Washington hilltop home on the edge of Los Angeles.[24] She and second husband, Ray Gottlieb, had just returned from their other residence high on the north shore of Lake Arrowhead, seventy miles away. As Marilyn, barefoot and wearing a red-and-white polka-dot top and khaki pants, brewed a pot of tea, I gazed at her collection of New Age paintings and statues, a giant purple crystal, and a huge stuffed bird. Late-morning sunlight reflected off the computer screen in her loft workroom, and Gulliver, the parrot, squawked in the background.

In the 1960s, Marilyn related, "I was a young mother [of three] in Houston. . . . I was also a naturalistic poet . . . intrigued with emerging science support for my intuitions."

As so she published a book, *The Brain Revolution.* (Actu-ally that was her second book. The first was *Champagne Living on a Beer Pocketbook,* all about "simple living on an elegant scale.") "To my surprise, scientists and researchers reacted with great interest."

So, in 1975, industrious Marilyn began publishing the *Brain/Mind Bulletin,* a monthly report on breakthroughs in learning, psychology, creativity, and brain function, among other topics. "The bulletin became a vehicle for pulling this information on mind and consciousness together . . . I became the 'eye of the hurricane' on this. . . ."

At this point, Gulliver—a "she"—suddenly and for reasons

known only to herself, flew off Ray's shoulder and smashed into the large picture window across the room.

After Gulliver's travels had ended and the bruised bird was reperched, Marilyn continued, telling me about the new book she and her husband were working on. "New York publishers are going nuts," she confided, naming a large sum Pocket Books had advanced, but pledging me to secrecy. The manuscript, titled *The New Common Sense*, "is on the secrets of a truly successful life. Overcoming the problems of life crises . . . compared to all this kooky stuff.

"Radical renewal is going on in every institution; that just needs to be nurtured. . . . People 'harboring the stream' are in every profession, every stair on the escalator. . . . They just needed the clue that they weren't crazy."

Marilyn Ferguson may be one of the most colorful exponents of New Age, but she's not the movement's only contemporary intellectual theorist.

They may not make the headlines, but a thorough assessment of the New Age should include thinker and channeler David Spangler, who had much to do with the founding of the eclectic Findhorn Community in Northern Scotland; transpersonal psychologist and editor Ken Wilber; mystic physicist Fritjof Capra; death-and-dying seer Elisabeth Kübler-Ross; and political strategists Mark Satin and Barbara Marx Hubbard—the latter a futurist and aspiring Democratic candidate for the vice presidency in 1984.

These and other channelers, honchos, and leaders of a rainbow assortment of communes and groups—like Werner Erhard of "est" (now the Forum); Native American mystic teacher Sun Bear; and Robert and Judith Skutch, publishers of the multi-volume metaphysical *A Course in Miracles*—will materialize in the following pages.

Some of the legendary New Age gurus already wait in the wings. . . .

7

Gifted Gurus

At the outset I need to say that my categorizing is arbitrary. Who am I to determine *the* gurus of the New Age? And what's a guru, anyway? Nearly anyone can be one these days. Frances Lear, ex-wife of Hollywood producer Norman Lear, launched a new magazine for the mature, upscale woman. What does *TIME* call her? "A Guru for Women over 40."[1]

Not many years ago, quipped Westmont College sociologist Ronald Enroth, Americans were likely to think a guru "was an exotic animal. Today . . . it is practically a household word."[2]

In religion, gurus are spiritual masters who teach and help the uninitiated and demand that their disciples totally surrender to their authority. Gurus are "said to be greater than God because they lead to God."[3]

For our purposes, we will go with a bit looser definition. Some New Age "top guns" could be classified as gurus, channelers, or simply celebrity leaders. Or a combination. Shirley MacLaine, J. Z. Knight, and Marilyn Ferguson are headliners because of their public prominence.

Gurus often start groups or communes. Some of these—like est, Scientology, and Hare Krishna—have become well established through the years or have moved beyond the immediate leadership or control of their founders. We'll consider some of these in the next chapter on New Age-related groups.

Remember, this is not a comprehensive list of contemporary New Age gurus. And some may not choose to identify themselves with the New Age movement. But they are representative.

Bhagwan Shree Rajneesh

In the summer of 1981, India's most controversial guru packed up his large commune in Poona and reassembled it on an immense, isolated cattle ranch in central Oregon known as "the Big Muddy." Within two years, the religion of Rajneesh and his $60 million empire had settled in: Crops covered more than 3000 of the 64,000-acre spread, watered from a huge reservoir. Some 250,000 square feet of permanent buildings dotted the brushlands, crowned by a five-wing "university" where orange-clad disciples absorbed a heady mix of Rajneesh-style Eastern mysticism and West Coast sensory therapy.

For years, Rajneesh had wanted "a new site, isolated from the outside world—a community to provoke God." This new commune, he wrote in 1979, would be "an experiment in spiritual communism . . . a space where we can create human beings who are not obsessed with comparison, who are not obsessed with the ego, who are not obsessed with the personality."[4]

But by late 1985 the commune was disbanded; Rajneesh had been deported; and many of his top aides, including tart-tongued Ma Anand Sheela, were doing time for crimes ranging from wiretapping to attempted murder (including mass poisoning of seven hundred people) to arson to arranging sham marriages in order to circumvent immigration laws.

The assessment of psychiatrist James S. Gordon is particularly enlightening because, as an expert in new religions for the National Institute of Mental Health, he had thoroughly investigated Rajneesh both in India and Oregon.

In an interview and in his book *Golden Guru*, Gordon sought to answer the perplexing question: Why had so many highly educated, successful people chosen to abandon their careers and families to devote their talents and lives to Rajneesh?

"Rajneesh was a catalyst, a teacher, if not a Master for me,"

Gordon said, conceding there had been "a moment" when he almost became a *sanyassin*, or initiated disciple. He was mesmerized by the dream of utopia, the creation of new human beings in new communities. But there was a "love of power there, a control that was potentially ugly and potentially dangerous." He admitted his disappointment:

"If this remarkably intuitive and intelligent man could not help people change," and if these "talented, smart, energetic, and cheerful *sanyassins* . . . could not make it . . . then it does not bode well for me or for others who might want to create and be part of loving and productive communities . . . Rajneesh . . . failed to live what he knew and taught."[5]

Yet the Rajneesh mystique lived on, despite his being booted out of twenty-one countries during a world tour after his U.S. deportation. Until his death in early 1990, about five thousand people—most of them Westerners—were attending the fifty-six-year-old guru's twice-daily discourses in the reconstituted Poona ashram.[6]

"I still see him as the wisest person I ever met," mused Sunshine, a former spokeswoman at the Rajneeshpuram compound in Oregon. She and Philip Toelkes, a lawyer who once served as Rajneeshpuram's mayor, expressed "gratitude" to Rajneesh, and Toelkes called him "the most innocent and the least innocent person I know."[7]

Elizabeth Clare Prophet

The Rajneeshnee exodus may have dismantled the portable housing at Rajneeshpuram, but the units were "reincarnated" 550 miles to the east at the New Age community of Elizabeth Clare Prophet, affectionately called "Guru Ma" by her disciples.

After pulling up stakes in Southern California (selling the $15.5 million headquarters estate to an American Buddhist group), the commune of 400—which temporarily swelled to 3000 during a 1987 celebration on the Fourth of July weekend—set up shop on the 33,000-acre Royal Teton Ranch near Yellowstone National Park.[8]

Prophet's Church Universal and Triumphant, with an estimated 10,000 to 25,000 members, stems from her teachings about the "ascended masters" and "light bearers" of the Great White Brotherhood. The church, active in 100 U.S. cities, embraces one of the most complex and syncretistic mixings of metaphysical beliefs in modern times.[9] Prophet and her late husband, Mark Prophet, who had founded the Summit Lighthouse in 1958 (its name was changed to the Church Universal and Triumphant in 1976) stitched Eastern and Western traditions together creatively. They relied heavily on recycled teachings from the "Mighty I AM" movement popularized by Guy and Edna Ballard during the 1930s, a group that swelled into the millions in the 1940s, then declined drastically.

Guru Ma, a strong-willed, middle-aged woman, has a penchant for expensive jewelry and "a very profound calling in Jesus."[10] As the "Vicar of Christ," she claims to be God's chosen earthly messenger for direct dictations (channeled messages) from a host of ascended masters including Buddha, Jesus, Saint Germaine, Pope John XXIII, Merlin the Magician, Christopher Columbus, and K-17, the "head of the Cosmic Secret Service."

Some rural Montana townsfolk, alarmed over a possible repeat of the Rajneesh fiasco in Oregon, have sought to have Guru Ma's growing, self-sufficient community expelled from their pastoral valley.

Baba Ram Dass

In the 1960s, a nascent guru was expelled from Harvard University for tripping out on LSD. Gaining notoriety, Bostonian psychologist Richard Alpert trekked to India where he studied with the late guru Neem Karoli Baba and donned sandals and beads. Reappearing with the name Guru Ram Dass, which means Servant of God, Alpert hit the American scene as the New Age was dawning. His newfound Eastern faith, superimposed upon a prestigious academic background, "made him the perfect symbol of the New Age," according to American religions expert J. Gordon Melton.[11] His popular books soon became a kind of bellwether of the movement's era of "tuning in, turning on and dropping out."

Now, Ram Dass's hair has silvered; his flowing beard has

been shorn, and he sports a neat mustache. He still practices Buddhist meditation but also sits in on trance channeling sessions. A few years back he was wooed by female medium Joya Santanya who claimed to be the conduit for his old Indian guru. In 1987, at age fifty-six, Dass was training volunteers to help AIDS patients and lecturing for a world-wide service group that runs an eye clinic in Nepal and a Native American health clinic in South Dakota.

"In the '60s," he told *Los Angeles Times* writer Carol McGraw, "I learned how to be, but not how to do." His focus now, he said, is on the Hindu practice of karma yoga—"using service to others as a path to transformation." He added with a laugh: "I had never thought of my humanity as a practice. I was too busy trying to become divine."[12]

Swami Muktananda

When Swami Muktananda Paramanansa died in 1982, one of the world's largest Eastern-oriented yoga movements, his SYDA Foundation, spiraled into administrative disarray and moral decay. But Muktananda remained one of the seminal New Age influences of the 1980s. His legacy lives on because he touched the lives of such notables as Werner Erhard, former California Governor Jerry Brown, singers Diana Ross and John Denver, musician Paul Horn, Puerto Rico-born actor Raul Julia, and actresses Marsha Mason and Olivia Hussey. Perhaps more than any other guru except Maharishi Mahesh Yogi of TM fame, Muktananda made yoga meditation accessible and fun to Westerners—particularly the Hollywood set.

To a casual observer, Muktananda was an old, brown-skinned man with a scraggly beard and tinted glasses perched on his wide nose. He habitually dressed in an orange pajama-like costume and a yellow knit cap. But to several hundred thousand devotees around the world who called him "Baba" (Hindi for daddy), he was the divine essence of the pure self—the manifestation of the God that he taught was in all of us. "God dwells within you as you; worship your Self," he said again and again as he crisscrossed the country with a message of self-renewal and established ashrams in twenty U.S. cities.

After Muktananda died, thirty devotees accused the guru of past sexual misconduct and left the movement in disgust. (Two told me firsthand details of sordid episodes in 1983.) Then Muktananda's appointed co-successors—a young Indian and his sister—had a falling out, and a struggle ensued for control of the SYDA empire. But the sister, Gurumayi Chidvilasananda, remained in charge through the South Fallsburg, New York, headquarters.

"Muktananda is still my teacher," averred a follower who would speak to me only on condition that I wouldn't reveal his name. He added: "Divinity is not the same as perfection. The whole is a perfection; the parts have defects."

Guru Maharaj Ji

In 1973, when he was fifteen years old, Indian guru Maharaj Ji claimed a following of six million, including thousands of flower-throwing young people and disenchanted counterculture dropouts. Prominent among them was antiwar protester Rennie Davis of the Chicago Seven. Devotees, called *premies*, clambered over each other to fall at Maharaj Ji's feet as he dispensed "the knowledge," or "getting it"— the "divine light" of inner peace.

His Divine Light Mission experienced meteoric growth in the early 1970s (284 U.S. centers), but donations fell off, devotees fell away, and the teenaged guru had a falling out with his mother. She objected to his marriage at sixteen to his twenty-four-year-old secretary and his ostentatious and worldly lifestyle. "In the eyes of the unregenerate," scoffed religious movements tracker Carl Raschke, "there was nothing particularly charismatic about the boy, who spoke halting English larded with clichés from the argot of hippiedom, wore natty and expensive clothes . . . rode Rolls Royces and motorcycles, and gorged himself on Baskin-Robbins ice cream."[13]

By the late 1970s the Mission in the United States had become nearly invisible and growth had all but stopped. In 1979 the Denver headquarters quietly moved to Miami

Beach, and Maharaj Ji and his wife and two children withdrew to a secluded hilltop estate in Malibu overlooking the Pacific. Now in his thirties, the Perfect Master occasionally circles the globe speaking to premies.[14]

Zen Master Rama

A more recent entrant into the guru supermarket was Frederick "Rama" Lenz, a curly haired, self-styled Zen Buddhist master who holds a doctorate in English. The laid-back Yuppie guru from Malibu mounted a massive ($850,000) advertising campaign during 1987 in major U.S. cities, announcing free public meditations, complete with free music, in rented concert halls and hotel ballrooms across the country. The ads showed a "smiling, bright-eyed Lenz, 37, dressed in a sports coat and a paisley tie, looking more like a young computer salesman than an ancient sage," recounted Katy Butler in the *San Francisco Chronicle*.[15]

But Rama Lenz abruptly canceled appearances after four former students publicly accused him "of pressuring women students into sex, giving LSD to one, and convincing others that they were possessed by demons and occult forces," the newspaper reported.

After studying under Indian mystic weight lifter Sri Chinmoy, Lenz began his career as a guru in the early 1980s in San Diego. He initially taught a Hindu meditation called "Atmananda" and the "last reincarnation of Vishnu." Later he moved to Malibu and thousands flocked to his "intensive Zen" series—which were not endorsed by any traditional Zen Buddhist teachers.

Benjamin Creme

Out of the metaphysical past of Alice Bailey's Arcane School and the Ballard's "I AM" activity, self-proclaimed way-shower Benjamin Creme appeared on the scene to announce the fulfillment of all the Messianic expectations of the world's great religions with the "reappearance of the Christ and the Masters of Wisdom." The white-haired British esotericist, author, and artist made his biggest splash in April of 1982 when his Tara Center organization took out full-page spreads in major papers worldwide declaring that "The Christ Is Here Now."

A month later, I attended a packed press conference in Los Angeles at which Creme claimed he had been singled out by "Lord Maitreya, the Christ," to inform the media that Maitreya was living in a Pakistani section of London, awaiting discovery by journalists. By early summer of 1982, Creme promised, the Christ's true identity would be revealed to everybody through a global radio-television broadcast. Then war and hunger would be forever ended and all religions unified. The *Los Angeles Times* was uninterested in dispatching me to London to find Maitreya.

Creme is still lecturing—to diminished audiences.

Swami Beyondananda

At least one guru is out to lighten up enlightenment. Swami Beyondananda, "the yogi from Muskogee," does live gigs featuring the "magical dance of Trudy Lite." The comic also specializes in tantrum yoga, speed suffering, and healing cars through autosuggestion. These spiritual practices are all discussed at "Yogi" Steve Bhaerman's one-nighters in spots like the Religious Science Creative Living Center in Orangevale, California.

Beyondananda, said to be a cross between Ram Dass and Häagen-Dazs, also has an advice column, published, among other places, in Sacramento's *Guide*, "A Calendar for the Whole Person," where I found the following typical exchanges.

Dear Swami:
What are your thoughts on reincarnation?

Ken-Adi Ring
Madison, Wisconsin

Dear Ken-Adi:
I am a firm believer in reincarnation. After all, if we're supposed to recycle, why shouldn't God? You might say I'm a born again, born again, born again Krishna and I subscribe to the born again Krishna credo, "You only go around 60 million times—so grab the gusto. . ."

Dear Swami:

How do astral projection and quantum mechanics relate?

Waylon Wall
Jerusalem, Israel

Dear Waylon:

It's simple. When you burn out a bulb on your astral projector, you find a quantum mechanic to fix it.[16]

8

Communes and Groups

You've come a long way, yogi!

Maharishi Mahesh Yogi—founder of the Transcendental Meditation Program (1957)—has indeed come a long way from the day he came West in the late 1950s to teach his popular and simplified version of Hindu meditation, later trademarked under the initials TM. The bearded, white-robed yogi, who studied under the famed Guru Dev, is founder of the Science of Creative Intelligence (1971), founder of Maharishi International University (1971), and founder of the Maharishi Technology of the Unified Field (1982).

By far the most successful and largest of the meditation groups, TM has been dubbed by author Adam Smith "the McDonald's of meditation." It offers a good basic meditation to chew on, says Smith.[1]

The TM organization and its affiliates have had lots to chew on in the intervening years since the diminutive Himalayan holy man hired PR agents, appeared on major talk shows, and courted sports, screen, and music celebrities, including the Beatles, Mia Farrow, and Joe Namath. In 1977, a federal court in New Jersey ruled—over Maharishi's strong objections—that the practice of Transcendental Meditation was really a religious exercise and therefore could not be taught in public schools. Although more than a million people had already taken the basic TM course, the decision slowed enrollments. (The courses are now taught under private auspices.)

In 1982, Maharishi announced the World Plan: The overall strategy is to set up 3,600 centers, one for each million people on Earth; each center is to have one TM teacher per 1000 people in the general population. As soon as 1 percent of the population practices TM, the world will be saved from war and strife, the yogi firmly asserts.

Meanwhile, his 700-student Maharishi International University in Fairfield, Iowa—where all students and faculty gather twice a day in the two "Golden Domes of Pure Knowledge" to meditate the TM way—is fully accredited and even offers four Ph.D. programs. Basic is Maharishi's "unified field-based education . . . of natural law, which students experience directly at the deepest level of their own intelligence."[2] TMers are promised decreased stress, increased productivity, heightened creativity, and overall peace of mind.

TM's claims to scientific substantiation have been challenged, and its "yogic flying," in which TM adherents apparently levitate from a sitting yoga position, has been debunked as nothing but a physical stunt.

Maharishi U. spokesman Mark Haviland conceded in the summer of 1987 that only "hopping" had been achieved so far, but he confidently predicted "hovering" and "actual flight" soon.[3] In any case, TM entrepreneurs in Fairfield were flying high (as we'll see in chapter 16).

While TM may be the most successful of the New Age religious groups to persist in America since the 1960s, the Hare Krishnas have been the most conspicuous—and the most resented.

Hare Krishna

"The International Society for Krishna Consciousness became for many people the symbol of the invasion of Asian religion into American life in the 1970s," observed J. Gordon Melton.[4]

With their bright saffron robes and shaved heads, chanting devotees pounded drums on street corners and hounded travelers in airports with "Back to Godhead" literature proclaiming that the transcendental bliss of Lord Krishna's paradise was the everlasting answer. Although these public displays have been replaced by more conventional lectures, fairs, and the building of ornate temples, Krishna followers still seek to realize the dream of a small holy man named A. C. Bhaktivedanta Swami Prabhupada.

When in 1965, at the age of seventy, the former pharmacist from Bengal sailed into New York Harbor on the deck of a tramp steamer, he was the sole embodiment of what burgeoned into a far-reaching fundamentalist Hindu sect. Before his death in 1977, Prabhupada had attracted as many as 10,000 hard-core disciples around the world and hundreds of thousands, if not millions, of followers. By 1981, forty Krishna temples had been established in the United States alone.[5]

Prabhupada's followers—many of them heirs of a counterculture disillusioned with materialism, and craving inner peace and awareness—embraced a whole new culture, worldview, diet, psychology, and geography foreign to most Westerners. The movement's ascetic essence is derived from accounts of Krishna's life on Earth five thousand years ago as interpreted by the Sanskrit scriptures known as the *Vedas*. Krishna consciousness aims at ending the cycle of continual birth and death caused by karma, a concept held by many New Age groups. By chanting the names of God, Krishna devotees believe they can attain spiritual bliss and finally break out of the slow and painful cycle and "go back to godhead," or Krishna.

Although Prabhupada planned for an orderly administration of the vast empire at his death, his passing provoked a leadership crisis and several abortive schisms led by guru underlings. Fewer new members were joining up in the mid-1980s, and Kirtinanda Swami Bhaktipada, head of the movement's palatial New Vrindaban Temple—a premier West Virginia tourist attraction—was investigated for arson, conspiracy, and mail fraud. He was ousted from the movement in 1987, and lesser devotees and former Krishnas were charged with crimes ranging from murder to drug running.

If TM and Hare Krishna are Indian imports, Scientology bears a definite "made in America" label.

Scientology

Scientology founder L. Ron Hubbard, a man of mystery born in Montana in 1911, became well-known for both science fiction writing and his system called Dianetics. The latter evolved into the Church of Scientology, which he incorporated in the mid-1950s.

Photos of the reclusive Hubbard, who died in 1986, hang in every Scientology center. "The face," as described by religion analysts Robert Ellwood and Harry Partin, "is fairly ordinary save for tiny, sharp eyes embedded in kindly crinkles. But from out of the mind behind those intense blue eyes has grown an initiatory procedure of fantastic complexity and effectiveness, a technique which challenges orthodox psychology, and a worldwide organization."[6]

The church of Scientology (which claims a worldwide membership of 6.5 million) offers near magical powers and the increase of mental and emotional achievement mediated through pop psychotherapy, Eastern philosophy, applied religious technology, and scientific-sounding jargon.

Hubbard, says new religions-watcher Brooks Alexander, "stripped away the gongs, incense, shaved heads and other culturally alien trappings and replaced them with business suits, electronic gadgetry and the jargon of self-improvement. At the same time, he retained the core values of the Eastern/occult worldview. Hubbard made the first systematic attempt to unite the search for self with the search for ultimate reality, and to present it in a Western technological package."[7]

Scientology, based on Hubbard's writings, teaches that all humans are *Thetans*—uncreated "gods" who are repeatedly reincarnated. But by the time they had evolved into human beings, they had forgotten who they were. Through costly counseling programs, Scientologists can eradicate the negative *engrams* accumulated from prior-life traumas and return to their true identity as "operating Thetans."

In recent years, Scientology has been immersed in legal hassles, and church operatives say enemies have infringed upon Scientology's religious freedom. In 1983, Hubbard's wife and eight other Scientologists were jailed for burglarizing offices of the IRS and other government agencies. Since then, the church has lost (and appealed) other major court cases and agreed to pay millions of dollars in out-of-court settlements.

Meanwhile, the Los Angeles-based group is pushing Hubbard's best-selling *Dianetics: The Modern Science of Mental Health*, and moving into corporate management consulting through subsidiaries WISE and Sterling Management.[8]

Other New Age human potential groups have borrowed heavily from Scientology concepts: notably, est, Lifespring, and MSIA (Church of the Movement of Spiritual Inner Awareness—pronounced "Messiah").

EST

Between 1971 and 1984, Werner Erhard, whom the *Wall Street Journal* has called "a guru of the Me generation,"[9] had enrolled nearly a half-million followers in his sixty-hour personal growth weekend training seminars. In 1985, est (Erhard Seminars Training) "underwent cosmetic changes and emerged as the Forum, designed for people who 'got it together' in the 70s and who are interested in 'making it happen' in the 80s," said sociologist Ron Enroth.[10] "Ested" personalities include Yoko Ono, Carly Simon, Diana Ross, and John Denver.[11]

The basic pattern is to jam large groups of people into one room for fifteen hours at a time with limited food and toilet breaks. Through a marathon of draconian "processes," including verbal abuse, trainees are caused to question and even dislodge their assumptions about every system of meaning. Exercises in visualization and self-hypnosis follow.

"When you get in touch with yourself . . . you will experience yourself as the creator of your own circumstance," says Erhard.[12] But Berkeley, California, psychologist Karen Hoyt analyzed est techniques and concluded they produced "a thought-reform program" resulting in "the loss of self, the loss of the human and the loss of freedom."[13]

Some of the more confrontive aspects of est have apparently been toned down in the Forum, and another 1984 Erhard spin-off, Transformational Technologies Inc., has become popular on the management training circuit (see chapter 15). But the metaphysical component still lurks just below the surface despite a "nonreligious" billing. Erhard, who began dabbling in yoga at age eleven, has said Scientology and Zen Buddhism were the most influential forces in est.[14]

Lifespring and MSIA

Lifespring, founded by John Hanley in 1974, is another human potentials and management training group that tears down the previous belief system of trainees. More than 250,000 Americans have taken Lifespring's five-day training course.

An offspring of Lifespring is MSIA, which enforces strict discipline during six-day courses. Students must not be late but cannot wear watches. They must abstain from alcohol, coffee, and sex throughout the week. Vomit bags are placed on the backs of the chairs where training is conducted.[15]

MSIA is led by the Mystical Traveler Consciousness—i.e., Sri John-Roger Hinkins, an educator-clergyman who founded the group in 1968 and an early leader in the Eckankar movement. By having "total awareness of all levels of consciousness," John-Roger "helps each person into a consciousness of his soul's perfection. . . . Such soul transcendence frees one from the wheel of incarnations."[16]

In 1984, MSIA claimed 250 centers in the United States, and Hinkins appeared regularly on national cable TV. New Age healing techniques, including "aura and polarity balancing," were a part of his related Baraka Holistic Center in Santa Monica, California. Barbara Streisand and other film personalities have boosted MSIA-related Insight Transformational Seminars.

Eckankar

There are more interconnections: MSIA adheres to the basic Eckankar teachings of the Sant Mat tradition of India. And Eckankar founder Paul Twitchell was a regular writer for a Scientology magazine, once worked for Ron Hubbard, and was among the first to achieve the Scientology level of "clear."[17]

"What is most controversial about Twitchell's involvement with Scientology, though," declares David Christopher Lane, an Eck defector turned anti-cultist, "is the fact that he blatantly *plagiarized* from L. Ron Hubbard's works."[18] Lane then provides convincing comparative samples.

Eckankar, "the ancient science of soul travel" and "astral projection," has a special connection also with India and Tibet. Twitchell, who died in 1971, claimed to have been taught by Tibetan lamas and to have been initiated by a neo-Sikh, Kirpal Singh.[19]

So maybe whatever goes around comes around. In any case, Twitchell's "rod of power" passed on to Darwin Gross, whose leadership of the growing organization ended in controversy. Meanwhile, earthly world headquarters for Eckankar's "soul travelers"—estimated to have dropped from a 1970's worldwide high of 50,000 to about 20,000—moved from Las Vegas to Menlo Park, California, and then to Minneapolis.[20] In 1981 Harold Klemp took over as the 973d Living ECK Master.

Self-Realization Fellowship

Another Hindu religious group whose popular founder brought it to Los Angeles in 1920 is the Self-Realization Fellowship, which looks to the Bible, the *Bhagavad Gita* and the *Autobiography of a Yogi* as its basic texts. Lately, the organization of the late Paramahansa Yogananda, which had forty-four U.S. centers in 1987, was pitching to New Age clientele, advertising that it teaches "scientific methods of meditation and life-energy" to harness the powers of the mind and achieve union with God in pure bliss.

Sounding very New Agey, the ad in *OMNI* magazine declared: "'Mind is the creator of everything,' explained Paramahansa Yogananda. 'If you cling to a certain thought with dynamic will power, it finally assumes a tangible outward form. When you are able to employ your will always for constructive purposes, you become the controller of your destiny.'"

In 1968, Swami Kriyananda, a former disciple of Yogananda, formed his own unique New Age community called Ananda Cooperative Fellowship. Nestled on 800 acres in the Sierra Nevada foothills northeast of Sacramento, California, the yoga-centered community unsuccessfully sought incorporation as a separate, theocratic city in 1982. It is one of the few religious and utopian communal experiments that has survived from the hippie heyday of idealistic flower children. The village of 40 homes housed 300 adults and 100 children in the summer of 1988 and was self-supporting. About 30 of its private and community-owned small businesses were thriving. Ananda members, who believe God dreamed the whole universe into temporary manifestations of nature, seek "superconscious attunement with infinite consciousness" through yoga exercises and meditation, vegetarianism, and simple, cooperative lifestyles. Kriyananda, also known as J. Donald Walters, is a prolific writer and musician-composer; he markets his books and tapes through Ananda's Crystal Clarity Publishers and Ananda satellite centers in six cities.

Sufis

Another commune within the New Age orbit is the Abode of the Message, founded by Pir Vilayat Khan of the Sufi Order. Pir Vilayat Khan conceived the Cosmic Mass to demonstrate the unity of all religions. Founder of eighty-eight Sufi centers in America, he is a respected speaker on the New Age circuit.

The syncretistic Sufis trace their roots both to Hinduism and to Muhammad, the prophet of Islam. Sufism stresses meditative techniques and dance movements (remember the whirling dervishes?) to open up the mind to cosmic dimensions and achieve union with the Absolute Being (God).[21]

The late Meher Baba, the "silent" guru who claimed to be "God personified" and made a hit with movie stars and counterculture kids of the 1960s, was firmly within the Sufi tradition, and scattered groups of "Friends of Meher Baba" persist today.[22] Baha'i, an activist faith of Persian background, began among the Sufis in the mid-nineteenth century. Enjoying a resurgence in America, Baha'i counts about 1000 U.S. Assemblies.[23]

And More

Among other communes identifying with the New Age movement are the Renaissance Community, also called the Fellowship of Friends. This reclusive metaphysical group in Northern California is led by Robert Burton, a devotee of Russian philosophers Georges Ivanovitch Gurdjieff (1872–1949) and Peter D. Ouspensky (1878–1947). There is The Farm, Stephen Gaskin's group in Summertown, Tennessee, rooted in Buddhist-Taoism. Then the movable commune of Da (Bubba) Free John, alias Franklin Jones, whose Dawn Horse Communion, then Free Communion Church, then Laughing Man Institute, then Persimmon—all located north of San Francisco Bay—was finally ensconced on Bubba's private Fijian island. And there is the 3HO Foundation (formerly the Healthy-Happy-Holy Organization), whose followers live the Sikh Dharma lifestyle of turban-wearing yoga master Yogi Bhajan. The largest 3HO concentration is in West Los Angeles, where Bhajan has his headquarters. An estimated total of 2,500 followers live in 125 ashrams and a rural retreat in New Mexico.

The Naropa Institute of Boulder, Colorado, and the Tibetan Buddhism of the late Chogyam Trungpa, Rinpoche (1939–87), should also be mentioned. Only his Vajradhatu organization—one of many among the various schools of Tibetan Buddhism established in the United State during the 1970s—has built a national network with local centers. Called *Dharmadatus*, they house several thousand students.

Unification Church

The eclectic-syncretistic Unification Church, founded by the Reverend Sun Myung Moon, received intense media attention during the 1970s and mid-1980s. The spotlight focused on controversial "Moonie" recruiting and fundraising activities, their involvement in conservative political and economic affairs, and the jailing of the North-Korea-born

Moon for tax evasion. While Moon aims to unify all religions in a restored "New Age," the group does not fit the New Age mold as easily as do other American new religions we have referred to above.

Unification Church theology reflects elements of both Oriental mysticism and traditional Christianity. But Moon's exposition of the "Lord of the Second Advent" in the group's guiding text, *Divine Principle*, is more an aberrant Christian teaching and reinterpretation of the Bible than the credo of an alternative religious movement. Devout disciples consider Moon the new Messiah of the Coming Advent who will achieve the salvation of the human race, which they believe Jesus failed to do.

The biggest theological upheaval in the church's thirty-four-year-history occurred in the spring of 1988 when Moon was reported to believe that one of his followers from Zimbabwe was the reincarnation of Moon's son, Heung Jin Nim, who was killed in an automobile accident in 1984. According to the *Washington Post*, the Zimbabwean was believed to be hearing and relaying messages from "Lord" Heung, and was traveling to church parishes worldwide, severely disciplining church members and elders by slapping and beating them.[24]

Christian Science and Mormons

While neither the Church of Jesus Christ, Scientist (Christian Science) nor the Church of Jesus Christ of Latter-day Saints (Mormons) is, strictly speaking, a product of the New Age movement, they do share common ground with present New Age thought.

Christian Science, as we discuss later, sprang from the Transcendental and New Thought movements. The Christian Science emphasis on "the overcoming of faith in matter" and "mortal mind"—and relying instead on the reality of "divine Mind"—is right in step with New Age metaphysics.[25]

Mormons insist their faith is thoroughly within the Christian tradition; and indeed, the *Book of Mormon* appears to be a kind of "Christian romance."[26] But the revelations of founder Joseph Smith (1805–44) developed in the *Book of*

Mormon were mediated through the occultic use of "seer stones." Smith said the stones were buried with the golden plates the Angel Moroni told him to unearth and translate. Jerald and Sandra Tanner of Salt Lake City, scholarly critics of Mormonism, have dug up a bonanza of historical material apparently documenting that "glass looker" Smith "not only engaged in money-digging but also . . . in the magical practice of divining with a seer stone."[27]

Mormonism's attachment to an essentially magic world-view—together with its teaching that "men may become gods" and, with many goddess wives, populate an infinity of spiritual planets—smacks of New Age esotericism rather than orthodox Christianity.

But, mysterious and exotic as the beliefs and practices of many New Age groups may be, it's hard to top the eerie phenomenon known as channeling. Let's tune in. . . .

9

Choosing a Channel

The TV camera zooms in tight on the squinting eyes and pleading lips of K. C. MacRoberts. He is beseeching viewers for large donations.

But it isn't MacRoberts speaking: It's the stilted voice of RamBash, a disembodied entity from the 27th Ray, using MacRoberts as a mouthpiece: "Indeed, that which is called money in your plane of existence is necessary in order for me to keep manifesting through the medium of television, as you call it. Putting it simply, darlin's, you create my own reality; we need $8 million from the lot of you by the end of the month of March, as you reckon it, to keep me on the air. Otherwise, blessed ones, the great Keeper of the Karma will call me home from your realm of consciousness, as it were, and recycle me into a three-toed sloth. Indeed!"

Channeling. It's yesterday's seance medium, palm reader, crystal ball-gazer, and fortune-teller dressed up in high-tech drag and often packaged by Madison Avenue.

As of this writing, there are no prime-time TV mediums or trance channelers rivaling the touted televangelists. The scene above is purely fantasy. But in New York you can flip on a locally produced cable TV program and watch dozens of amateur channel-it-yourselfers imitate big-timers like J. Z. Knight, Kevin Ryerson, and Jach Pursel.[1] And in Los Angeles, Gerry Bowman channels John the Apostle every Sunday at midnight on radio station KIEV.

Channelers—often simply called a channel—go into a trance state to establish contact with a spirit, ascended master, off-planet being, higher consciousness, or even an evolved animal entity. The channel then receives and repeats the messages and impressions from the "other side."

The channeling spectrum includes receiving information through "automatic writing," such as the Ouija board; "dictated" poetry, art, and music composition from the "mind pool" of the masters; and "physical channeling"—such things as table-tipping, levitation, and the materialization and movement of objects without physical contact.

Since the New Age channeling craze hit—with a big assist from Shirley MacLaine—these mediums have multiplied like hobbits. Mundane requests jam the ethereal wavelengths.

Maria, a California attorney, says she uses channeling to create a parking space at the courthouse.[2] The New York clients of channel Gerri Leigh ask her spirits for mink coats, BMWs, summer homes in the Hamptons, and cabs at the curbs in rush hour.[3] When Sharon Gless won an Emmy for her role in "Cagney and Lacey," she announced in her September 1987 acceptance speech that she owed her success to Lazaris, a disembodied entity channeled by Jach Pursel, the retired Florida insurance supervisor who is one of the fastest-rising channel superstars.[4] At the time, Lazaris had a two-year waiting list for private consultations—at $93 an hour.[5]

Other upscale channels:

Kevin Ryerson, the medium on MacLaine's TV miniseries whose expanding repertoire of other-worldly entities includes John, a Middle East scholar from Jesus' day, and Tom McPherson, an Irish pickpocket who served the English diplomatic corps during the Shakespearean era.

Penny Torres-Rubin, who came up to medium stardom from housewifery by channeling to the Hollywood decaf coffee-klatsch crowd. She represents a highly evolved "entity from the seventh dimension" named Mafu who last incarnated in A.D. 79 as a leper in Pompeii.

Former illustrator-designer Darryl Anka, channel of Bashar, an extraterrestrial humanoid from Essassani, a civilization roughly five hundred light-years in a future time line "in the direction of the Orion constellation."[6]

Brazilian Luiz Antonio Gasparetto, who runs a "spiritist center" for the poor in São Paulo, airs a weekly psychic TV show and claims to channel about fifty "Old Master" artists, including Renoir, Picasso, Goya, Van Gogh, and Toulouse-Latrec. They reputedly mix the colors, put them in Gasparetto's hands, and rapidly move his arms and hands over the paper or canvas while he paints furiously—with his eyes tightly shut.[7]

And there's the Rev. Neville Rowe, a graduate electrical engineer, who channels dolphins as well as Soli, an off-planet being from the Pleiades.

Two of the best-known mediums of the recent past are Jane Roberts (1929–84) and Edgar Cayce (1877–1945). Roberts's books about a highly intellectual "energy personality essence" known as Seth were a breakthrough because they were published by a respected major-market house (Prentice-Hall). Cayce, whom New Age writer Jon Klimo has called "one of the biggest stars in this unusual firmament,"[8] was idolized as "the Sleeping Prophet" by millions because he diagnosed ailments and prescribed remarkably helpful cures during a sleeping trance state. Some 30,000 case histories of his work were amassed during his lifetime. Cayce also practiced telepathy, clairvoyance, and fortune-telling, but always spoke in his own voice.

"Mediumship" dates to the Spiritualist movement of the second half of the nineteenth century. New Age enthusiasts, however, claim that trance communication has been present throughout history and that early Egyptians, Greek oracles, Moses, the Hebrew prophets, and Jesus and the Gospel writers brought forth spiritual information through channeling.

Jesus is still speaking, according to the many who channel him: "Death is the creation of humanity, not of God. This is the simple truth," he said through channel Virginia Essence.[9]

"Our Lady of the Roses"—the Virgin Mary—purportedly speaking through ultra-traditionalist Roman Catholic channel Veronica Leuken of Bayside, New York, has revealed that radical Jesuit priest Teilhard de Chardin (1881–1955) is in hell and that the late President John F. Kennedy is in purgatory "for his mishandling of the missile crisis in Cuba."[10]

The basic messages of the channeled entities exhibit a striking commonality:

- Death is unreal.
- All is One in the synergy of Deity.
- We are Divine Beings but have chosen to exist as physical humans.
- In this life there are no victims, only opportunities.
- We can control reality through the powers of Universal Mind.

"Channeled material tells us that when we die, the intact higher frequency of our nonphysical being moves on to a new realm," explains Stanley Ralph Ross, narrator on a "how-to-channel" tape. "Through channeling millions of people are discovering experiences—their own and others'—that satisfy their hunger for meaning."[11]

Ross uses the TV analogy to describe what happens in channeling: Imagine, says he, that you and all other humans are like TV stations, sending out and receiving signals, but only on channels 1 to 13. At the same time, UHF and other signals are coming in though you're not receiving them: "They're just not on a frequency you're tuned to." But if you adjusted your equipment, you could receive them. Channeling is like that, says Ross. It is receiving signals you don't normally receive with your five senses.

But who or what is sending out those signals? And how do you tune into them?

There seem to be at least six alternatives:

1. The entities are real and are telling the truth about themselves.
2. The entities are demonic and lie about their real nature.
3. The entities don't exist, and the channelers resort to fakery and/or acting to simulate their reality.
4. The entities' messages come from the intuitive, subconscious mind of the channeler.
5. The entities are the products of hallucinations and/or their messages are induced under a hypnotic state.
6. The entities are not objectively real but are a part of the "Higher Self" or what psychoanalyst Carl Jung called the "Collective Unconscious."

Checking the Channels

During nineteenth-century mediumship almost all the sources being contacted were considered to be spirits of deceased human beings.[12] There seems to be convincing evidence that some accurate information has been transmitted from beyond the grave, and that the mediums through which it was communicated could not have otherwise known about it. Psychic researcher Colin Wilson cites numerous examples in *Afterlife*.[13]

For example, he tells of a medium who passed on a message to a Professor Hyslop from a spirit calling himself William James. James, who had been a friend of the professor, had died some years earlier. The two had agreed that whoever died first should try to communicate with the other. The medium's message to Hyslop was to ask him if he remembered some red pajamas.

At first, the professor drew a blank. Then suddenly he remembered, reports author Wilson: "When he and James were young men, they went to Paris together, and discovered that their luggage had not yet arrived. Hyslop went out to buy some pajamas, but could find only a bright red pair. For days James teased Hyslop about his poor taste in pajamas. But Hyslop had long forgotten the incident. As far as he could see, there was no way of explaining the red pajamas message except on the hypothesis that it was really James who had passed it on."[14]

Other accounts from people I know and trust also seem plausible but equally difficult to prove. H. Newton Malony, director of programs integrating psychology and theology at Fuller Seminary in Pasadena, California, told me about a 1977 investigation he and several of his students conducted into the Rev. Richard Zenor and his Agasha Temple of Wisdom in Los Angeles. At the time, a spirit guide supposedly spoke through Zenor to one of Malony's students. The message apparently duplicated exactly the tone of voice, accent, and wording of terms of endearment that the student's deceased lover had used.[15]

J. Gordon Melton, author of the *Encyclopedia of American Religions*, told me he had seen and heard things that were "either genuine clairvoyance or amazing coincidences." He said these included a medium's ability to correctly state Melton's grandmother's name and the unusual circumstances of Melton's father's death. The medium, in Melton's opinion, could not have known that information before the unscheduled "reading." Nevertheless, Melton added, the reading did not offer convincing evidence of life after death.[16]

Much channeled information, however, is filled with inaccuracies or communication so vague as to be inconclusive; or if it contains verisimilitudes, it is, at best, a bit of lucky guesswork. And most channeled material is simply unverifiable, especially reports about persons being "regressed" into "past lives."

F. LaGard Smith, the Pepperdine University lawyer who wrote *Out on a Broken Limb*, was admittedly out to "get" channeler Kevin Ryerson. Smith tells of purposely misrepresenting that his mother was no longer living. Ryerson's entity "wrongly assumed the truth of that misrepresentation," Smith gloated, adding: "Wouldn't the Akashic Records [the energy records of all that has ever occurred, according to New Age belief] *know* whether or not my mother were still on the earth-plane?"[17]

Conservative Christians often equate channeled entities with evil spirits or demons. In this view, the entities are real but are lying to us.

"Impersonation is one of the central ploys in the Adversary's [Satan] inexhaustible arsenal of devious strategies," wrote cult critic Robert Burrows in the *Spiritual Counterfeits Project Journal*. [A]ttributing the 'revelations' to God or Christ himself . . . is the height of demonic hubris, a direct and brazen assault—like robbing a bank dressed up as police and Brinks security guards."[18]

Some channeled material identifies the possessors as "lower" or bad" spirits, entities waiting to gain control over human bodies or resume some form of human existence. Most channels warn that using a Ouija board can be the entry point for these entities. The voice said to speak through J. Z. Knight during the hometown prayer meeting alluded to earlier in this book identified itself as a demon named Demias, according to an alleged witness.[19]

So if all entities are demons, then sometimes they lie, sometimes they don't.

Another alternative is that channelers are perpetrating a hoax for material gain or fame, or both. James "the Amazing Randi," the magician who has debunked various faith healers and parapsychologists, summarily dismisses channels as "actors," while there is no doubt about LaGard Smith's view of channeler Ryerson: "Kevin's act is simply one of the best road shows in America." He adds: "If someone *wants* to believe that he or she has lived before it's easy to imagine it!"[20]

Then there is always the possibility that some channelers are sincere but have blurred the line between grand imagination and unclouded reality. In other words, the medium is the message.

"Perhaps they are pretending," suggested Dr. Joseph Barber, an expert on hypnosis and a psychiatrist at the UCLA Neuropsychiatric Institute in Los Angeles. "Maybe trance channeling is a form of self-hypnosis. . . . Anyone can learn to do it if you make up your mind to do it. . . . A person's wishes and beliefs and expectations play a big part."[21]

Ray Hyman, professor of psychology at the University of Oregon and a member of the Committee for Scientific Investigation of Claims of the Paranormal, said 95 percent of psychics are "not conscious frauds. Some are split personalities. Everyone has the potential. People have enough information to act out hundreds of personalities with details. Creative artists and writers have learned to tap this. Most of us haven't."[22]

In a lengthy article on channelers in the October 1987 issue of *OMNI*, Katharine Lowry tells of spending time with amiable, bearded Jach Pursel, Lazaris's channel, in Beverly Hills:

> [E]ven when Pursel is just being Pursel, he's clearly well-read, exceptionally bright, articulate and funny—a lot like Lazaris. This leads me to suspect that Lazaris is simply a "higher self" or unconscious part of Pursel's mind which he has learned to tap into. The other possibility, of course, is that he's consciously making this all up. . . . When we talk for an hour alone . . . he is friendly, relaxed, helpful, and seems genuinely modest and kind. But whenever I ask about Lazaris or the mechanics of channeling his eyes—those windows to the soul—slide this way and that.[23]

Penny Torres-Rubin, who channels Mafu, was unabashedly egotistical in her assessment of whether Mafu is a fraud. "What if I am an actress?" she said in a *Life Times* magazine interview. "Those things used to terrify me . . . because I was afraid that there was some part, a subconscious part of me, creating this. My answer to that is that if this is coming from me, then I think that I am absolutely incredible! And I'll take all the credit that they want to give me!"[24]

What about the role of intuition and the subconscious mind?

Could channeling tap into the vast resources of a shared primordial memory—the so-called Akashic Records, or the "Universal Mind"?

The theory of new religions expert Carl Raschke is that most channels, after considerable study in metaphysics and meditation techniques, attain a heightened sensitivity to their own unconscious minds. He also thinks a form of "mass hypnosis" often occurs in group channeling sessions: "A process of collective suggestion and transfer of unconscious content" takes place.[25]

Concurs channeling counselor Stanley Ross: "Much of what you receive may come from you, although it may seem to come from something other than you."[26]

The entities communicate their information by thought-transference, according to Los Angeles medium Lyssa Royal, who channels Raydia, a multi-dimensional consciousness system. "Therefore, in communicating with you, they form a link with your Higher Self (your higher consciousness, so to speak) and your Higher Self provides many of the answers that they share with you."[27]

In the view of New Ager Jon Klimo, channeling "is the growing awareness of any part of the one Being that it can access any of the rest of itself." In other words, he says, "we are all of the one Universal Being; or, as some say . . . we are God."[28]

Perhaps in the final analysis it's immaterial who or what these trendy channeled spirits are. The fact that so many people believe in them and become emotionally dependent upon their often banal and sometimes dangerous "advice" should concern us all in our most rational and lucid moments.

10

UFOs and ETIs

Brad Steiger's 107 books on psychic phenomena—with sales topping 15 million—have struck a nerve. Americans are desperately curious about such things as Unidentified Flying Objects (UFOs) and Extraterrestrial Intelligence (ETIs).

Most New Age libraries contain at least a dozen of Steiger's works, including *The Promise*, which traces the UFO connection and the "sky people"—"our cosmic cousins"—throughout history; or *The Fellowship: Spiritual Contact Between Humans and Outerspace Beings*, a "breakthrough book" picked up by major publisher Doubleday; or possibly *Aquarian Revelations: Channeling Higher Intelligence*, which tells how to work with multidimensional beings and experience a "peaceful" UFO encounter.

Many New Age channelers like Darryl Anka believe in UFOs. Anka says he first spotted Bashar, an extraterrestrial from the Orion constellation, when he (Anka) and some friends "had close, broad daylight, physical sighting of Bashar's spacecraft over Los Angeles."[1]

Ruth Norman, whom *People's Weekly* calls "the grande dame of New Age spiritualists," owns sixty-seven acres outside San Diego, where in the year 2001 she expects "33 interlocking spaceships to land, each carrying 1000 'other planetary dwellers,' ushering in the age of UNARIUS (Universal Articulate Interdimensional Understanding of Science)."[2]

Medium Patricia-Rochelle Diegels of Sedona, Arizona, who wears six giant gemstone rings on her fingers, often "sees UFOs" in people's minds during their "immortality consultations." At a November 1987 New Age workshop in San Francisco, she said she had performed more than 35,000 of the readings at $144 each—a lot of $ightings.[3]

Shirley MacLaine has put the stamp of the stars on UFOs. She believes flying saucers from the Pleiades constellation may have brought spiritual guides to Earth. And her book, *It's All in the Playing*, closes with her vision of a huge gray UFO that hovers over her head. The craft vanishes, replaced by a "spectacular ocean of liquid crystal shimmering in front of me."[4]

In *Out on a Limb*, MacLaine "sees" vehicles full of ETs which she says are found in the Book of Exodus when the Hebrew people moved out of Egypt and crossed the Red Sea (Exodus 14:19–22); she also sees a spaceship in Ezekiel's vision of the wheels (Ezekiel 1 and 10).

A lot of folks, from top government officials down, see a close encounter of the third kind as a distinct possibility. A 1987 Gallup Poll showed that 50% of Americans believe UFOs exist—the same number who think extraterrestrials are real—and one in eleven reported they had seen something they thought was a UFO.[5]

The late Margaret Mead (1901–78), one of the century's most colorful and influential anthropologists, gave a detailed rationale for UFOs in a column for the September 1974 issue of *Redbook* magazine. "Yes, there are unidentified flying objects. . . . There is no reason to deny the reality of psychic phenomena we cannot yet explain," she concluded.[6]

UFOlogy has been boosted by Stephen Spielberg films like *E.T.* and *Close Encounters of the Third Kind*, in which the outer space visitors are amiable types, wise and benevolent.

But tales of malevolence have also soared. Fantasy writer Whitley Strieber's *Communion* was high on the best-seller lists during the summer of 1987. The sinister story, which Strieber insists is true, is his account of being spirited into a spaceship by a horde of three-foot-tall aliens.

Another horror story, *Intruders*, by Budd Hopkins, details how 135 people claimed to have been abducted by extraterrestrials. Hopkins, who says he himself saw a UFO near his

Cape Cod home, found near-identical experiences among the self-proclaimed abductees. "They were abducted by small, gray men with large, almost triangular, heads, and large, black eyes. Blue lights floated above them into the spacecraft, where the creatures performed [bizarre and macabre] medical examinations on them."[7]

A typical scenario of UFO contact, pieced together from multiple accounts gathered since UFO-mania first broke out in mid-century, goes something like this:

A spaceship brings beings from another planet to investigate, save, conquer, or harass and confuse earthlings. The ETs make contact with an ordinary and often totally unsuspecting human being, usually in an isolated location.

If they are of good will, the space brothers and sisters seek to steer our civilization toward higher things. They do this by taking the earthling on board their spaceship where they communicate through telepathy, explaining the technology of the spaceship itself and space travel. Then they share their wisdom about the higher society from which they come. This "wisdom" material is often transmitted by an older man who assumes a shamanic role, or a beautiful young woman who takes on goddess proportions.

The ETs predict dire events that will overtake Earth soon because of human failures and environmental disasters caused by such things as pollution and atomic testing. These threaten life on other planets as well, they say.

The earthling is told he has been singled out for an important mission. Religious analysts Robert Ellwood and Harry B. Partin round out the scenario. Success of the mission "is crucial, for it will allow earthlings to avert catastrophe and to live in peace and plenty. The contactee initiates a campaign giving lectures and writing books in order to get the message across, although he is certain to be greeted with skepticism and ridicule, for he has little or no proof of his encounter with 'saucerians.'"[8]

Just before the amazed and bewildered earthling is released to terra firma once again, his hosts promise they will return and that he will be their channel for further communication.

Although some UFO groups have obviously been influenced by Theosophy as well as fundamentalist Christian "rapture" theology, most UFO buffs reflect what Ellwood and Partin call "a new and direct discovery of symbols of mediation in the fabric of American life. The wise ones come as American Indians, Spirit Doctors, departed relatives, or from futuristic technology."[9]

Messages from outer space also seem to fall into a recognizable pattern. According to Brad Steiger, George King of the Aetherius Society, and other UFOlogists:

1. We are not alone in the universe. It is egocentric to think that Planet Earth is the only inhabited sphere in the vast cosmos. Highly cultured beings, who are light years ahead of us spiritually and scientifically, inhabit other planets.
2. All things are interconnected and interrelated; what affects one, affects all.
3. We are poised for a quantum leap forward on both the biological and spiritual levels. (This is also a teaching of Harmonic Convergence, which we will explore in the next chapter.)
4. The shifting of these energy fields will not be without pain, stress, and change. We are entering the "last days"; the Age of Aquarius is the "Age of the Apocalypse."
5. Cosmic intelligences have come via UFOs to guide us into the New Age, teaching us to rise to higher levels of consciousness. The ETs are aware this will cause birth pangs, but once reached, this higher state will only be the beginning of a golden age of peace and prosperity.
6. Death is an illusion, merely a doorway to another existence.

George King, the Englishman who is the leading light of the Los Angeles-based Aetherius Society, claims to have been contacted by "Master Jesus" and a multitude of space intelligences. He predicts a "New Master" will come "shortly and openly . . . in a Flying Saucer."[10]

King has also devised "Spiritual Energy Batteries," which he claims are able to store energy from prayers for later discharge through "specialized radionic equipment . . . at the right Karmic moment . . . in the event of catastrophes. . . .

Since 1978, every Sunday morning, during a Spiritual Push, a certain amount of the Prayer Power energy contained in our Batteries is discharged through our Spiritual Energy Radiator and manipulated by Satellite No. 3."[11]

The Aetherius Society has branches throughout the world and a College of Spiritual Sciences in London.

Smaller UFO groups have also emerged, including Gabriel Green's Amalgamated Flying Saucer Clubs of America and the Urantia Foundation. Then there is the Bo and Peep cult, sometimes called "the Two." In the mid-1970s this mysterious couple proclaimed that in order to escape coming catastrophe, believers were to sell everything, desert family and friends, and hang out with Bo and Peep until spaceships descended and sucked them all up into an astral vortex of safety.

So what about these giant spaceships and gray-skinned spacelings? The scientific community remains skeptical of both, and the U.S. government officially denies the existence or danger of UFOs. Not all officials agree, however.

True UFO believers accuse the feds of a cosmic Watergate conspiracy. They say this cover-up suppresses the results of a number of military and space agency investigations in the late 1940s, 1950s, and 1960s.

Several years ago Peter Gerston, a New York criminal lawyer, sued the government under the Freedom of Information Act and won. Based on the several hundred pages of UFO documents he was awarded, Gerston said he could "go into a criminal court at this moment ... and conclusively prove that UFOs exist."[12]

Other UFO buffs, when asked for evidence of UFO claims, cite the existence of ancient structures like the Great Pyramid, the Mayan ruins, and Stonehenge. Modern technology can't duplicate those feats of engineering today, they say, thus proving that a higher civilization than our own built them. And, points out Irving Hexham, religious studies professor at Calgary University, archaeologists can't figure out the purpose of these structures, which UFO defenders say "only becomes clear when we see them in terms of space travel."[13]

Once these other-civilization myths are accepted as fact, UFOs are also believable. They are the chariots of the gods.

The UFO flap first lifted off in 1947 when Idaho businessman Ken Arnold, while piloting a private plane over the Cascade Mountains, said he spotted nine gleaming discs racing along at speeds of 1000 miles an hour near Mount Rainier. Arnold told a newspaper editor that the objects moved "like saucers skipping across water"; the wire story that went round the world and ignited public excitement called them "flying saucers."

Martin Gardner, a fringe-science debunker who writes for the *Skeptical Inquirer*, says forty years have gone by "without finding a single nut or bolt from a flying saucer."[14] Unverified sightings and contacts and a few fuzzy photos have fallen far short of the hard data scientists demand.

As in the supposed instances of communications from the dead, a minority of cases evade explanation: These are sightings that cannot be attributed to misperception of *known* natural occurrences. Indeed, the content of UFO messages seems nearly identical to that received through the centuries by mediums and mystics.

Some conservative Christian groups believe UFOs and ET contacts are caused by demonic activity (the same explanation they give for channeled entities)—what cult-watcher David Fetcho referred to as "demonic spirits which have gained the power to actually perform materializations in the physical realm."[15]

Meanwhile, many UFOlogy advocates have switched to an untestable view: UFOs are "ghostlike things from some higher plane of reality, perhaps illusions created in our minds by alien superbeings."[16]

John Keel, a UFO researcher who claimed to be an agnostic, noted that "over and over again, witnesses have told me in hushed tones, 'You know, I don't think that thing I saw was mechanical at all. I got the distinct impression that it was *alive*.'"[17]

As long ago as 1959, psychoanalyst Carl Jung published his controversial but insightful book, *Flying Saucers: A Modern Myth of Things Seen in the Skies*. Its thesis was that UFOs were not physical craft but "visionary rumors" that had psychological and religious, rather than interplanetary, significance.[18]

So we are again back to square one: Who or what causes UFOs and ETI? Is anybody out there? Do we have company?

Are otherworldly visitors who have transcended the known laws of physics—*extradimensionals*—hovering in our midst, occasionally blipping into dimensions we can see and measure?

Or is the elusive mystery truly in the mind of the beholder?

11

Harmonic Convergence

harmonic: in agreement with each other
convergence: to come together at one point

It was billed as "a planetary operation." The "cosmic trigger" would be pulled when 144,000 "rainbow" humans created a "human battery through resonant attunement" along a psychic grid of earthly acupuncture points. The goal: world peace and harmony.

The faithful rallied on August 16 and 17, 1987, at more than 350 "sacred sites"—from New Mexico's Chaco Canyon and California's Mount Shasta to Machu Picchu, Peru, and the Great Pyramids in Egypt; from 83rd and Central Park West in Manhattan and Haleakala Crater in Maui to the Temples of Delphi in Greece and Stonehenge in England—all to "synchronize the Earth with the rest of the galaxy."

Harmonic Convergence founding father Jose Arguelles promised massive UFO sightings as well as "great, unprecedented outpourings of extraterrestrial intelligence that will be clearly received."[1]

As it happened, however, there were no official sightings of UFOs, and no ETIs were known to have landed during the forty-eight-hour extravaganza of worldwide humming, chanting, dancing, hugging, and hand-holding at Harmonic Convergence "be-ins." Turnouts at what had been hailed as the

"Woodstock of the '80s" were considerably less than predicted (the worldwide total was estimated at 20,000).

But predictions can always be adjusted in retrospect. A month later, Arguelles, a Colorado art historian, amateur archaeologist, and author of *The Mayan Factor: Path Beyond Technology*, declared: "The timing was exquisitely correct. When Woodstock happened, the time was absolutely perfect. There was a juncture of different energies occurring for the Harmonic Convergence. Whether people understood it or not, they felt the signal—it was on the level of when a species gets a signal to change its migration pattern. The message is that ultimately peace will come through [and we will] return to a respect for the Earth and the ways of nature."[2]

The media sensed the signal for sure. Suddenly Harmonic Convergence grabbed front-page attention across the land. It was written up in the *Wall Street Journal*, satirized in Gary Trudeau's "Doonesbury" cartoons ("B.D." called it "moronic convergence ... sort of a national fruit loops day. Lots of windchimes ... [and] a crafts fair"), and put down as the "maximum bummer" by *People's Weekly*.[3] Talk-show host Michael Jackson suggested wryly that it would be better if 144,000 New Agers "donated one hour a week to work with the homeless."[4]

The Arguelles vision for worldwide resonance came into focus on December 4, 1983, when he was motoring down Wilshire Boulevard in Los Angeles to return a rental car: *At sunrise on August 16, 1987, 144,000 people would gather to participate in "ritualistic surrender" to the Earth.* By early 1987 Arguelles had fleshed out the dream: His book speaks about a confluence of astronomical and chronological phenomena making August 16 and 17 an unprecedented "turning point" in human history.

This would be "the first Mayan be-in for—well, for a long time," he told *Los Angeles Times* writer Dick Roraback.[5] "Kind of sexy. We represent the hot, luminous tip of a galactomagnetic vortex."

The convergence, Arguelles elaborated, was lined to Mayan and Aztec calendars, and the 144,000 convergers (which interestingly corresponds to the 144,000 elect servants of God described in the seventh chapter of the biblical book of Revelation), were needed to "create a field of trust, to ground the new vibrational frequency." The Mayans, according to Arguelles, were really extraterrestrials.

The Aztec calendar, with thirteen cycles of heaven and nine of hell, came to an end on August 16, 1987, according to Arguelles—the date he said Aztecs had circled on their calendars for the second coming of Quetzalcoatl, the god of peace. According to Hopi Indian legend, that was also to be the day 144,000 enlightened Sun Dance teachers were to "dance awake" the rest of humanity. And, according to Arguelles, who holds a Ph.D. in art history from the University of Chicago, the time was also ripe because on convergence weekend, nine planets were aligned in an unusual configuration called a grand trine.

Finally, the Mayans' "great cycle," which runs from 3113 B.C. to 2012 A.D., is nearing an end. This "galactic beam 5,125 years in diameter through which the planet passes" will phase out in 2012 and we'll slip into a "galactic synchronization phase," in Arguellean lingo. Exactly twenty-five years before that—August 16, 1987—was the critical "cosmic trigger point when we shift gears or miss the opportunity" to save humanity through "vibrational toning."[6]

As this cycle draws to a close, to spin out the Arguelles agenda, humans are to launch a new world order. By 1992, he wrote: "[T]he phase shift transiting civilization from a military state of terror to a de-industrialized, decentralized, post-military planetary society will be complete at least in its foundations. Present governmental and political structures will by and large be replaced by vast numbers of bioregional local cells. Information will be ... presented as *edu-tainment*: video and ritual participation that informs as much as it affords pleasure."[7]

Some, like Detroit astrologer and New Age bookstore owner Bob Thibodeau, envision an age of cosmic communications as well: "The possibility is there now for anyone to receive a personal WATS line to their own god or goddess," he said enthusiastically.[8]

But Harmonic Convergence drew instant fire from those who didn't groove on getting it together with their divine sparks.

Paul Kurtz, a philosopher at the State University of New York at Buffalo called Harmonic Convergence a "non-event

. . . a hodgepodge. . . . It's like the ancient Hopi rain dance. The only thing that will bring on rain is if enough Hopis sweat, the water will condense."

The Hopis themselves weren't having any truck with Harmonic Convergence, thank you, and Mayanist Rosemary Joyce, assistant director of the Peabody Museum for Harvard University, said Arguelles's Mayan theories were "truly out to lunch. And I'm being polite."[9]

"Summer madness," opined James Cornell of the Harvard-Smithsonian Center for Astrophysics.

"It's really crazy to extrapolate from the Mayan and other mesoamerican traditions," added Berkeley anthropologist John Graham. "It's a game that has become popular with amateur archaeologists."

New Age sympathizers, for the most part, were only slightly less critical of the wobbly foundations of Harmonic Convergence.

Sy Safransky, editor of *The Sun*, a "magazine of ideas," said Arguelles struck him as "a brilliant trickster who delightedly mixes cosmic wisdom and whimsy, kneeling before the mysteries with a rascally twinkle in his eye."[10] Safransky was kinder toward those who were drawn to the gatherings: "I don't question the deep longing," he editorialized, "the wish to reach out to others in the gathering darkness of a troubled time, the yearning for communion and for a resurrection of hope. But as an event . . . it represented the worst kind of spiritual showmanship. Elitist, flamboyant, bewitchingly unreal, it parodied the New Age better than any satirist."[11]

But even "If all these Second Coming scenarios are nothing but metaphorical spurs to get us to live as if they were true," New Age votary Marilyn Ferguson told *Wall Street Journal* reporter Meg Sullivan, "they can be an inspiration to get our act together."[12]

Jean Callahan, a onetime editor of the *New Age Journal*, rose well before dawn to celebrate the Harmonic Convergence on Mystery Hill in the southern New Hampshire Woods. "There was an undeniable feeling of peace and joy in that gathering," she said, then wondered aloud whether expectations have anything to do with creating reality.

"Isn't it better," she concluded, "for us to expect a new age to dawn, an age that will bring us from hunger and ignorance and war to peace and plenty and tranquility? Isn't it better for us to work and hope for that than simply to live our lives believing in nothing at all?"[13]

Believing in a myth, however, is something else again. As Safransky pointed out in his editor's note, the linchpin of Arguelles's Harmonic Convergence is the theory of the Hundredth Monkey, which suggests that when enough members of a species notice a new idea, it triggers a change in the consciousness of the entire species.

To Arguelles, the 144,000 individuals linked together through "resonant attunement" represented "the minimum human voltage to leap the imagination" of 550 million persons, or 11% of the total world population. This, said he in obfuscatory language, is the "minimum critical mass of humanity" needed for "the significant turn-around stage for establishing the infrastructure of a new world order."[14]

So how, in Arguelles's arcane reasoning, was he making monkeys out of convergers?

The Hundredth Monkey theory is based on a 1953 study of a troop of macaque monkeys on the Japanese island of Koshima. To attract the apes and thus make them easier to observe, they were given sweet potatoes. Before eating them, Imo, one of the female monkeys, began washing the dirt and sand off the potatoes by dunking them in the sea; soon her playmates and mother learned this trick. According to researcher Lyall Watson, after a certain critical number of the macaques—for sake of example, he said it was 100—had copied this behavior, suddenly *all* the monkeys in the colony began the practice. Apparently they had crossed a new threshold, or achieved a "critical mass."

The habit then seemed to spread spontaneously in a kind of miracle to colonies on other islands and even the Japan mainland, according to Watson's account in his 1978 book, *Lifetide*.[15]

This tale and its implications were so catchy and persuasive, said Ravi Dykema, writing in Colorado's New Age-related publication, *Nexus*, that it spawned a million-copy bestseller (*The Hundredth Monkey* by Ken Keyes), a film, and three articles in semi-scientific journals.

Ever since, New Age social-change leaders have been using the myth as though it were scientific evidence, drawing upon it to support their theory that when awareness of an idea reaches the critical level, it spreads exponentially and becomes universal.

But Watson, who also wrote on occult themes, was guilty of faking his findings, and journalists eventually blew the whistle on his monkeyshines.

"It is a metaphor of my own making," admitted Watson in the fall 1986 issue of the *Whole Earth Review*, "based . . . on very slim evidence and a great deal of hearsay. I have never pretended otherwise."[16] Only a few of the primates washed potatoes; the practice never spread to a whole colony, let alone unrelated colonies, according to primatologist Masao Kawai.[17]

Quite aside from the bogus nature of the Hundredth Monkey motif, if something becomes "true" for a "critical mass" of people, does that make it true for *everyone*? The inference is that when a myth is shared by large enough numbers of people, it becomes a reality. More likely, suggests Tim Farrington, "it simply becomes a widely shared myth."[18]

Myth taken as truth can be scary indeed. The hundredth Nazi "monkey" believed Hitler's super-race myth. The "final solution" had reached critical mass.

The rest is history.

12

Crystal Consciousness and Pyramid Power

If the cross is the classic symbol of Christianity, the crystal is the quintessential talisman of the New Age.

The crystal-conscious hang the rocks of ages around their necks and suspend them from their ceilings; they wear them on their fingers and in body pouches; they place them on their coffee tables and window ledges and around their pets' necks; they stash them in their pockets, purses, and briefcases; drop them in their toilet tanks and bathtubs; affix them to their carburetors and bedposts; and use them for meditating and relaxing, focusing energy, and finding soul mates.

Some true believers even drink powdered rock crystals in an energizing elixir dubbed the "gem and tonic." And they want you to know that crystals can cure toothaches, allergies, face wrinkles, and toenail fungi.

All that, the proponents say, is possible because crystals molecularly can develop shapes in harmony with the internal structure of the human body, thereby helping us amplify and balance our energies.

New Agers—and a lot of other people, too—are fond of quartz crystals. They come in sizes minuscule to mammoth (up to a ton or more) and they can be as clear as water (preferred by many), milky or smoky, or dazzling shades of rose, blue, and violet. Gemstone favorites also sell well these days at psychic fairs, trendy boutiques, and New Age bookstores. The sought-after baubles include amethysts, rubies, emeralds, sapphires, topaz, onyx, jade, lapis lazuli, tourmaline, and moldavite, a translucent, green meteorite gem—and, of course, diamonds. Some New Agers even have an obsession with obsidian.

You don't need a crystal ball to see that all this demand has pushed up the price of gemstone jewelry and crystals like . . . well, like magic. (We'll take a closer look at this commercial angle in chapter 15.)

Crystals and their alleged mystic properties were known and taught about in Hindu scriptures thousands of years ago, said Swami Sivasiva Palani, editor of *Hinduism Today*.[1] Precious minerals played an important role in the religious practices of biblical times as well, and figured prominently in the pagan rites of astrology.

Though a waggish critic proclaimed the New Age fascination with crystals "an epidemic of lost marbles," the undeniable beauty and alleged special powers of the hexagonal shapes of silicone dioxide have glittered in the eyes of the stars as well as lesser lights.

A veritable cache of crystals was on parade at the 1987 Academy Awards—not surprising, given their popularity among such celebrities.

Actress Jill Ireland wears a crystal necklace and ring and keeps crystal clusters on the tables and in the gardens of her Malibu and Los Angeles homes. She first meditated with pieces of quartz following her mastectomy when her doctor recommended the therapy to reduce stress.

"I'm not saying crystals cure cancer, but when you have the disease, your peace of mind is damaged as well, and that's where they work for me," she told *Los Angeles Times* writer Carol McGraw.[2]

Singer Tina Turner reportedly holds a crystal for a few moments when she's on tour and enters a strange hotel room. The properties of the crystal seem to calm her and purge the loneliness.

Shirley MacLaine wears quartz pendants, and her solid-gold triangular pendant is registered "No. 7" by the firm that will see *you* one just like it for $250.[3] Bandleader Herb Alpert loves his 750-pound slab of quartz which he bought at a Manhattan fossil and mineral shop. And Alan Talansky, owner of a Manhattan investment company, explained the therapeutic comfort he feels radiating from the 600-pound quartz that sits on a lighted pedestal in a corner of his office: "When I'm in a big hassle, I turn and look at this thing that has been around for millions of years, and it makes the problems seem less."[4]

It's true that quartz has been around a long time; it is, in fact, the most common mineral on the planet, comprising about 12% of the Earth's crust. Yet rock power has dug its own substratum within the New Age movement.

The inventory of titles on crystal consciousness at the Bodhi Tree, one of Southern California's best-known metaphysical bookstores, doubled to forty in just six months between 1986 and 1987. The Whole Life Expo shows, which in years past had only a handful of crystal dealers, now limit the number because of overcrowding.

Joan's Crystals in Venice, California (where you get a free crystal just for dropping by), sells "gourmet crystals at fast-food prices." Not far away is the home of Abraham's Atlantia Quartz Crystal Temple Bell Bowls, which come in five sizes and a variety of tones and are produced from pure quartz-crystal sand. The bowls give off good vibes and ring well at the cash register ($150 up, mallets not included). "Fill a room, fill a canyon, fill a universe" with the dulcet tones, sounds an advertising flyer.

In late 1987 Abraham was also creating "crystal wizard's hats which theoretically raise your consciousness and intelligence with cone energy. It's the same principle as the dunce cap," he said, "a tool to make you smarter."[5]

Abraham is no dummy; he's also been tapping into knowledge about "sacred geometry" from a pyramidologist-mystic. Together, they make quartz pyramids with superpowerful paranormal properties. The angle is the age-old belief that the pyramid form emits magnetic energy that can be harnessed to control events.

Ramtha, you may remember, first came to channeler J. Z. Knight through pyramid power. Knight tells one version of the story (it differs somewhat from other accounts she has given in media interviews) on a videotape distributed to her followers. She began placing small pyramids of different colors and sizes throughout her home, she says, and was amazed when a pyramid was able to create a "petrified cockroach." Then one day in 1978 she decided to hold a polka-dotted pyramid to her brain. The results were immediate. An entity appeared in her kitchen, saying, "I am Ramtha, the enlightened one. I have come to help you over the ditch. I have come to teach you to be a light unto the world."[6]

But Ramtha's not the only pyramid scheme.

"Pop-together" open-frame portable pyramids kits can be purchased for under $100 from Universal Mind, complete with a compass for proper alignment with magnetic north. According to assorted pyramid promos, the objects are acclaimed for such things as sharpening razor blades, stimulating exceptional plant growth, purifying water and killing bacteria, preserving and dehydrating foods, mellowing inexpensive wines, lowering electric bills, heightening awareness, raising vibrational levels, and amplifying thought, meditation, and astral projections. (And, I suppose, we should add petrifying cockroaches.)

What about these claims? As usual, the answer is cloudy rather than crystal clear.

Scientists know that tapping or squeezing a crystal produces a minute electrical charge, called the piezoelectric effect. The compression forces the negative and positive ions together, creating the tiny current which flows in one direction; when the pressure is released, the ions return to their original position, giving off a charge flowing in the opposite direction. This ability has been harnessed by industry, particularly in the field of electronics.

From the simple quartz crystal "cat's whisker" radios that some of us remember assembling when we were children, to crystal-controlled frequencies, computers, watches, lasers, and the amplification of phonograph recordings, the crystal's vibrational constant is highly valuable.

So, wrote Jake Page in *OMNI* magazine, "it does not seem too great a leap of imagination to believe that a crystal could respond piezoelectrically to the electric field of a human being, augmenting such signals or somehow restoring a distorted (diseased) field to harmony and balance."[7]

Except for one thing: The crystal's current only flows during "deformation or recovery," says Page; constant pressure produces no continuous current. And any current produced is minutely weak, with almost no amperage.

It seems unlikely that anything more exciting, electrically speaking, could come from a crystal than one could get from a tiny squeeze-type flashlight cell. But even if a perceptible current were generated, how could that influence health, happiness, or the future?

When New Agers say that crystals correctly synchronized, or "programmed," to the body vibrations of their owners can enable them to tap into past lives and future events, earth scientists sputter.

Anthony R. Kampf, curator of minerals and gems at the Los Angeles County Museum of Natural History, says: "With people assigning metaphysical properties to certain minerals, it's shades of the Dark Ages, when there was a certain amount of mysticism associated with minerals. . . . I can see a lot of people out there who have become quite enamored with certain minerals to which they are assigning these properties, which in scientific terms, the minerals don't have."[8]

"It's as close to poppycock as you can get," added Samuel Adams, a director of the Geological Society of America and head of the Department of Geology and Geological Engineering at the Colorado School of Mines.[9]

But crystal devotees leave no stone unturned.

Quartz miner Jimmy Coleman first beamed his light on a gigantic "super crystal" in 1972 as he dug into a cavern sixty-five feet deep in his mine in the Ouachita Mountains of Arkansas. An ancient earthquake had dislodged and exposed what he considered to be the rarest crystal in the world. Standing thirty-nine inches high and weighing seven hundred pounds, the quartz beauty was perfectly formed and milky white. Sensing a mysterious destiny, Coleman wrested the single-pointed "Earthkeeper" (so called because it is purported to possess a remarkable protective power and knowledge) to the surface and stored it.

Then, in July 1987, Almitra Zion, a "scout" for the Saiva Siddhanta Church, a Hindu group based on the island of Kauai, trekked to Arkansas in search of a crystal she said she had seen in a vision. She found it at Coleman's mine— although he had never told anyone about finding the behemoth crystal, according to a monk at the Hindu monastery near Kauai's famed Fern Grotto. The scout persuaded Coleman to sell the rare crystal, and on Harmonic Convergence

Day (August 16, 1987) it was installed in Kauai's San Marga temple.

Light focused from a laser beam was "sanctifying" the crystal, the orange-robed monk told me during a visit in May 1988. The Earthkeeper, which the faithful believe is a "planetary knowledge storage device," was to be enshrined as the main icon of the San Marga sanctuary, overlooking lush meditation gardens above the Wailua River. The stone will be "adored as the . . . naturally formed mark of God Siva," the monk said.[10]

"The worshiper receives the vibration field of this crystal and attunes to it," he continued as the pungent aroma of incense wafted through the temple. "It is God pervading and being all souls, all universes in the rarefied psychic vibration it constantly radiates. It is God unmanifest in its . . . image of the undefinable Absolute. It is the type of awesome behold-ing that dilates the eyes' pupils while the mind stills into its own superconscious depths seeking to fathom what it sees."

New Age practitioners also consider smaller slivers of mineral Earth to have equally awesome and wondrous properties.

Brett Bravo, a pleasant lady who speaks in soothing tones and instructs her clients to place crystal jewelry on specified acupuncture meridians of their bodies for healing, claims stones heal through "the tuning fork effect." Crystals and people both have electromagnetic fields around them deter-mined by their vibratory rates, says the Solana Beach, California, parapsychologist.

"The crystal or gemstone is the first tuning fork and transmits its vibration to the human being as the receiving tuning fork that begins to vibrate at the same frequency as the crystal. This is the healing/harmonizing effect!"[11]

If this is really so, why not use manufactured tuning forks?

Retired IBM scientist Marcel Vogel, who has studied crystals as well as less exotic subjects like fiberoptics, looks to mysticism for the answer. He has set up a million-dollar lab in San Jose to find out whether cut crystals can accomplish such feats as easing arthritic pain or purifying water. He believes a "divine" force *like* electromagnetism operates—but in a different plane—and crystals can help align that energy. He also thinks patterns of this force are stored in bones, and that vibrations from crystals can replace a bad pattern.[12]

However, since scientific inquiry, as we now know it, cannot measure spiritual or divine energies, any objective proof or crystal healing of pyramid power eludes us.

Materials Engineer Lawrence Jerome, of the Committee for the Scientific Investigation of Claims of the Paranormal, concluded that "the energies and powers they claim to use and capture in crystals have nothing to do with the everyday electromagnetic, chemical, or other energies we ordinary humans are familiar with."[13]

Popping a crystal in your pocket may make you feel lucky—like rubbing a rabbit's foot. Your anxieties might even melt away if you clutch the crystal's smooth, angular surface and think positively.

But if very much is wrong with you, better call the doctor.

13

Native Americans and Shamans

A tall young man in jeans and a fringed buckskin jacket holds a football-sized quartz crystal, pale purple and translucent, above his head. Peering through his small round gold-rimmed glasses, he gazes past the crystal into the misty gray sky and offers a prayer to the Great Spirit. Then he kneels and places his special rock on the rim of a large circle marked on the grass.

Nearly a hundred other participants carefully position similar stones along the perimeter of the sacred medicine wheel as they sing, "The dawning of a new time is coming." The ceremony is over. Just in time! The skies open in a drenching downpour, and the worshipers run for cover.

Medicine wheels of stone once spread across the North American continent. Constructed by the original native inhabitants, these wheels were ceremonial centers, high energy areas where the people sought knowledge and sensed the forces of the Earth and the cosmos.

In 1980, Sun Bear, a Chippewa Indian teacher and medicine chief, had a vision that medicine wheels should return as places for teaching, sharing, and "channeling love and healing energy to the Earth Mother."

On Halloween 1987, I was one of several hundred people—a mixture of ages and races, Indians and New Agers—who attended a Medicine Wheel assembly in Southern California's Malibu Mountains. This was the twenty-fourth two-day event of its kind sponsored by Sun Bear's teaching and healing community, Bear Tribe. Tucked away in the wooded hills of eastern Washington, Bear Tribe is a center for publishing, organic gardening, and the training of contemporary medicine men and women.

"This modern Medicine Wheel gathering," explained Singing Pipe Woman, director of the gathering, "brings together Native American medicine people, Hawaiian kahunas, and other sacred teachers to share their traditional philosophies, ceremonies, and prophecies." Added Sun Bear, a friendly hulk of a man who has been a stunt man and a consultant for western films: "You begin to realize your interconnectedness with the Earth and with all other life."

Sun Bear's medicine wheel consists of thirty-six stones (not counting those placed around the perimeter by participants); each stone represents a part of the universe. The ceremony begins by smudging, a purification ritual for those approaching the sacred wheel. Pungent smoke from burning herbs such as sage and sweetgrass is wafted around each person by an attendant who waves an eagle feather back and forth over the incense as it smolders in an iridescent abalone shell.

Next, participants make prayer "ties" by placing pinches of tobacco into small colored cloth squares and wrapping them with string. The ties are hung around the edge of the circle, with the four colors segregated according to the directions of the compass. Thirty-six preselected participants enter the wheel, one at a time, and honor the powers that each of the stones represents. After blessing the stones with cornmeal, participants "become" their power by acting out its representation—for example, "coyote the trickster," or "the frog clan" (water). Sun Bear leads off by placing a buffalo skull in the center of the wheel to represent the Creator, the central power object and the "hub of the universe." The colorful ceremony is topped off with singing, dancing, drumming, and chanting.

Sun Bear is one of an increasing number of modern-day medicine men and women—*shamans*—who combine reverence for the circle of life and traditional native healing methods with New Age technologies and assumptions.

The way of the shaman (pronounced SHAH-maan) is spiraling beyond the Native American circle, however. For couched inside this magical worldview is a sophisticated and powerful cosmology that appeals to spiritually adventuresome Americans who seek transcendence. Many want "something a little closer to home than, say, Tibetan gong meditation."[1]

I first became aware of the resurgence of Native American tribal religions in 1985 when I was researching a story about the clash of foresters and Indians in the rugged Six Rivers National Forest of Northwestern California.

I discovered that ceremonial sites for traditional religious dances, long unused, were being reconstructed at spots with exotic names like Ishi Pishi Falls, Weitchpec, and Kota-Mein. The latter, in Karuk language, means "center of the world." In the summer of 1984, the Yuroks—for the first time since 1939—held the sacred Jump Dance, part of the tribe's World Renewal ceremonies intended to stabilize the Earth and preserve the human race from catastrophe and disease.

Some Native American youth, formerly embarrassed by their Indian heritage, are now seeking to reestablish their cultural and religious roots. Part of that quest involves trips into the high country wilderness to "receive power" in visionary experiences. Those in training fast and meditate in sacred spots like Medicine Mountain and Doctor Rock, where their ancestors talked to the "Great Spirit" and prepared to be medicine women and men.

The crisis came when logging interests wanted to develop paved roads through these sacred sites, forcing local tribes to consider ways to preserve Indian identity and religious practice. It also awakened the long-slumbering beat of the primitive American medicine drum.[2]

"The outer rituals may have been lost, but the knowledge wasn't; it's still within the vibrant nature of this land," Jack Norton, a Hupa Indian dancer and professor of Native American Studies at Humboldt State University, told me during a visit in his Indian-style home in Hoopa, California.

Many Indians believe these ceremonies, practiced thousands of years before the first contact with the white man, were initiated by prehuman spirits, or "Beforetime People," who inhabited the world and brought all living things and cultures to mankind. These elaborate rites, taught by the "Immortals," were repeated in precise fashion by priests and "spiritual specialists" in ritual centers scattered along the steep canyons of the Klamath, Trinity, and Salmon rivers near the California-Oregon border.

Other tribes throughout America have remarkably similar traditions. In many, the death and rebirth of the world are reenacted by building sacred structures, such as dance arenas and underground sweat lodges, and by creating sacred fires, rock walls, and medicine wheels related to the acquisition of power by shamans. Noted ethnologist Mircea Eliade has described these individuals as "technicians of ecstasy and the sacred."[3]

Norton told how seekers of "mystical visions" open themselves to "cosmological forces" in high country training, often fasting and dancing for hours at a time while shouting to the "spirits": "Sometime during that time on the mountain, there will be a visitation, a confirmation. A song might come to you on the wind, and this, though yours, could be given for the healing of the tribe. . . . If you are very fortunate, a white [albino] deer would come before you, or a pileated woodpecker."[4]

Many anthropologists and historians of religion see these rites as an integral part of a Western society that has teetered on the edge of extinction, and which, like the condor, must be saved. Indian artifacts serve as "a hidden symbol of a raped and decimated culture," says Jon Magnuson, a Lutheran campus pastor and cochairman of the Native American Task Force of the Church Council of Greater Seattle. It is a symbol that raises questions "about the price we have paid to reduce religion to art, spirit to craft, ceremonial mask to museum display."[5]

In recent years various church bodies have confessed participation—much of it unconscious—in the past destruction of Native American religions and the forced assimilation of Indians into white culture. During his September 1984 swing across Canada, Pope John Paul II told a group of Indians near Quebec City of his concern for native peoples and urged them to preserve their cultural identity. The message followed a papal letter to Canadian tribal peoples asking forgiveness for the insensitivity and presumption of generations of missionary effort.

The rise of Indian tribal self-consciousness coupled with

the vogue of penitence by conscience-stricken non-Indians for sins of exploitation and neglect comes at a propitious time for the New Age movement. For affirming native spirituality is more than the "call to justice" envisioned by Magnuson.[6] It is also the belief that the secret power of the high places has not passed away but only awaits the New Age we are now entering.

But, as Robert Ellwood and Harry Partin point out in *Religious and Spiritual Groups in Modern America*, the spiritual affinity the New Age culture feels with Native Americans is not a "new primitive shamanism" but "a rediscovery of certain motifs of shamanism as effective counters to the values of a technological, rationalistic culture in historical time. . . . The new shaman's role is to serve as charismatic center of a cultus, around which a new symbolic cosmos, and ultimately transformed world (through processes really mystical or apocalyptic rather than historical), will form itself."[7]

New Age shamans include Carlos Castaneda's Yaqui Indian sorcerer-warrior Don Juan, who imitates many of the attributes of the age-old shamanistic lifestyle. The largely fictitious Don Juan testifies that a warrior must be an expert in visions and obscure arts, and he must contend with the mysterious energies and dangers of the invisible world through power places and power animals and spirit guides. That is not unlike the shaman's legendary role to safeguard the tribe against disasters, unexpected evil forces, and enemy attacks, as well as to use magic power to heal sickness and ensure good hunting and plentiful crops.

But the neo-shamans seem more intent upon individualistic endeavors in a pluralistic society that offers them no clearly defined social roles. These latter-day shamans, says Brooks Alexander, "are psychospiritual soldiers of fortune, seeking wisdom and power. They are both autonomous and rootless."[8]

Even so, the cultural influence of neo-shamanism is pervasive.

Shamanistic body-mind healing techniques are promoted by Michael Harner, an anthropologist at New York's prestigious Academy of Science. In his widely influential book, *The Way of the Shaman: A Guide to Prayer and Healing*, Harner gives explicit directions to those who wish to become "professional shamans." This instruction, he says, should include "wilderness wandering, the vision quest, the shamanic experience of death and resurrection, the Orphic journey, shamanism and afterlife, journeying to the Upperworld."[9]

Environmental psychologist Jim Swan edits *Shaman's Drum*, a New Age journal that explores the ecstatic and altered states that "transcend all cultures." Paid circulation jumped to 18,000 within two and a half years of the publication's start up, Swan told a New Age gathering.[10]

And Leslie Gray, a Cherokee who holds a Ph.D. in psychology from Harvard, has blended ancient native wisdom with Western technology in her "shamanic counseling" practice. Her "Speaking with Spirit Tongue" workshops are popular on the New Age circuit.

Shamanism in the 1980s and 1990s "is what Zen and yoga were in the 1960s and '70s," she says, adding that "the United States, not the Himalayas or Tibet, is the Holy Land. . . . Now I can tell people I'm a shaman and they understand what I'm talking about."[11]

In the early 1980s, Harley Swiftdeer, of mixed Cherokee and Irish descent, founded the Deer Lodge and its related teaching unit, Dreamweavers, for serious students of the Native American spiritual path.[12] And then there's Rolling Thunder, an aging medicine man born in the Cherokee nation, a favorite of show biz and music personalities such as Bob Dylan, the Grateful Dead, James Coburn, and Candice Bergen. Rolling Thunder travels about spinning Indian yarns and promoting shamanistic healing.

But Native Americans aren't the only ones taking shamanistic journeys these days.

Lynn Andrews, known as the "Beverly Hills medicine woman" and the "female Carlos Castaneda," has put legions of upscale suburban women on the path to Native American spirituality. Though not an Indian herself, Andrews spent the better part of fifteen years as an apprentice to indigenous women shamans, all the while gathering material for her five best-selling books on adventures of enlightenment, which one reviewer categorizes—along with the Castaneda series—as a new genre: "visionary autobiography."[13]

When she's not at her Benedict Canyon cottage, where she writes and gives private spiritual counseling at $150 an hour, Andrews is apt to be with her Native American teachers—especially Cree medicine woman Agnes Whistling Elk and Ruby Plenty Chiefs, in Manitoba, Canada.

Andrew's shamanistic journeyings do stretch the imagination, as do her counseling techniques, which include the use of rattles and bells "to balance the electromagnetic energy field surrounding the body."[14] Some Indians resent her "crash course" in shamanism, saying it takes nearly a lifetime to become expert. Others think she exploits Native American spirituality and shouldn't charge specific fees for her services.

But Andrews, a former art dealer and documentary producer, says the wampum comes with the territory. Anyway, she insists, Agnes Whistling Elk told her to spread the word. And, says she, her brand of urban shamanism is a vital link to the ancient, mystical knowledge of female consciousness, a link that ties in well with the growing feminist or goddess element of the New Age movement.

"Power is female. That's always the first lesson of shamanistic training," tutors warrioress Andrews, adding that the obligation of all women is the education of men.[15]

Meanwhile, back at Calamigos Ranch—only a few short miles away on the other side of the Santa Monica Mountains—Sun Bear's Medicine Wheel gathering had moved inside the lodge to escape a cold driving rain. There, "Grandfather Sun" was teaching some Native American chants and songs; most were unfamiliar to the largely non-Indian crowd.

What happened next was an example of the ability of the descendants of our nation's first inhabitants to keep a moccasin in both worlds without taking either world too seriously.

Strumming his guitar softly, Grandfather Sun warbled "The Forty-Nine Songs," a lengthy ballad about fifty warriors who go out to battle and only one returns. Halfway through the song, Grandfather suddenly began swiveling his hips and belting out the lyrics made immortal by Elvis Presley: "you ain't nothin' but a hound dog!"

It almost brought down the lodgepole.

14

Goddesses and Neopagans

The Earth is our Mother, we must take care of her. Hey younga, Ho younga, Hey young young. Her sacred ground we walk upon with every step. . . . Hey younga, Ho younga, Hey young young.
—Medicine Wheel Chant to Honor the Earth Mother

The Goddess of Pele was on a rampage!

A fiery deity, the volcano hissed her anger, spewing molten lava and sulfurous ash over the heaving sides of Kilauea.

Those who worship Pele say her five-year snit of eruptions began the very day the first geothermal permit was issued in 1983. The Department of Land and Natural Resources wants to drill into the mountain's sides to tap geothermal energy.

In a First Amendment case reminiscent of the clash between loggers and Indians in the northwest corner of California, the attempted harnessing of Kilauea in Hawaii's Volcanoes National Park has touched off an inferno of controversy. Proponents think the geothermal energy within Kilauea's hissing heart could supply power for the entire chain of oil-dependent islands. But Pele's devotees, who see her as a living Goddess, believe the plan not only violates their religious rights, but is destroying the object of their worship.

"They are punching holes in what we consider her body," Lehua Lopez, a member of the Pele Defense Fund, explained angrily. "She has eaten 58 houses already. She's causing people to be sick. She's mad."[1]

Pele worshipers, said to number in the thousands, aren't the only ones who see a direct connection between earthly catastrophe and deitific displeasure. Harmonic Convergence insiders grimly predicted that human failure to generate enough positive energy on August 16, 1987, could call down Earth Mother's wrath.

"There may have to be some cataclysmic events," Zena Starfire of Mill Valley, California, warned darkly. "There has to be some way for the Earth to blow off her negativity."

This is a familiar theme in the New Age scenario, where Earth is actually a goddess whose ancient name is Gaia (from Greek mythology). The goddess "has been seriously 'wounded' by the expansion of human civilization, and now there must come a universal atonement for these many millennia of grief on 'her' part through an event or process New Agers cryptically and ominously call 'the cleansing,'" according to a paper on the New Age movement.[2]

"The recent upsurge of volcanic action, earthquakes and unusual weather patterns," reasoned Regina Ryan and John Travis in their *Wellness Workbook* "may well be messages from Gaia, calling us to pay attention to her needs. If we continue to ignore her communications, there may be even harsher outbursts as Gaia is forced to take more drastic action to regain balance."[3]

The "Gaia hypothesis," while based in ancient mythology, has enjoyed a recent revival inspired by the environmental activists and New Age aficionados of the 1980s and 1990s. It squares with the New Age worldview that the Earth is a conscious, living entity with a "mind" that in turn participates in some universal or cosmic Mind.[4]

New Age writer George Seielstad summarizes the cosmic ecology of the Gaia hypothesis:

Life, acting as a collectivity and over a global basis, actively regulates and modulates the environment in just such a way as to optimize the very conditions under which that life can flourish. Earth's biosphere (life) is not independent of the atmosphere (air), hydrosphere (oceans), or lithosphere (soil). Instead, all are parts of a coherent whole. Insofar as that whole maintains a constant temperature and a compatible chemical composition—in short, a benign homeostasis—within a constantly changing setting, it can be considered alive.[5]

Life, said Ilya Prigogine, Belgian chemist, Nobel laureate, and a prop for New Age science, "is the supreme expression of the self-organizing processes that occur."[6] (We'll return to Prigogine and other New Age scientists in chapter 20.)

In addition to their roots in Greek and Roman mythology, the themes of the Great Mother and the Great Goddess are grounded in Eastern religions. For example, the Sanskrit root *ma* (or *matr*), meaning "production," underlies the belief that everything is the product of the Great Goddess, the One whose body is all manifestation.

The Great Goddess Kali of India, observed New Age psychologist Ken Wilber, "when viewed in her highest form as wife of Shiva, is a perfect example of the assimilation of the old Great Mother image into a new and higher corpus of Great Goddess mythology . . . which serves actual sacrifice in awareness, not substitute sacrifice in blood."[7]

Nature-based religion, particularly that of the Goddess and of Wicca (or "witchcraft"), is strong within the New Age strand often referred to as "ecofeminism." This feminist spirituality began to flower during the radical cultural movement of the 1970s. It views men as brutalizing women through sexual violence and pornographic exploitation, and dominating them through a stern, overbearing, male "sky-god."

Female fear and resentment further festered through what feminist cultural historian Charlene Spretnak has called the "patriarchal culture with its hierarchical, militaristic, mechanistic, industrialist forms."[8] As a result of prominent attention paid to these views, feminism and feminine consciousness have flourished.

Another factor in the development of feminism within the New Age movement has been the recent focus on various forms of neopaganism extracted from Western and pre-Christian "primal" cultures.

According to new religions expert Robert Ellwood, women—exhilarated over the discovery of a religion that exalts the female role—now realize that many of the Eastern religions "have been repressive in many ways. They [those religions] don't have the appeal they did in the 1960s."[9]

Intertwining female homage with the divinity of nature especially appeals to the ecofeminists. In a speech at a conference on ecofeminism, Spretnak, a leading New Age spokeswoman, said:

> We would not have been interested in "Yahweh with a skirt," a distant, detached, domineering godhead who happened to be female. What was cosmologically wholesome and healing was the discovery of the Divine as immanent in and around us. What was intriguing was the sacred link of the Goddess in her many guises with totemic animals and plants, sacred groves, womblike caves, the moon-rhythm blood of menses, the ecstatic dance—the experience of *knowing Gaia*, her voluptuous contours and fertile plains, her flowing waters that give life, her animals as teachers.[10]

Feminist spirituality has captivated many women dropouts from traditional Christianity. Twelve of seventeen former nuns who left their orders to embrace lesbianism now practice neopaganism, according to the book, *Lesbian Nuns: Breaking Silence*. These "New-Age nuns" are into "astrology, Goddess imagery, tarot, dreamwork, I Ching, herbal healing, meditation, massage and body . . . and psychic work. We are creating communal rituals for solstices, equinoxes, and full moons."[11]

A group of Quaker women, relating to the vision of one of their number who saw a Goddess fall "as a star from Venus to Earth," worship and meditate upon their star Goddess.[12]

On the radical edge of New Age feminism is the serious proposal of Deena Metzger that "holy prostitutes" be reinstated as the conduit for the sacred. Beyond the temple attendants, she advocates that all women become prostitutes "as a means for resacralizing the body and regaining spiritual power lost with the advent of patriarchical religion."[13]

Others, like Beverly Hills "medicine woman" Lynn Andrews, are less radical. She speaks of balancing the male and female aspects within each of us, rather than asserting sheer female power. Healing the feminine consciousness within men as well as within women will lead to a "sacred androgyny," she believes.[14]

But by most measures, "female energy" is where it's at in New Age circles: Sun Bear's *1987 Bear Tribe Catalogue*, for instance, lists sixty-four books on the topic—including connections to the Goddess, making magic in sex and politics, and using the witches' cabaia. But only six books on "male energy"—one of them being Herb Goldberg's *Hazards of Being Male*—are in the catalog.[15]

In addition to feminine Goddess worshipers, neopagans include among their numbers Celtic revivalist witches; creators of Greek, Egyptian, Norse, and Druid revivals; and those who experiment with various forms of ceremonial magic (often spelled "magick" to distinguish it from the stage-show version), sorcery, animism, divination, and witchcraft.

"Neo-pagans think of their religion as based on what one does, not on what one believes," declared Margot Adler, the popular New Age author of *Drawing Down the Moon: Witches, Druids, Goddess-Worshippers, and Other Pagans in America Today*. Adler is a priestess in a coven of witches (usually a group of thirteen) and conducts workshops on contemporary neopaganism titled "Magic, Wicca, and Goddess Spirituality."

She added in a Unitarian-Universalist magazine article: "Most Neo-pagan religions have few creeds and no prophets. They are based on seasonal celebration, the cycles of planting and harvesting, on custom and experience rather than the written word."[16]

Practitioners of New Age witchcraft are coming out of the broom closet. Religion experts estimate there are perhaps 50,000 witches in the United States, although the figure could be higher since many still choose anonymity.[17]

The practice of modern witchcraft has soared as witches have successfully exorcised the "Inquisition image" the craft has borne for centuries, and as New Age syncretism has enfolded a panoply of spiritual paths all said to bring equal access to the divine One. "Sky-clad" (nude) ritual ceremonies are fewer in most neopagan groups of the 1980s than a decade or so earlier. Also, practicing "black" magic, sacrificing animals, casting evil spells, and engaging in voodoo rites and sex orgies are downplayed, and most witches deny that they believe in—much less worship—Satan. That is not to deny, however, the existence of satanist groups (we'll consider them later under the topic of evil and the demonic in New Age religion).

The great majority of people who call themselves witches, says Gordon Melton of the Institute for Study of American Religion at Santa Barbara, "follow the nature-oriented polytheistic worship of the Great Mother Goddess," whose names include Diana, Isis, Demeter, Hecate, Cubele or Demeter, as well as Gaia.[18]

Miriam Starhawk, one of the best-known propagandists for Wicca, writes and lectures widely about witchcraft and is on the faculty of an institute in spirituality at Holy Names College in Oakland, California. Harvard Divinity School has offered courses on neopaganism and hosted meetings of witches, according to Westmont College sociologist Ron Enroth.[19]

There are Goddess bookshops and jewelry stores; pagan Alcoholics Anonymous meetings and performance theaters; witches' newspapers, computerized information networks, and professional societies. And even a witches' cemetery was dedicated near Los Angeles not long ago.[20]

Full Moon meditations—rollicking celebrations of Goddess worship and ritual symbols of nature—draw heavily from the circles of the well educated and affluent, with the majority of participants being female. Indeed, some of the rituals are open only to women.

Robert Ellwood and Harry Partin classify neopaganism into the magical groups, influenced by the activities of notorious magician Aleister Crowley (1875–1947) and others, and the "romantic" nature-oriented groups who "prefer woodsy settings to incense and altars" and who "dance and plant trees." Wicca covens, cast in the middle between the two, typically worship a Horned God (Pan) and a Triple Goddess (Virgin, Great Mother, and Crone).[21]

Though widely diverse, these neopagan ideas about the deities—from Pele to Pan—relate to some kind of "connectional" and symbolic "experience" that is part of the totality of Nature and the Oneness of divine Reality. The spirit of magick, then—which the New Age prefers to call "spirituality"—is expressed in terms of self-empowerment. It is receiving what we need from our "Higher Selves" within and from the universe without—what Jack Pursel's channeled entity Lazaris fondly refers to as "God/Goddess/All That Is."[22]

The New Age magick is, in fact, the Edenic longing for godhood through a certain and secret wisdom that disperses limitations and suffering with the wave of a wand.

PART III

THE LONG REACH OF THE NEW AGE

15

Commercial Appeal

"At the Celebration of Innovation, you'll find Fortune 500 business consultants, visionary artists, pioneering scientists, futuristic architects, psychologists studying hallucinogenic drugs, inspired musicians, clowns, and maybe some visitors from other planets and dimensions."

So beckoned a brochure advertising a three-day "psychic fair" in downtown San Francisco in the fall of 1987, one of dozens of such New Age cosmic expos springing up with increasing regularity around the country these days.

"Just walking in the door may change your life as you encounter the rich exhibit environment and more than 200 exhibit booths," the brochure tempted. "After sampling the ambience, sit back and dine on some gourmet [vegetarian] food and drink. Then try spending an afternoon with medicine man Rolling Thunder or listen to Dr. NakaMats describe his 'seven pagoda' method of inventing, or trip out on Michael Pinder, founder of the Moody Blues."

Science fiction, shamanism, synthesizer music, sacred architecture, megavitamins, spoon-bending engineers, and brain-stimulating devices—why bring these together under the New Age big top?

"Creativity is what puts magic into life and enables us to evolve into higher levels of peace and health," answers Jim Swan, who directed the Celebration of Innovation and edits *Shaman's Drum*, a magazine that explores esoteric pathways to spiritual power. "This exposition will get your creative juices flowing and inspire the genius to come out in all of us."

Four or five thousand souls—ranging from the committed to the curious—paid $10 for a one-day pass and $20 per workshop, to partake of this smorgasbord. And for a special $100 rate, there were a limited number of passes that included four workshops, entrance to the concourse all three days, a free bodywork session, preferred seating at the Saturday night concert—and a VIP badge.

While many New Agers profess to eschew mainstream materialism, the movement itself strongly intersects with Madison Avenue merchandising and capitalistic commercialism. Perhaps it's simply a matter of taking advantage of the heady market for psychic goods and services that will naturally rise and fall with New Age faddishness.

But there is, unmistakably, what *TIME* called "a slightly greedy tone" to the movement.[1] More than a few ads that promise healing, growth, and transformation also appeal to the pocketbook: "How to use a green candle to gain money"; "The power of the pendulum can be in your hands"; "Make money doing what you love."

Indeed, some New Age entrepreneurs are getting rich selling enlightenment. Author Gita Mehta calls it marketing "Karma Kola."

J. Z. Knight, according to ABC TV's *20/20*, can earn up to $200,000 in a single appearance channeling Ramtha, the controversial 35,000-year-old warrior. Her weekend retreats bring in $400 to $1,500 per person. Knight's Yelm, Washington, spread includes a $1.5 million brick mansion ("It isn't nearly as nice as the Pope's house," she explains); Arabian horse stables ("nicer than most homes") complete with crystal chandeliers; fancy clothes; and a late-model powder-blue Rolls Royce.[2]

Shirley MacLaine, wealthy as a superstar well before her entrance into the world of New Age, charged 1,200 seekers $300 a head to attend a spirituality session in the ballroom of the New York Hilton Hotel. That was the going rate for a seventeen-city, sell-out national tour in 1987, calculated to garner $1.5 million for a 300-acre, state-of-the-art meditation retreat center MacLaine planned to build in Southern Colorado.

"I want to prove that spirituality is profitable," she said.[3] "I've liked moderate success, but I've . . . not wanted gigantic success. I'm changing now. I want gigantic success," she told another interviewer.[4]

MacLaine, and other New Agers interviewed for this book, defend the crossover from spiritualism to materialism as being a part of religion in general.

"After all," demurred one practitioner, "look at television evangelists and their millions. And what about those Tammy Faye Bakker dolls that sold for $650?"

Beverly Hills shaman Lynn Andrews, author of bestselling wilderness adventure books telling of her fanciful searches for female consciousness (*Medicine Woman, Flight of the Seventh Moon, Jaguar Woman, Star Woman,* and *Crystal Woman*), connects spirituality with health and wealth, and unabashedly insists money is just a medium of exchange that should not be resisted.

"We have chosen to be born into a world where we have to make money to survive," she says. "But there's no reason why we can't also be spiritual."[5]

Or consider circuit speaker and former Religious Science minister Terry Cole-Whittaker. By the early 1980s she was out front with lapel buttons that blurted: "Pro$perity—Your Divine Right!"

Writer Carol McGraw notes that the enterprising often capitalize on the New Age message: "Madison Avenue sells everything from shoes to lottery tickets using New Age lingo. Neiman-Marcus is pushing fetish dolls described as 'representatives from another dimension.' A Club-Med ad features a student telling his yoga teacher that his is going on vacation: The ad concludes, 'Perfect climate for body and soul . . . but hurry—Nirvana won't wait.' Creator Lynn McGrath of N. W. Ayer Co. in New York got the concept from her yoga instructor."[6]

Nowhere has the nearly unquenchable thirst for New Age knowledge and technologies been more apparent than in the book and tape industries.

"It's a ripe time for books with a metaphysical view of everything from crystals and channeling to business, baby's future and AIDS," enthused David Tuller in *Publishers Weekly*, the trade magazine of the publishing industry.[7]

Bantam Books, sensing the swelling tide as far back as 1980, was the first major publishing house to create a New Age book division and published such classics as *The Way of the Shaman* and *The New Physics*. Bantam also went out on the limb of what turned out to be a money tree by publishing MacLaine's mystic-journey books after another publisher turned them down. (Sales of *Out On a Limb* weren't hurt a bit by the inclusion of juicy details of MacLaine's torrid love affair with a heavily disguised member of British Parliament whom she called "Gerry.")

Bestsellers like those of MacLaine, Knight, Marilyn Ferguson, and New Age physicist Fritjof Capra prime the pump for even wider interest in New Age titles. MacLaine's books alone had sold 8 million copies by the end of 1987—an estimated gross of $40 million annually.

Noted Bantam vice-president Stuart Applebaum: "Metaphysical books are "one of our strongest categories" and are "getting even stronger."

Masterworks Publishers of Friday Harbor, Washington, must have known the strength of the market when it arranged for a special 2000-copy hardcover, limited "keepsake edition" of *Genies Are Usually Green* to be "elaborately presented, numbered and signed by J. Z. Knight" for $30 a copy.[8]

The cover story of the January 1988 *American Bookseller* magazine, "Read the Signs of a New Age," described at length promotional and merchandising ideas for the burgeoning New Age book trade. Nationwide, at least 2,500 bookstores specialized in New Age books (twice the 1982 number); and 25,000 titles were in print, accounting for more than a billion dollars in sales in 1987 (up 30% over 1986), according to industry figures.

By the end of 1987, most major publishers were getting in on the action. Harper & Row published a first-run of 40,000 copies of *Channeling, the Intuitive Connection*, by William H. Kautz, with a foreword by Kevin Ryerson, one of MacLaine's foremost channelers. Warner Books came out with *State of Mind*, the autobiography of J. Z. Knight. Nor was the greening of New Age lost on St. Martin's Press, which in late 1987 ran a healthy 250,000 first printing of Linda Goodman's *Star Signs*, her first book in ten years.

As a promo flyer from Waldenbooks reminded, "Linda

Goodman is, of course, the superstar astrologer who gave us the 7-million-copy bestseller *Linda Goodman's Love Signs*. In *Star Signs*, . . . Goodman covers virtually every facet of the New Age smorgasbord—from numerology and reincarnation to holistic healing, the power of sound, and ghosts and gurus. There's even an astrological guide to financial security. As for Linda Goodman, she divides her time between her homes in Colorado and California. And, for you astrology fans out there, she's an Aries."

The buyer for Waldenbooks' metaphysical titles said that, following the MacLaine phenomenon, sales of News Age titles jumped from 25 to 900 a week. And B. Dalton Books reported a 95% increase in occult book sales during the week of MacLaine's "Out on a Limb" TV miniseries in January 1987.[9]

Marcia Gervase Ingenito's *National New Age Yellow Pages Directory* debuted in 1987 as an annual sourcebook of publishers, goods, and services such as New Age artists, New Age dentists, New Age churches, New Age resorts, and even New Age subdivisions.

Meanwhile, the occult bookshop, often ensconced in a seedy part of town, has gained prominence and respectability. One of the largest in California is the Bodhi Tree (named for the fabled spot of Buddha's enlightenment), which occupies a block of buildings housing a mind-boggling array of New Age literature and a clearinghouse-posting of seminars, lectures, and other events.

Most mystic oriented bookstores have added sections for New Age music, tapes and videos, tarot cards, board games, incense, crystals, jewelry, and greeting cards.

New Age books for children are increasingly popular. *The Tao of Pooh*, by Benjamin Hoff, was a featured cover-display item in the 1987 holiday catalog for Yes! Bookstore in Washington, D.C.

Need a gift for Dad? Try *The Tao Jones Averages: A Guide to Whole-Brained Investing* by Bennett W. Goodspeed. It was out just in time for Black Monday on October 19, 1987!

Who buys these books? asks religion-watcher and historian Martin Marty. "Clearly they are beamed at highly educated and well-off people, people who can afford $300 weekend seminars and complex equipment and expensive books; this is not a populist revolution."[10]

And, of course, the large Christian book industry also sensed the trend and stepped up its output of counter-New Age literature.

Celestial Entertainment Unlimited

New Age music has also turned up the volume at the cash registers. According to *Publishers Weekly*, the New Age music category is growing "at a rate even faster than printed and spoken materials, and a comprehensive listing of these recordings would simply overwhelm the [magazine] issue."[11]

I was surprised to find a rack of New Age music tapes next to the cashier's counter at the local car wash. But what better time to listen to "Music for an Inner Journey" than while driving to work. Frazzled in freeway gridlock? Step "Through the Portals of Infinity," or try the "ambient psychoacoustics" of Thunder Storm." Or how about "Sailing," the sound of "splashing sea, gulls and creaking mast"?

The Institute for Human Development in Ojai, California, added a line of subliminal tapes in 1987: "Our new Tropical Ocean format is the most relaxing, soothing ocean we've heard yet," burbled the Winter-Spring catalog.

Pregnant women who want to prepare their unborn children for the outer world can turn to Prenatal U. of Hayward, California. This organization offers manuals and cassettes to guide parents-to-be through exercises said to stimulate and even educate the child while he/she attends "in utero university."[12]

Effective Learning Systems of Edina, Minnesota, markets "The Love Tapes," touted to teach "how to use your mind to do anything you choose." Regular tapes cost $9.98; subliminals, $11.98.[13] Sybervision of Newark, California, which advertises extensively in airline magazines and calls itself "the leader in personal achievement technology," markets audio and videocassettes on everything from excelling in sports, to weight control and self-discipline and self-defense, to language learning and successful parenting.

Lectures and exercises for achieving altered states and,

yes!—even channeled wisdom from Elvis Presley—abound on tapes and videocassettes. Popular video categories also include instruction on yoga and martial arts and "be-it-yourself" mediumship—although discerning metaphysical bookstore managers are cautious about the latter.

"You have no idea how many channeling videos I refuse to carry," says Jamie Michaels of Bodhi Tree. "There are more channels in L.A. than there are TV sets."[14]

Still, tens of thousands of Americans shell out from $10 to $300 an hour to seek counsel from channeled beings (including at least one dolphin); and profits from channeling tapes, seminars, and books range from an estimated $100 to $400 million annually.[15]

New Age radio stations are proliferating, with most major U.S. cities offering round-the-clock "planetarium music," spinning off the popularity and profitability of New Age artists like Grammy Award-winning Andreas Vollenweider, the Swiss harpist.

Mass entertainment shows strong penetration by the New Age. Films and television programs with occult and mystical themes have caught on well, as box-office receipts and Nielsen ratings attest.

One of the most familiar, of course, is George Lucas's *Star Wars*, which tells of Luke Skywalker's initiation into a league of Jedi knights by mastering the "'force' that animates the cosmos, dwells within, and is tapped intuitively through feelings. . . . Sights and sounds from the Star Wars trilogy are rattling around in the brains of millions of Americans," points out New Age researcher Robert J. Burrows.[16]

Harrison Ford's Indiana Jones was such a smash hit that it called for a sequel. In *Indiana Jones and the Temple of Doom* the handsome hero combats a Tantric yoga sect for possession of a primeval talisman called a "shankara stone."

The popular cycle of recent horror films, many of which contain occult and metaphysical themes, traces from *The Exorcist* in 1974 and *The Omen* in 1976. Other box-office favorites include *An American Werewolf in London* and *The Amityville Horror.*

Product Profitability

As we saw in the chapter on crystals and pyramids, these "energy fields" have become de rigueur talismans for New Agers, resulting in a bauble bonanza.

New York-based Crystal Resources says Americans spend $100 million a year on crystals. Nationwide, prices can run from a couple dollars for a small slice to $150,000 for museum-quality crystals. That's as much as 1000% more than ten years ago.[17]

But if New Age rocks are on a roll, pyramid power is exponential.

At the Celebration of Innovation in San Francisco, Paradyne Systems of Laguna Beach offered a choice of five wire pyramids, all about a foot long at the base and slightly less in height. Curiously, the largest, the VITAMID, was the least expensive. For $10 show's price ($11.95 regularly) the VITAMID was said to "generate the negative ion effect . . . and extend the shelf-life of vitamins." Prices quickly escalated from the PYRADOME ($19) to the FIREDOME ($20), RAYDOME ($30) and POWERDOME, which was a show-time-only bargain at $99.95 (regularly $120). The POWERDOME was billed as being "omnidirectional" and "100 times higher than a normal pyramid" in power.

Other benefits/selling points were listed above stacks of the wire POWERDOME triangles:

• Increases attention span and high concentration
• Decreases appetite
• Expands psychic ability
• Stronger detoxifier
• Negative ion effect for euphoric feeling
• Increases vitamin absorption

In Van Nuys, California, Nick Cariglia has appointed his Rubicon Realty offices with crystals and pyramids to smooth transactions. He encourages clients to strike crystal Tibetan bowls to create calming tones and focus their energy as they approach the close of a deal. And he provides his brokers with subliminal audiotapes to inspire sales. Cariglia, who sets his net worth at $10 million, "has merged the two quintessentially Californian preoccupations of acquiring property and attaining enlightenment, and the marriage has worked," observed Steve Chawkins in the *Los Angeles Times*.[18]

"It's not that unusual these days," remarked social psychologist Michael Ray, "to see enormously successful, hard-core corporate types doing biofeedback and using crystals."[19]

Harvard Business School graduate Mason Sexton has 1,500 subscribers who pay $360 a year for his biweekly newsletter of stock market predictions, which are based on unorthodox and New Age concepts. Those who took his advice of October 2, 1987, were well-rewarded: Sexton warned investors that the stock market would peak later that month and that they should bail out.

A significant number of stockbrokers consult astrology charts, and one investment banker with a $100,000-a-year salary talks about her previous life as a monk. Joe Sugarman, president of JS&A, a direct-mail marketing firm, says he profits from occult advice on negotiating deals, personnel decisions, and product promotion. And financial astrologer Arch Crawford, formerly an analyst for Merrill Lynch, charges $250 for a subscription (ten issues) of his newsletter; for an additional $2,500 a year, subscribers can phone the Wall Street psychic for advice anytime.

Steep? Yes. But *Timer Digest*, which rates trade newsletters, ranked him the second most accurate forecaster of 1986.[20]

For a mere $99.95, however, you can buy a computer software program called AstroTalk: "your own personal astrologer with daily forecasts, accurate horoscopes and pick-a-date features." Just phone your order to 1-800-PLANETS.[21]

For half that price, *The Mystic Trader* in Coeur d'Alene, Idaho, will sell you four tapes on "The Mastery of Money" by the catalog's creator, metaphysician Stuart Wilde. These "[p]ractical consciousness aligning techniques . . . will allow you to step effortlessly into abundance. While not judging others, you move to creating the wherewithal that you need to express the special individualized God Force that you are. You will begin to get the things in life that you have always wanted."[22]

While some millionaire celebrities retain their own private

gurus who make house calls, the travel industry, New Age style, will take you to Enlightenment—for a price.

Wildland Journeys of Seattle (1-800-345-HIKE) features worldwide nature and cultural explorations supporting conservation and community development. Travelers can choose from Inca Trail Preservation, Himalayan Tree Planting, Ladakh Prayer Wheel Restoration, Costa Rica Cloud Forest Protection, or Kenya Wildlife Conservation.[23]

Janie Gabbet, a writer for Reuters wire service agency, spied an ad that said, "This year, don't just take a vacation; take an adventure—a Shaman's Tour of Peru."

"I said to myself, 'Goodbye Club Med, hello Peru.' I sent my money in," she reported.[24]

Shamanistic journeys to Mexico and Guatemala are also available. Singing Pipe Woman of Springdale, Washington, offered a two-week pilgrimage ($2,450) in early 1988 that included studying with 108-year-old Huichol Indian shaman Don Jose Matsuwa and Bear Tribe teacher Sun Bear. According to the description, the tour explored the "sacred power" of ancient Mayan sites.

A "mystical adventure to Egypt," presented by the Center for Applied Intuition and Quest Tours, runs a little more: $2,795 a person (in March 1988). Wilderness vision quests (limit ten people) offer transition experiences for a week in isolated places like Last Chance Range and Death Valley.

Can't break away from home or job? Not to worry. "Spend a little time relaxing at Altered States and you'll swear you just returned from Maui," entices the Altered States' Float Center in West Hollywood, California. The brochure promises "an oasis of tranquility where, in the comfort of a flotation tank or using a device in our MindGym [trademarked], you'll discover your youthful energy. Your own Fountain of Youth!"

And after you enjoy a sixty-minute vacation float, the MindGym allures with such cosmic contraptions as the hemisync (produces altered mental states through pulsing headset tones of different frequencies), the synchro-energizer (combines flickering lights, pulsating sounds, and vibrating electromagnetic impulses), the Graham Potentializer (a massage table that slowly rotates in a counterclockwise motion, and the mind mirror (a biofeedback device designed to reproduce a yogi's brain state).

But be warned: These are big-buck items! It takes $1,700 to "reduce your biological age" by sleeping in a magnetic cocoon, $5,795 for a flotation tank, $6,500 for an lpha Chair," and $3,700 for the brain-sync machine, according to price sampling at the Whole Life Expo in Los Angeles in the spring of 1988. Those with unlimited capital might go for the "crown jewel of mind-expansion technology"—the $65,000 "Brain-Mind Intensive Dome." A brochure tempts: "Imagine yourself revolving slowly on a platform inside a geodesic dome [surrounded by] 32 specially engineered speakers."

"I did," reported Al Seckel of the Southern California Skeptics, "and the image of a baked potato turning slowly in the microwave popped into my head."[25]

The list of New Age products is seemingly endless: Color, Sound and Fragrance kits; ChiPants, which feature a gusseted design to "free your crotch" for ease of movement in yoga and other therapies; the Crystal Flute, a "breakthrough . . . under $300" gadget to "empower your dreams and let them change you" by electrically amplifying the "thoughts you program into your quartz crystal."

Alisha Summers of Angel Fantasy in Langley, Washington, has created special "fabric angel" costumes, presumably for women and girls, that Alisha describes as "a gateway to the Angelic Kingdom, the temple of the most high Goddess within your soul."

But my favorite is Earthrise Spirulina, sold by "the leader in aquaherbals" in San Rafael, California. Spirulina "talks" to readers in *Body Mind Spirit*, America's largest-circulation (160,000) New Age magazine.

> I am the immortal descendant of the original photosynthetic life form. Over three billion years ago, blue-green algae produced the earth's oxygen atmosphere so life could evolve. . . . Your own technology and lifestyle threaten you. Pollution, toxic chemicals, radiation, disease, stress, drugs and processed foods attack your immune system. Damage to your body and its cells can cause premature aging and cancer. . . .
>
> But my whole food spirulina vitamins and minerals are easily absorbed. . . . DNA molecular codes in natural foods contain genetic memories of successful life forms for millions of years. I have rejuvenated myself since the beginning. My three billion years of cell memories can help your body remember its

powers and renew itself. . . . I flourished in the nutrients of the original primordial soup. . . .

So, partake of my immortal body each day. Eat three billion years of cell memory and a concentration of protective nutrients. Renew your health, renew your connection with your sisters and brothers in the Third World, and with your origins of life.[26]

Quality Control

Commenting on the "blatant commercialization" of the New Age movement, historian Christopher Lasch quotes the lament of San Francisco philosopher and theologian Jacob Needleman: "There's no Better Business Bureau" for spiritual shoppers. "Let the buyer beware."[27]

Needleman's rule: You should be open-minded, but not so open-minded that your brains fall out.

The *New Age Journal*, alarmed over the lack of quality control in the psychic supermarket, warned about a New Age version of the old-fashioned pyramid scheme disguised as a seminar in abundance. The Airplane Game, also known as the Infinity Process Seminar, works like a chain letter. And it has what Ravi Dykema called "a New Age veneer that does little to conceal the old-fashioned avarice that drives it."[28]

The rules call for "realizing your unlimited possibilities for peace, joy, love and abundance on this planet." But at its peak, according to the *New Age Journal* and the *Boston Globe*, some two thousand players spent as much as $2 million to join a "plane" that needs fifteen persons to "take off."

When the seats are filled, the pilot "pilots out" with the passengers' money and the plane divides, with each copilot in charge of a new plane and each passenger advancing to the rank of crew. The new pilot and crew seek fresh passengers who are told they, too, can pilot out if they have enough "positive energy, belief, cooperation and integrity."[29] But winning gets tougher and tougher as more and more people must be persuaded to play in order to keep the game airborne.

Responsible New Age leaders have warned that this is not the way to fly, adding that the scam tarnishes the nobler goals of the movement, such as personal and social transformation, justice, and global harmony.

That focus on quality of life is apparent in what New Age architect Marilyn Ferguson calls "a new paradigm based on values." In her pace-setting opus, *Aquarian Conspiracy*, she writes that the shift is reflected "in changing patterns of work, career choice, consumption ... evolving lifestyles that take advantage of synergy, sharing, barter cooperation, and creativity ... the transformation of the workplace, in business, industry, professions, the arts, innovations in management and worker participation, including the decentralization of power ... the rise of a new breed of entrepreneurs ... the search for 'appropriate technology.'"[30]

Ferguson believes this synergy has opened up new sources of goods and services, cooperatives, and mutual-help networks. These are, says she, "modern urban counterparts of quilting bees, barn-raisings, and farmers' co-ops."[31]

One of the most visible manifestations of the synergy Ferguson is talking about is in Fairfield, Iowa. Here, the disciples of former Beatles' guru Maharishi Mahesh Yogi have produced what *Newsweek* called "a white-collar boomtown ... the karma of capitalism."[32]

The Transcendental Meditation master, who planted his Maharishi International University in Fairfield, has preached that spiritual enlightenment is the key to corporate success. And by mid 1987, Fairfield was headquarters for nearly 300 disciple-owned businesses, including Fred Gratzon's Great Midwestern Ice Cream Co. (with sales of $3 million in 1986) and Lincoln Norton's Corporate Education Resources, leading maker of computer software for tracking the careers of executives.

Some non-TM disciples have been coaxed by the town's success, and Iowa Governor Terry Branstad praised Fairfield's unorthodox entrepreneurialism as "an important part of the future of Iowa."

Though bankruptcies and lawsuits have involved a few Sidha (TM) executives, personal income in the once economically depressed region rose 55% between 1980 and 1984. More than twenty meditators made fortunes, and Fairfield remained "bullish on the maharishi effect"—the TM belief that if enough meditators do their thing simultaneously, they create a powerful force that can accomplish anything from ushering in world peace to driving up the stock market.

Businesspeople comprise the group most receptive to New Age transformation and human potentials techniques, believes Marilyn Ferguson. Top executives seem to have a gut knowledge of what's involved in transformation, she says, adding that an impact in the business sector "would seem to have a huge portent for the society as a whole."

Speaking to an interviewer for *New Age* magazine, Ferguson declared:

> [W]hen businesspeople come in and start opening up to the process, there's nobody who changes faster, and I think there are several reasons for this. First of all, when you're dealing with top-level executives . . . these are people who have entrepreneurial minds, which means they are risk takers. Also, various studies have shown that business executives tend to be right-brained, or at least quite spontaneous, creative and intuitive in their thinking. And they are also extremely pragmatic: They're interested in anything that works.[33]

One entrepreneur who has made New Age tech work big is Chris Majer, founder of a multi-million-dollar Seattle corporation called Sportsmind. And herein lies a tale of how the theology of "creating unlimited potential" is sweeping the management training ranks of corporate America.

16

Corporate Entities

Chris Majer motioned toward the large picture window in his hilltop penthouse, framing a myriad of Christmas lights twinkling in the distance on the far side of Puget Sound. It was a raw December night, trying to snow, and Majer, who had just jetted back to Seattle from a quick business trip to Salt Lake City, was relishing the vacation he and his wife would begin the next morning. "Hawaii," he said.

Sipping from a can of diet Minute Maid orange juice, Majer, a muscular and affable man who fits all criteria for the Yuppie label, pointed to the freeway far below. During his student days at the University of Washington in the early 1970s, he said, he had led antiwar marches on that very stretch of highway.

But now, at thirty-six, Majer heads a glossy management training and motivation firm staffed by retired military officers, psychologists, physiologists, and MBAs. Just six years after he and a sports psychologist founded Sportsmind in 1981, Majer's company landed a two-part, $4 million contract with AT&T. The goal: Teach 3000 AT&T managers how to achieve peak human performance.

As I turned the conversation to New Age and what had made it so appealing to so many, Majer seemed a little uncomfortable, shifting in his overstuffed chair.

"The term New Age has been so bandied about that I'm not sure anyone knows what it means anymore," he began. "It could mean anything from crystals to rainbow hair to anything that Jerry Falwell doesn't like." Allowing that his company wanted no part in New Age theological discussions, he nonetheless ventured a little Sportsmind philosophy.

> What we do is to allow people to retouch that spiritual foundation within themselves. . . . Much of this work is about spiritual stuff, but we don't ever say that because people start getting nervous when you talk about that. It's about the human spirit, the energy or human spirituality that is in us all. It's about touching that uniquely human capacity of feeling, a space of heart-felt concern, and from there creating futures and outcomes that we all want. . . .
>
> Sure, there's the danger of Jim Jones and some of those "crazo-cult" things, but that's an over-reaction to some New Age stuff. So what if people want to commune with crystals, get guidance from rocks, consult channelers? What is it we're afraid of in all that?[1]

Sportsmind, as the name implies, began when Majer applied aspects of peak performance and team cohesion to the training of athletes, including the U.S. ski and rugby teams. But the company soon found a niche in training U.S. military personnel and corporate America. With more than 8000 graduates, Sportsmind has helped executives in hundreds of major companies to achieve high performance through a combination of motivation training, physical experiences, and focused energy.

"Our stance is that people are unlimited in their individual abilities, that as humans all of us are infinitely able to do anything we want . . . [and] that all of us desire to express a greater wholeness and to be consciously in charge of our lives," Majer explained. He added that typical programs for executives include relaxation and "centering" exercises, outdoor simulation games "which are a mirror of the way people live the rest of their lives," and modified martial arts.

The U.S. Army was so impressed with Sportsmind's success with athletes and corporate entities that it hired Majer to shape up listless troops. First there was a $50,000 training program in 1983 at Fort Hood, Texas, then a $350,000 program to train Green Berets. In both cases morale shot up and sick calls plunged.

"We amazed them. . . . We pushed all sorts of boundaries of

human performance," Majer summed up, adding that meditation techniques helped military Special Forces stay hidden in enemy territory for long hours.

That wasn't the first time the government cooperated with transformation innovators, however. Research projects on meditation, biofeedback, psychic phenomena, and alternative medical approaches have been funded by the Department of Defense since the 1970s.[2] Also, in the early 1980s officers at the Army War college in Carlisle, Pennsylvania, did a study aimed at creating a New Age Army."[3]

According to participants, the study envisaged training soldiers in meditation, extrasensory skills, magic, and "neurolinguistics," a hypnosis technique. Army officials later said the program had been canceled.

Another project, known as the First Earth Battalion, was the brainchild of an untraditional military think tank called the Delta Force. "The battalion, also called the Natural Guard, was projected to be a New Age militia of warrior monks attuned to resolving conflict through yoga, meditation and the martial arts. . . . Although the Delta Force is now out of commission, it did inject New Age ideas into the military."[4]

Sports psychologists have long known that visualizing an event in the controlled dream state summons body involvement at the deepest levels, and that imaging athletic skills before taking part in an event can result in superperformance. Bruce Ogilvie, the first psychologist to work with large numbers of athletes, often relies on the technique of self-talk, in which athletes "rescript the language they use in approaching other players, the racket or club, or even the ball."[5]

OMNI magazine interviewed a dozen top sports psychologists as well as some of the athletes who have excelled using their methods, then distilled their complex techniques into sixteen exercises which the editors listed under "Mind Control: How to Get It, How to Use It, How to Keep It." In addition to visualization, the techniques include stimulating right-brain alpha waves, generating flow states, and entering controlled dreams.[6]

For 160-pound, vegetarian, nonbodybuilder, spiritual adept Sri Chinmoy, meditation is said to provide a fountain of limitless strength. The 56-year-old Indian master, who has run "ultramarathons" and reputedly lifted elephants and airplanes, also directs meditations for peace at the United Nations. One of his greatest feats was lifting 7,063 pounds with one arm.[7] The lift was unofficial, however, and took place in his specially outfitted exercise room.

Meditation techniques can be applied to any sport, and Vasanti Nienz, who in 1986 was the first German woman to swim the English Channel, has said that "someday meditation will be considered as essential to optimum performance as diet and training schedules."[8]

Physical and mental fitness and team cohesion. Unlimited abilities. Being in harmony with the universe. These are the staples of Sportsmind and a passel of other human potentials management organizations increasingly in demand by corporations that want to gain and hold the competitive edge.

Pete Saunders, head of Success Potentials Unlimited, a division of his nonprofit psychic organization Free Soul, says the "psychic foot in the door" to corporate America has been stress management. "Business equated psychic with weird . . . but they understood stress and . . . needed help with that. When they saw how effective our mental dynamics worked for stress they said 'Give us more.' So now you talk about psychic attunenment and expanded mental states, and they say, 'How can I use that in my business?' "[9]

California Business magazine reported in 1986 that a survey of 500 company owners and presidents found that more than half had used some form of "consciousness-raising" technique.[10] The figure squares with a 1984 survey conducted by Richard Watring, former personnel director of the Budget-Rent-a-Car Corporation in Chicago. His poll of 780 personnel directors showed that 45% had "seen or used" one or more psychotechnologies of consciousness-raising.[11]

In July 1986, representatives of some of the nation's largest corporations, including IBM, AT&T, and General Motors, met to "discuss how metaphysics, the occult and Hindu mysticism might help executives compete in the world market."[12]

One major petrochemical company provides regular workshops in stress management for its employees and hired a "faith healer to read auras of ailing employees and run her hands over their fields of energy."[13] Other corporate giants who have signed on New Age consultants include Procter & Gamble, TRW, and Polaroid.

Anna Wise of the Evolving Institute of Boulder, Colorado, reported that a Wall Street executive hired her to do a corporate brain profile of his forty employees "to determine what creative training programs each needed."[14]

And to increase efficiency, firms such as Merrill Lynch, Ford, Westinghouse, RCA, Boeing, Scott Paper, and Calvin Klein have sent employees to seminars conducted by groups like Innovation Associates, Lifespring, Energy Unlimited, and Transformational Technologies (a 1984 spinoff of Werner Erhard's est) to develop their "motivation for success."

By the end of 1987, Transformational Technologies had licensed fifty-eight small consulting firms for a $20,000 fee plus 8% of the gross—selling Erhard techniques to dozens of Fortune 500 companies.[15]

These major New Age inroads into management training are not surprising in light of the popularity of courses like "Creativity in Business" taught by social psychologist Michael Ray at Stanford University's prestigious Graduate School of Business. Ray invokes Zen, yoga, and tarot cards and includes chanting, "dreamwork," and a discussion of the New Age Capitalist" in his class, which has a long waiting list.

Techniques of humanistic psychology and Eastern mysticism are often incorporated into management training in terms more acceptable to those who might be put off by New Age language. But even these often conjure their own glossary of arcane lingo.

And sometimes, as a corporate statement of principles worked out for Pacific Bell by consultants of New Age trainer Charles Krone attests, the alternate language can become downright "bafflegab." For example, the statement defined "interaction" as the "continuous ability to engage with the connectedness and relatedness that exists and potentially exists, which is essential for the creations necessary to maintain and enhance viability of ourselves and the organization of which we are a part."[16]

"I see training consultants employing the very same techniques that promote New Age transformation but for different reasons," Watring, the Budget-Rent-a-Car executive, said in a telephone interview. "Meditation techniques are recommended for stress management, and visual imaging for improving intuitive faculties, creativity, and to get employees to accept greater responsibility for themselves. . . . But along with that come some side effects. . . . If you practice a New Age technique often enough with intensity you'll have this mystical experience . . . and accept the worldview beliefs that support it."

Elaine Smith, a pioneer in developing transformational techniques for businesses and the peace movement, said as much during a panel discussion on "Creativity in Business" given in San Francisco in the fall of 1987.

To help a CEO "connect with the level of consciousness where all truth exists, you don't have to teach him kundalini yoga," she explained, adding that "creative juices" can be tapped rather like slipping a drinking straw into a pool of creativity.

Another panelist, Brad Brodsky, publisher of a listing of New Age businesses called "Open Exchange," agreed, saying that trainers shouldn't initially use "certain phrases or concepts" and that they shouldn't make employees feel they are being indoctrinated into a form of "company religion."

Is religion an issue in corporate leadership development programs? It is and it isn't.

Chris Majer says that over a seven-year period, only one couple, who had "newly converted to some fundamentalist beliefs," declined to take a Sportsmind course.

However, hundreds of workers objected to a 1987 Pacific Bell training program called "Kroning," some on religious grounds, provoking a scolding of the company by the Public Utilities Commission. The watchdog agency found the program enormously expensive (at least $40 million) and recommended that $25 million of the cost be charged to stockholders instead of tacking it onto customer's phone bills. (About 15,000 of Pacific Bell's 67,000 employees took the Kroning program before the company halted it and ordered its own study.)

Although the company claimed that productivity increased by nearly a fourth after employees were Kroned, several disgruntled Bell workers said that the exercises were, in fact, mind control sessions based on the teachings of Georges

Gurdjieff, a controversial Russina mystic.[17] One called Kroning "a mental dress code."[18]

New Age human potentials training "may prove to be a livelier First Amendment workplace issue in the next few years than traditional questions such as the right to take off on the Sabbath of your choice," predicts John J. Reilly.[19] In another widely reported incident, a car dealership sales manager in Tacoma, Washington, was fired because he refused to complete a course called "New Age Thinking to Increase Dealership Profitability." In a lawsuit, Steven Hiatt claimed that the course, offered by The Pacific Institute of Seattle, emphasized the concept of self-will rather than God's will.

Pacific Institute materials are confusing on that point, though the program's originator, Louis Tice, a former high-school football coach of Roman Catholic background, has denied that Pacific has any New Age connections.

"It's just good old common sense," Tice says of the training materials.

The Tice materials used for Rockwell aerospace employees approvingly quote William Penn: "Man must choose to be ruled by God or he's destined to be ruled by a tyrant and then might makes right."

But on another page in the same manual is this trainee affirmation: "I choose to treat myself with dignity and proceed to move toward full love, wisdom, freedom and joy, knowing that *I am the authority over me*" (emphasis added). The Tice manual for Rockwell relies heavily on self-image psychology and says that the campus is "conveniently located inside yourself."[20]

Tice, an internationally known educator and author who charges $8,000 a lecture, numbers among his clients General Motors, the Internal Revenue Service, the Central Intelligence Agency, the U.S. Army, Navy, and Air Force, and many fire and police departments. And during 1987, Pacific Institute turned $20 million in sales.[21]

Tice tells trainees to frequently repeat positive self-talk slogans such as "I am a super salesperson and grow every day in every way"; "If it's going to be, it's up to me"; and "Imagination times vividness equals reality on the subconscious level." The courses, like Krone training, create an insiders' vocabulary with key concepts such as "scotomas . . . cultural trances . . . flat worlds," "lock on-lock out," and "reticular activating."

The Anaheim, California, chapter's ten-hour management program for Rockwell titled "New Age Thinking" was retitled "Investment in Excellence" in October 1987—perhaps because of bad publicity the New Age label had attracted in some management quarters.[22]

Ron Zemke, senior editor of *Training* magazine, assessed New Age efforts to transform people on an organization-wide basis:

> If we're talking techniques that claim to work miracles on large groups of people and a philosophy of life that insists on the growth of the individual as well as the success of the organization, we're talking motherhood and apple pie. If that's the New Age, who could object? . . .
>
> The good news, apparently, is that some evolving procedures—psychotechnologies, if you like—may be effective tools for making fundamental changes in peoples' attitudes and thinking. The bad news is . . . well, the same as the good news: Meditation and guided imagery and Suggestopedia and affirmations may indeed be effective tools for changing people.[23]

In other words, the problem may be not that New Age psychotechnologies don't work, but that they work all too well.

17

Education, Music, and Art

Spinning Inward, a handbook by Maureen Murdock, tells teachers and parents how to use guided imagery to enhance children's imagination, learning, and creativity. The title is an apt description of the New Age focus in education and the arts. From learning theories and classroom techniques, to the new breed of electronic and acoustic sounds, to visionary paintings and spiraling architectural design, New Age looks inward—and Eastward.

Children's-book buyer Tim Campbell at Book People in Austin, Texas, says he goes out of his way to find New Age books "that tell kids you *can* take control of your life." Most of these titles are aimed at first to third graders. And along with an ongoing fascination with Eastern spirituality, Campbell sees a resurgence of interest in Native American literature.[1]

Parenting in the New Age "becomes a spiritual journey taken by parent and child, one teaching the other in reciprocal agreement," says Harriette Davis, a trance therapist teacher in North Hollywood, California, who conducts Rainbow Bridge workshops for parents and children who may have "trouble integrating on this Earth plane." The classes, which include "past life regression" and "psychic awareness," tap into the normal frustrations and guilt often produced by parenting responsibilities.

Children in the Los Angeles City School System have been taught to imagine they are one with the sun's rays. In doing so, they are told, they are a part of God, "they are one with Him."[2]

Overt New Age educational philosophy has made sporadic advances into public schools, with an accent in California and parts of Colorado. The wider arena of what is known as "values clarification," which teaches children to discover and clarify their own values rather than having them imposed by outside authority, is compatible with New Age thinking on "confluent education." This New Age theory posits the equality of individual values because everyone has the wisdom of the universe within. Or, as Shirley MacLaine puts it: "We already know everything. The knowingness of our divinity is the highest intelligence."

The chief architect of confluent education, the late Beverly Galyean, described it as a holistic approach using thinking, the five senses, feeling, and intuition.

In an interview with religion researcher Frances Adeney in 1980, Galyean summed up her beliefs: "Once we begin to see that we are all God, that we all have the attributes of God, then I think the whole purpose of human life is to reown the Godlikeness within us; the perfect love, the perfect wisdom, the perfect understanding, the perfect intelligence, and when we do that, we create back to that old, that essential oneness which is consciousness."[3]

Galyean developed three federally funded education programs for the Los Angeles Public Schools—using guided imagery and meditation. In the early 1980s, the similarly New Age-oriented Project GOAL (Guidance Opportunities for Affective Learning) was developed with federal and state funds to help handicapped children in Irvine, California, as well as nonhandicapped students in fifty-four school districts.[4]

Marilyn Ferguson approvingly notes such "subtle forces" at work in education:

> For example, tens of thousands of classroom teachers, educational consultants and psychologists, counselors, administrators, researchers, and faculty members in colleges of education have been among the millions engaged in *personal transformation*. They have . . . begun to link regionally and nationally, to share strategies, to conspire for the teaching of all they most value: freedom, high expectations, awareness, pat-

terns, connections, creativity. . . . Even a tiny minority of committed teachers, counselors and administrators can set off seismic shocks with programs that work.[5]

Complaining that American educational institutions have limited and fragmented students and the learning process— "relentlessly turning wholes into parts"—Ferguson identifies a malaise that has exasperated many educators: "Whereas the young need some sort of initiation into an uncertain world, we give them the bones from the culture's graveyard. Where they want to do real things, we give them abstract busywork, blank space to fill in with the 'right' answers, multiple choices to see if they can choose the 'right' answers. Where they need to find meaning, the schools ask memorization; discipline is divorced from intuition, pattern from parts."[6]

But the times are a-changing in the teaching of the traditional "three Rs." Pat Boerger, an instruction consultant in the Los Angeles City Schools, says that visualization "is becoming a big part of critical thinking. In relationship to problem solving, it is essential and is just now beginning to impact our schools. Children are taught to visualize alternatives that are the most reasonable for a given problem situation. Reasoning needs to come before the math problem, or the language session. . . . [With visualization techniques] children begin to see the broad implications of an answer, not just a narrow, 'fill-in-the-blank' approach."[7]

And now a New Age curriculum is abroad in the land of higher education—a curriculum that takes altered states of consciousness and human qualities of transcendence seriously. For example, Citrus Community College in Azusa, California, has given credit for self-hypnosis classes and parapsychology courses that teach about ESP, telepathy, clairvoyance, how to see and interpret auras, how to recognize out-of-body experience, and how to harness the secrets of spoon-bending through psychokinesis.[8]

Sexual counseling derived from Tantric and Taoist practices is offered at the California Institute of Integral Studies in San Francisco through a class designed to meet the human sexuality requirement for the California psychology license.

The school is accredited by the Western Association of Schools and Colleges and grants a Ph.D. in psychology and a master's in anthropology, philosophy, and religion. The institute's weekend workshops have included "Ethnobotany and Shamanism: Psychedelics Before and After History" and "Towards a Psychological Archaeology and the Forgotten Nose."[9]

Other alternative-style universities in the San Francisco Bay area alone include the Rosebridge Graduate School of Integrative Psychology (the Ph.D. combines "western psychology with the wisdom of the body, mind and spirit of the East"); Antioch University (M.A. In Somatic Psychology and Education, which covers "bioenergetics, primal therapy, gestalt, various forms of Reichian therapy and a host of lesser known modalities"); and John F. Kennedy University (master's programs in psychology, holistic health, and arts and consciousness, promoted as "The graduate school for the study of human consciousness. . . . Come home to the whole of yourself").

Although in 1977 a federal court declared Transcendental Meditation—introduced into New Jersey public schools in 1975 with government funds—to be a violation of church-state separation because of its Hindu undertones, meditating on the Inner Self, often in conjunction with yoga, is taught at some state universities.

According to New Age leaders, however, what is taught at the university level now needs to filter down to the elementary classroom and kindergarten—and even to "mother's knee."

"We have to realize once and for all that there is no separation between the sacred and the secular, so it will be natural for our children to assume this," says educator Gay Luce, who has been a consultant to the National Institute of Mental Health and the President's Scientific Advisory Committee. She adds that she fully expects meditation techniques involving "the body's energy chakras" to be taught in kindergarten soon.[10]

In his award-winning essay, "A Religion for a New Age," John Dunphy declared: "I am convinced that the battle for humankind's future must be waged and won in the public school classroom by teachers who correctly perceive their role as the proselytizers of a new faith: a religion of humanity that recognizes and respects the spark of what theologians call divinity in every human being."[11]

Sights and Sounds

New Age education is getting help from films, television, and popular music.

In the movie *The Dark Crystal*, produced by the Muppets' creator Jim Henson, good and evil are transcended and cosmic unity returns after a lost shard once split off from the planet's magic crystal is restored. The lovable Mystics do not win over the evil Skecsees, but the two fuse into one group; ultimate reality is beyond good and evil, writer Douglas Groothuis says of the plot.[12]

New Age music also transmits values and transports souls into a kind of cosmic connectedness, proponents say, while at the same time uniquely touching spontaneous chords in individuals. Largely instrumental, this music is unstructured and circular in form, with a blurring of tones; often there is no ending or resolution to the melody.

Critics call it "yuppie Muzak," "aural wallpaper," and "audio valium." Those who like it say it echoes the ambience of natural environments, helps them relax and meditate, or elicits a joy that energizes and brightens them.

Whatever else it is, New Age music is diverse, part of a complex cultural trend, and appeals to a growing cross-section of Americans that extends far beyond the core of identifiable New Agers. It includes the sounds of plant vibrations, animal and nature noises, Celtic harps, gourd-shaped sitars, tunable tabla drums, drone-generating tambouras, and digital synthesizers. It can even be produced by a sheet of steel balanced on a balloon submerged in water.[13]

New Age music is also a hot industry. Windham Hill, whose serene, introspective recordings first sold in health food stores in the 1970s, had parlayed an initial $300 investment into more than $35 million in sales during 1987.[14] The Palo Alto, California-based company also cut the first New Age record ever to go platinum (George Winston's

classic *December*) and created a special division to license
New Age music for use by advertisers.

New Age sounds can be heard on several nationally
syndicated radio programs. "Music from the Hearts of Space,"
which signed up forty stations during the summer of 1986,
was reaching more than two hundred public stations by early
1988.[15]

But is New Age music really new? Some commentators,
like former *Journal* editors Peggy Taylor and Rick Ingrasci,
trace its emergence to the late 1960s and early 1970s with
recordings such as Paul Horn's solo flute album "Inside the
Taj Mahal" and Brian Eno's minimalist electronic "Music for
Airports."

"As the genre emerged it was generally restricted to
meditative, ambient music. . . . [T]he idea caught on, and a
growing number of listeners began using the better-quality
recordings to create a peaceful, introspective atmosphere for
reading, massage, relaxation or meditation."[16]

By the time it had become a bona fide marketing category,
New Age music had broadened to include everything from
the blending of polyrhythmic ragas from the East with
contemporary rock rhythms from the West, to pastoral,
impressionistic New Age chamber concerts. And then there
are eerie tribal sounds and "Earth music," produced on
ancient instruments. New Age music artist Elisabeth Waldo
of Northridge, California, for example, has a collection that
includes llama bone flutes, ceramic whistles, fruit shell
rattles, and two rasps fashioned from human bones.[17]

Beethoven once noted that "music is the mediator between
the life of the senses and the life of the spirit." This seems
particularly apt in regard to New Age music. For while there
is nothing overtly theological about it, many New Age music
superstars (such as Japanese synthesist-composer Mansanori
Takahashi) consider their music to be part of their spiritual
path and a means to express New Age values and to shape
culture.

Not everyone is moved by New Age music, of course; some
find it tedious and boring and the victim of cheap imitations.
Iconoclastic rock musician Frank Zappa objects to New Age
music being promoted as therapy. "As far as I'm concerned,"
he says, "music has better things to do than find one drone

chord to help you achieve your mantra. If it's therapy, let's not call it music."[18]

Indeed, meditational/space musicians like Steve Halpern have collaborated with physicians and music therapists to create stress-reduction music designed to help people cope with sickness or face terminal disease. Hospitals throughout the country use Halpern's series of "Anti-Frantic Alternative" tapes.

"Who knows," quipped Pamela Bloom, a contributing editor to *High Fidelity* magazine. "Before too long, your yearly check-up might turn out to be a tune-up."[19]

Iasos Inter-Dimensional Music, creator of "angelic music," claims that its *Angels of Comfort* record was selected at a conference of persons involved in "near-death experiences" to be the music most similar to the "heavenly music" they heard while "on the other side." Many said that's what they would like to be hearing when they make the "transition known as death."[20]

Some ethereal music, like that of Emmy Award-winning Emerald Web artists Bob Stohl and Kat Epple, is packaged in video albums, combining the sounds and sights of New Age. The latter include moving mandalas (visual symbols used as meditation aids), swirling lasers, and electro-kinetic abstract images.

Visions and Visionaries

New Age has also influenced the visual arts. For example, computer-generated art, including "Fractal Fairy Tales," simulating the branching, twisting organic shapes found in nature, is a popular New Age art genre.

"These mathematically inspired pieces of art, with their fine detail and dazzling colors, reveal the richness and complexity that are hidden in even the most elementary equations," says Bruce Schechter, suggesting that the border between art and science is not only less clearly marked than previously thought, but also that their commingling holds immense potential for exploring the mysteries of creativity.[21]

The nondualistic dimension of existence, seen as underlying all of life, reverberates powerfully in New Age art and architecture. It also represents a reaction to the depressing

"aloneness," profound isolation, and numbing violence inherent in the themes of much contemporary abstract art.

"New Age art is an attempt to create a safe, fantasized
environment, with its friendly animals like unicorns, trees,
landscapes and castles," says Karen Hoyt, a psychologist and
artist who has studied and written about the New Age
movement. "New Age art focuses on 'the universe next door'
. . . but it is escapist and narcissistic. It depicts contact with
spirits—other beings who are like you—but you are not in
relationship with them."[22]

Gilbert Williams, considered to be a quintessential Visionary painter, exemplifies these themes in canvasses filled with
the subjective imagery of transcendence: moons and temples,
goddesses and gateways, groves and guardians, lakes and
light "beings" shining with bright color and intricacy.

In similar fashion, New Age architecture is "art for the
people": "It has to do with earth-sheltering homes, solar-
powered homes, and hand-built homes. The new wave
concerns itself with log homes and Buckminster Fuller's
geodesic domes. The latest in technology, in energy-aware
physics, is being combined with the pervasive belief that
homes are to live in, that they should be comfortable, that
even if a wood-burning stove spoils 'the line of a wall,' it can
be tolerated."[23]

Thus New Age architect Eugene Tsui of Berkeley, California, says his work is "expressive of the supreme intelligence
and spiritual powers manifest in Nature."[24] He designs
houses like the one he did for N. Starr in Baja, Mexico, which
floats in the ocean and is partially anchored to a coastline rock
outcropping. A bridgeway connects the music studio/patio
with the main portion of the house, and a screened aviary tops
the seven-story structure.

And Camden, Maine, tentmaker Bill Moss, who looks upon
his work as "functional sculpture," designs "perfect pitch"
tents that are all hoops and peaks; their graceful, sweeping
curves "resemble crustaceans or caterpillars more than home
sweet home."[25]

New Age artist Sharon Skolnick, who is fond of painting
surreal images within images of San Francisco scenes, sums it
up well: "Making art for me is a day trip into my primal self
and the collective selves where we all join in a kind of divine
molecular dance-prayer."[26]

18

Holistic Health and Healing

To begin with, there's the problem of spelling. Is it "wholistic" or "holistic"? Jack Gordon, editor of *Training* magazine, says it depends on what you're talking about: "If they bring in a motivational speaker who tells you how to accomplish anything you set your mind to, at work or in life, that's wholistic, with a "w." If they bring in an Apache medicine man and a live eagle, that's holistic."[1]

Holistic medicine, to say the least, is a complex and controversial topic that includes a baffling grab bag of quasimedical therapeutic techniques. But it is also an emerging force in medical practice, based on the concept that body, mind, and spirit are interconnected and that true health—being whole, from the Anglo-Saxon word *haelen*—results from the proper interaction and alignment of all three.

New models of wellness and healing are being popularized by many in the mainstream medical professions and by people who are sick and tired of finding conventional medicine all too impersonal, expensive, and ineffective.

Even in the 1970s, the mushrooming of holistic health centers and networks testified to the vulnerability of traditional health care. In her 1980 book *Aquarian Conspiracy*, Marilyn Ferguson noted that "Within a few short years, without a shot's being fired, the concept of holistic health has been legitimized by federal and state programs, endorsed by politicians, urged and underwritten by insurance companies, co-opted in terminology (if not always in practice) by many physicians, and adopted by medical students. Consumers demand health, a whole new assortment of entrepreneurs promise it, and medical groups look for speakers to explain it."[2]

The Association for Holistic Health describes the holistic approach as "person oriented rather than disease oriented," having "full vibrant health (positive wellness), not symptom amelioration" as its objective, and "primary prevention rather than crisis intervention" as its focus.[3] And the American Holistic Medical Association reported that 2%, or about 10,000, of all doctors in the United States practice some form of holistic medicine.

"Our approach is to do the least that we can, and to have the patient do the most that he can," said Steven Finando, associate director of the Wholistic Health Center in Manhasset, New York, which reportedly treats 1000 patients a month. Finando told a *Forbes* magazine interviewer that the treatment "might involve diet, biofeedback to control stress, acupuncture. We prescribe medicines, but that is seen as a dramatic thing, something not done lightly."[4]

The cause of holistic healing was given a major shot in the arm by the classic case of Norman Cousins, well-known editor and publisher of *Saturday Review*. Writing in the *New England Journal of Medicine*, Cousins told the world how he was apparently cured of a strange Asian disease by megadoses of love, laughter, Vitamin C, and the will to live. Every other method failed until he began viewing his favorite film comedies from his hospital bed and reading books on humor.[5]

"The belief system is a prime physiological reality," Cousins wrote. "The greatest force in the human body is the natural drive of the body to heal itself—but that force is not independent of the belief system which can translate expectations into physiological change."[6]

When health practitioners talk about such things as "the natural healing powers of one's intuitive mind" and "the healing depths of one's own soul," they are—whether they know it or not—treading on the edge of New Age concepts about the mind, body, and cosmos.[7] For the underlying assumption of a host of new diagnostic and curative consciousness techniques is that reality is one and manifests itself as universal spiritual energy in the body. That perception is also as old as the most ancient system of mind-body healing known to humans—the shamanic methods of persons previously known as witches, witch doctors, medicine men, sorcerers, wizards, and magicians.[8]

Said to be omnipresent, spiritual energy supposedly flows from the universe into living beings, circulating within them in an orderly and discernible pattern, and then flowing out again. In Eastern religions this impersonal energy, or life force, is the equivalent of "God." The Chinese call the dynamic energy field "Chi"; the Japanese call it "Ki." It is known as "prana" by the yogis, and by a variety of names in other cultures.[9] However, New Age strategists seeking to import the concept into the West prefer the term "bioenergy" because it avoids the Eastern mystical connotations.

Whatever you call it, it is not a recognizable force like gravity or electromagnetism. Supposedly it is generated by the interplay of the "yin" and the "yang," which represent the opposing male and female dimensions in the Eastern religion of Taoism.

Thus, in Eastern medicine, pain is understood not as a symptom but as an accumulation of energy in some part of the body, which, if correctly redistributed, can restore health and harmoniously "balance" the body. "Energy—psychic energy—corrects or balances organic wrongness."[10]

While not all holistic health practitioners base their work on thoroughgoing New Age concepts of energy and the mind, most of the popular holistic therapies are predicated on a spiritualistic understanding of psychic powers. The following are but a few examples:

Dolores Krieger, a nurse and Ph.D. professor at New York University, teaches her system of Therapeutic Touch to a wide following of care givers, and the method is explicated through continuing education courses across the nation. Krieger centers on a "compassionate intention to heal" by achieving a meditative state. She moves her hands over or just above the patient's body, hovering where she senses "accumulated energy." Then, she tries to transmit a feeling of well-being to the patient, channeling "prana" and redistributing the patient's energies.

Acupuncture and its related therapies of acupressure

(shiatsu) and reflexology also make use of the belief that energy flow can be redirected to balance healing energies by inserting needles (acupuncture) or by applying pressure (acupressure and reflexology) to specific points on the body.

Certified "acutherapist" Mark Fingert advertises free energy-balancing seminars that promise to teach "amazing techniques" to:

- Balance all the body's acupuncture meridians, neurolymphatics, neurovasculars, chakras, and more . . . *within 2 minutes*
- Eliminate on-the-job-stress within minutes
- Eliminate wrinkles
- Eliminate environmental negativity
- Increase the white blood count to fight infections
- Save $3000 on orthodontics

But, Fingert advises seekers attending a seminar at the American Red Cross building in San Francisco: "Bring your checkbook: Many unique health/consciousness products will be available."[11]

Reflexology rests on the assumption that the foot is the window into internal body parts, and that massaging a precise point on the foot will bring fast inside relief just where it's needed. Increasingly popular, reflexology is now as common at fairs and exhibit conventions as the booths of palm readers and handwriting analysts; for $10, walk-weary sightseers can enjoy a fifteen-minute foot massage that does wonders for the feet—whether or not it balances their bile.

Iridology, or iris diagnosis, is based on the belief that observation and intuitive skills can discern a person's physical condition and ailments. If the eye is the mirror of the soul, the theory goes, then gazing into the iris can detect what's wrong—or going to go wrong—with a person's gall bladder or whatever. The theory is that each area of the body has a corresponding locus within the iris that undergoes a "microinflammatory" change corresponding to changes in the disordered organ.[12]

Reading the auras, or etheric electromagnetic color fields—thought by many New Agers to surround every living thing—is another holistic crowd-pleaser at psychic fairs. Health psychics claim they can remedy nearly any ailment by reading the sufferer's aura and then prescribing the correct massage, aroma therapy (the use of scents for healing), color therapy (application of colored lights, clothing, or crystals to restore proper vibration and balance), or . . .

Then there's cymatic therapy, developed by British osteopath Peter Guy Manners. Believing that each part of the body vibrates at a unique audible frequency, he devised an instrument which, when placed directly on the body, reputedly transmits the "correct" sound frequency of health to a diseased organ.[13]

Yoga, Reiki, Rolfing, and a host of other "bodywork" therapies are based on the assumption that the body needs alignment of its physical parts and vibrational energies. Rolfing, a sometimes painful, deep massage technique, is said to release the negative energies stored in the physical body by tuning it with the Earth's gravity field. It also appears to attune many people with the New Age movement by helping them get in touch with their "own physical vehicle and with the past which is stored as energy in it," says John F. Miller III.[14]

The regime of vitamins and minerals, natural foods (often including a vegetarian diet), and homeopathic remedies (small doses of natural medications to stimulate the body's immune system) form additional spokes in the well-oiled holistic wheel of health. The revolution has juiced up business for the nation's more than 6000 natural health food stores, which had sales estimated at $3.3 billion in 1987.[15]

New Age health spas have also been sprouting with a fecundity akin to that of the ubiquitous bean sprout. At Anne-Marie Bennstrom's upscale New Age spa, The Ashram, in Calabasas, California, the schedule is rigorous.

"The day includes yoga, a three-hour hike, fruit juice for lunch, more hiking, weight lifting, swimming, a vegetarian dinner. Then clients meet in the meditation hall for health programs. There, Bennstrom tells her students: 'Your body is crystallized thought. . . . If you are in harmony and at peace with yourself, it doesn't matter what you eat, even chocolate cake.' She concludes, 'One day food will give you up, and you will live in the fire of your prana [spiritual life force].' "[16]

Of course, the self-help philosophy that eating the right

stuff will make you live longer, avoid cancer, have a five-star sex life, and get ahead faster at the office isn't a maxim confined to hard-core New Ageism. Nor is the use of hypnosis, biofeedback, yoga exercises, or visualization techniques. For example, biofeedback can be effective in helping lower blood pressure, control headaches, and overcome muscular tics and insomnia. Or vegetarianism may be adopted as a way of life because of nutritional or ecological concerns.

However, these become manifestations of the New Age when they are seen as being regulated by some form of mystical, spiritual energy, or when they are adhered to because of a belief in reincarnation and pantheism. Take vegetarianism: If the soul is on an eternal journey progressing through many life forms, then it is wrong to eat the flesh of animals that share a common bond with man in the universal life force or "congealed energy" that is "God."

"If this is indeed true, then to kill an animal is to tamper with a soul," says John F. DeVries.[17]

One of the more controversial holistic therapies is the treatment Dr. and Mrs. Carl Simonton of Fort Worth, Texas, employ on cancer patients. Using relaxation, meditation, and visualization, the Simontons teach that a person's "active imagination" can prod the body's immune system into destroying even widespread malignancies.

"Force yourself to mentally picture the cancer," says the doctor's voice on a cassette used to instruct patients. "Picture your body's own white blood cells—a vast army that was put there to eliminate the abnormal cells. . . . See the white cells attacking the cancer cells and carrying them off. . . . See the cancer shrinking. . . . See yourself becoming more in tune with life."[18]

Simonton does not eschew conventional methods of cancer treatment, but sees his work as a supplement. Underlying his brand of psychotherapy as an alternative to surgery is the idea of personal responsibility for one's illnesses. The view that persons cause their own sicknesses and injuries in order to learn a lesson in this life, or from a past life, is fairly common among New Agers.

Although critics scoff, Simonton maintains: "If we are going to believe that we have the power in our own bodies to overcome cancer, then we have to admit that we also had the power to bring on the disease in the first place."[19]

The list of the most mysterious and controversial approaches to holistic medicine would also have to include psychic diagnoses and healing through trance channeling and shamanism, as well as psychic surgery. These procedures and rituals that critics label "fringe medicine" share much common ground with the paranormal.

Parapsychologists Alberto Villoldo and Stanley Krippner have detailed their visits to six healers and shamans in Brazil, including Edson Quieroz, a licensed M.D., who practices psychic healing and operates with a rusty knife and no anesthesia. According to Villoldo and Krippner, there had been no reports of any infections or deaths resulting from Quieroz's practice.[20]

Techniques such as these are the most open to exaggeration, fraud, deception, and quackery, yet there is little doubt cures have been effected. How? is the question.

Placebo power, answer many.

New York psychologist Larry LeShan tells about a woman who once telephoned and asked him to perform a long-distance meditative healing that evening. The next day she called back to say her relief had been immediate. But LeShan had forgotten to do the healing![21]

Dr. Wayne Oates, professor and author, reported on thirteen double-blind studies, in which one group of chronic-pain patients received a placebo while another group received an active pain medication. In the studies, 35% of chronic-pain patients on placebos received at least 50% relief from pain "because they believed they were getting the real thing."[22]

Oates and others speak about endorphins, a range of natural pain relievers, or analgesics, that the body manufactures.

"There is a hypothesis," Oates declares, "that the placebo, thoroughly believed in, kicks on the endorphin system . . . and changes the capacity of the body to actually heal itself. And so now our physicians are talking at med school about the 'biology of belief.' "[23]

Many New Agers, like Marilyn Ferguson, carry this out to the fullest degree. The mind, she says, is "primary or coequal in *all* illness. . . . Whether cancer or schizophrenia or a cold [all] originates in the bodymind."[24]

Others, like scientific investigator Karl Sabbagh, would say it differently: When they do work, these New Age therapies create psychosomatic improvement through belief in the therapy or the therapist, "enhanced by the full panoply of unusual devices and charts, pseudoscientific terminology, and single-minded concern shown by the therapist for the patient."[25]

Albert Schweitzer reportedly remarked that "the witch doctor succeeds for the same reason that all the rest of us [doctors] succeed. Each patient carries his own doctor inside him. They come to us not knowing this truth."[26]

Community mental health centers in the state of New York have used spiritism as a supplementary healing system since the mid 1980s. And in the Southwest, Navaho shamans have been allowed to enter hospitals to work with Native American patients, often using herbs and chants.[27]

Whatever questionable items are in holistic health's bag of mystical medicine, a promising development is the growing concern in traditional health care circles for "promoting prevention and life-style changes rather than merely treating symptoms or picking up the pieces when the body breaks down."[28]

New Age advocates point to what they see as responsible efforts to link traditional and alternative styles of medicine. Examples include the Plane Tree Unit at Pacific Presbyterian Hospital in San Francisco, where a model thirteen-bed wing combining the two approaches was under evaluation in late 1987 by the University of Washington[29] and American Biologics Hospital and Medical Center in Tijuana, Mexico. This licensed, full-service facility advertises itself as "the world's first total assembly of all major metabolic/nutritional and eclectic modalities."

Holistic health may be the most potent force to emerge from the New Age movement.[30] The market for the products, as well as for techniques of chiropractic and massage, is likely to endure and grow as more and more Americans become concerned about self-care, wellness, and ever-rising costs of professional health systems.

19

Psychology: Outside In

They spend the day precariously groping their way, helping each other inch their feet along parallel ropes strung a dizzying fifty feet above the ground. Many report exhilaration on the far side of fear—a "breakthrough experience" when feelings of self-limitation dissolve into the belief they can do anything they set their minds to.

The next day, however, the group of nearly fifty AT&T executives divides into teams to play the Samurai game, a simulation exercise of warrior martial arts where things don't go well at all.

"Essentially everybody loses," said Chris Majer, whose Sportsmind, Inc., was teaching 3000 of the huge utility's managers how to realize their creative potential. "The idea is to find out how you behave when you and your team lose."[1]

Seekers of full human potential also play the Samurai game at Esalen Institute, the Northern California bastion of once-shocking consciousness-raising techniques. But at Esalen, the Samurai simulation focuses strongly on death.

Participants are invited to "enter the state of consciousness of a medieval samurai, to live intensely in the moment, and to experience symbolic death and rebirth." And before returning to the office on Monday, wrote Alice Kahn, "we were to join in 'a symbolic battle to the death . . . to experience the ultimate futility of war and the value of every moment of existence.'"[2]

Esalen, cradle of the human potentials movement and
known in the countercultural heyday of the 1960s as the wild
frontier of the touchy-feely and the primal hot tub, has come
of New Age. Through the years Esalen has attracted such
celebrity intellectuals as writers Aldous Huxley and Alan
Watts, historian Arnold Toynbee, scientists Linus Pauling
and Fritjof Capra, architect R. Buckminster Fuller, theologian
Paul Tillich, former California governor Jerry Brown, and a
host of psychologists—Carl Rogers, Fritz Perls, B. F. Skinner,
Rollo May, and Abraham Maslow. (The latter, lost in a dense
fog one night during a vacation trip, mistook Esalen for a
motel and ended up forging a long, symbiotic relationship
with the institute.)

Some of Esalen's outlandish excesses have been curbed,
and less extravagant claims are being made there these days.
But the meat and potatoes seminars are still meditation,
psychotherapy, Eastern religion, and massage and bodywork—the core of New Age consciousness. And since Esalen
was founded in 1962, many of its concepts have gradually
permeated nearly every YMCA and university extension
program in America.

Psychology—under a kaleidoscope of mutant schools and
theories—has shaped the modern world, molding its beliefs
and lifestyles as no other influence. Most of this has happened only since World War II. But to understand all this,
and how the universal "oneness" seeped into the collective
unconscious of the New Age, we need to go back to Freud,
the famous creator of the psychoanalytical school of psychology.

Sigmund Freud (1856–1939) believed that strong and often
competing subconscious forces and instincts are the engine
for the human mind. He used trance induction and hypnosis
techniques to ferret out repressions from the unconscious,
holding that sexual repressions were the basis for most
human ills.

According to Freud's theories of determinism, these biological instincts constantly clash with the moral standards
imposed by society. Freud, who was familiar with occult
literature, also thought that belief in God was a sign of
neurosis and that man was a being neither different from nor
superior to animals.

Not all of Freud's disciples totally agreed with their brilliant and eccentric mentor. One of them, Swiss psychoanalyst Carl Jung (1875–1961), questioned Freud's tying of all human behavior to selfish and infantile sexual impulses, and Jung embraced spirituality as a vital component of personality. Thus, in Jungian psychology there was room for religious thought and mystical experience.

Jung also posited the "collective unconscious," which has been defined as "a reservoir of psychological images and forces accruing through all history and shared by all people."[3] These experiences, Jung said, are "the primordial images which have always been the basis of man's thinking—the whole treasure-house of mythological motifs."[4]

Psychiatrist M. Scott Peck calls the collective unconscious the theory "in which we inherit the wisdom of the experience of our ancestors without ourselves having the personal experience."[5]

Some identify the channeling phenomenon as a way of tapping into the pool of this shared, or collective group memory. Religious studies professor Carl A. Raschke notes: "At one remarkable stroke the notion of a 'collective unconscious' became, for Jung, a construct which for the first time in the history of mainline thought could be cited to warrant not only the claims of mystics, but the odd and often convoluted metaphysical statements of seers, spiritualists and Gnostics. . . . He insisted that the meaning of human history actually was to be found outside of history—in the collective unconscious."[6]

But we hasten on to the next major stages in the psychological drama: humanistic psychology and transpersonal psychology.

One of the chief architects of the humanistic school was Abraham Maslow (1908–70), whose concept of "self-actualization" became a buzzword in the human potentials and pastoral counseling circles of the 1970s. Self-actualization, or growth values, were at the top of Maslow's totem of human needs. And capping them all was transcendence: a person's ability to reach out beyond individuality and become united with the whole of reality.

Since our "inner nature is good or neutral rather than bad," Maslow wrote, "it is best to bring it out and encourage it rather than to suppress it. If it is permitted to guide our life, we grow healthy, fruitful and happy."[7]

This seemed like good news for those who wished to assign humanity a slot one notch above the animal kingdom and quash scientific determinism by restoring freedom of choice, dignity, and responsibility to the human equation. But Maslow's transcendence was the universal potentiality of human nature, not the supernatural breaking in via a transcendent and personal God.

Before long other psychologists were building upon Maslow's assumptions that persons are good by nature and that human potential is unlimited. Among the best known and most influential of the human potentials psychotherapists was Carl R. Rogers (1902–87). One of Rogers' chief contributions was his belief in not making diagnoses—a technique known as "client-centered" therapy. The approach stemmed from Rogers' assertion that individuals always hold within themselves the answer to any problem, and therefore the role of the counselor is simply to create the proper environment for the solutions to emerge. This is done by simply reflecting back the client's feelings rather than guiding or directing him or her.

Because, in Rogers' view, human experience is the center and source of meaning, self-realization can be accomplished apart from responsibility to other persons, tradition, or an objective God who makes moral demands. One is only responsible to one's own feelings. Only you can judge your values, Rogers said.[8]

Elevation of personal growth as the highest good has been sharply criticized on grounds that its assumptions ultimately lead to a psychology of narcissism, asocial irresponsibility, and personal license. Nevertheless, humanistic psychology and transpersonal psychology, the most recent entrant in the human potentials lineup, have made enormous impact on Western culture. And the New Age script has copied, line for line, their basic tenet: One can realize infinite potential—become enlightened—because personal experience equals reality, and reality can be created by focusing on the self.

Ken Wilber, a leading New Age exponent and figure in transpersonal psychology, traces the stages of psychological growth through fourteen levels which mirror the seven Yogic chakras of Eastern mysticism. At the "most realized state," he maintains, a person experiences higher consciousness—the goal of mystics through the ages, the essence of Maslow's "peak experience," and the apex of transpersonal psychology. At this stage, says Wilbur, "we are in touch with the divine; the physical is lost in the spiritual; we become enlightened."[9]

One of the most potent popularizers of the old/new concept of spiritual growth through oneness with deity is Scott Peck, whose *The Road Less Traveled* emerged from feeble beginnings to reign almost two years as number one on the *New York Times* bestseller list.[10]

What does God want of humans? Peck asks in the book. What are we to grow toward? What is the goal of evolution?

> [N]o matter how much we may like to pussyfoot around it, all of us who postulate a loving God and really think about it eventually come to a single terrifying idea: God wants us to become Himself (or Herself or Itself). We are growing toward godhood. God is the goal of evolution. It is God who is the source of the evolutionary force and God who is the destination. This is what we mean when we say He is the Alpha, and the Omega, the beginning and the end. . . .
>
> It is one thing to believe in a nice old God who will take good care of us from a lofty position of power which we ourselves could never begin to attain. It is quite another to believe in a God who has it in mind for us precisely that we should attain His position, His power, His wisdom, His identity.[11]

As the human potentials movement migrated east from California, it had by the end of the 1970s already spawned 8000 different "therapies," Alvin Toffler wrote in *The Third Wave*. We can only briefly tour a few New Age psychotechnologies here. But notice the "divine within" in all of them.

• Down the coast from Esalen is a half-sister, Elysium Institute, known for its "clothing optional" seminars and hydrotherapy pools. Elysium offers sessions on the "New Age Focus," featuring such leaders as psychic Robbie Jacobson: "She will help you to focus on yourself, to capture the source of your own abundance, to tap into the power of universal consciousness, and to create your future by developing your own clairvoyant techniques."[12]

• Shakti Gawain, who leads workshops on visualization at

the Shakti Center in Marin County, California, talks about
trusting intuition above reason:

> At first you may find that the more you act on intuition, the
> more things in your life seem to be falling apart—you might
> lose your job, a relationship, certain friends—your car might
> even stop working! You're actually changing fast and shedding
> the old things in your life that don't fit you anymore. As long as
> you didn't let go of them, they imprisoned you. Now, as you
> continue on this path, things will just fall into place. Doors will
> open in a seemingly miraculous way.[13]

• Composer-musician Robert Fritz has developed a program
called Technologies for Creating which teaches that persons
can create the results they want in their lives. Fritz assumes
that the so-called superconscious—also called "higher self,"
"inner teacher," and "spiritual guide"—can be activated. By
tapping into the superconscious we allow the deeper, spiritual side of ourselves to emerge, he says.[14]

• In the Hawaiian process of Ho'oponopono—classes are
regularly presented throughout the world by The Foundation
of I—"Self-I-Dentity consists of the three aspects of the Self
or Mind in partnership with the Divine Creator. The SELF—
subconscious, conscious and superconscious ... exists in
every atom and molecule of Creation." The Self-I-Dentity
process is not limited to humans, according to the foundation's brochure, but may be used for both animate and
inanimate objects and applied to "any problem or situation."
Note the Jungian concept in Self-I-Dentity: "If we can accept
that we are the sum total of all past thoughts, emotions,
words, deeds and actions and that our present lives and
choices are colored or shaded by this memory bank of the
past, then we begin to see how a process of correcting or
setting aright can change our lives, our families, and our
society."[15]

• The Cauldron of Thoth journey of empowerment with
Nicki Scully induces altered states of consciousness "in
which previously inaccessible information becomes available
from our internal wellspring of the collective, our Cauldron."[16]

• The concept of "progressive deepening" through "process
meditation" has also been widely popularized by the national

"Intensive Journaling" workshops of psychotherapist Ira Progoff. (We'll say more about him in chapter 22.)

Indian mystic Bhagwan Shree Rajneesh, whom we met earlier in our Who's Who of New Age gurus, has been one of the most successful mixers of Eastern philosophies with Western psychotherapeutic techniques. He combined dance and bioenergetics, Gestalt and hypnotherapy, encounter and sensory awareness, and created dozens of new and hybrid groups. Pushing therapists to the limit, Rajneesh admonished them to trust their intuition.

"If they were stymied, they were to relax, breathe deeply, touch the *mala* [bead necklace with the guru's picture pressed in a locket], or summon up their Master's image. He would be there, with the appropriate response, working through them."[17]

The goal of the spiritual pathway along which he sent his disciples, said Rajneesh, was for them to disappear into the oneness of God: "The enlightenment happens only when the ego has disappeared. The ego is the darkness of the soul, the ego is the imprisonment of the soul, the 'I' is the barrier to the ultimate . . . *You* will never encounter God. If *you* are there, God is not there because the seed [ego] is there. When you disappear, God is there; so there is no encounter, really."[18]

That process is akin to various forms of *tantra*, a ubiquitous form of New Age "transcendence into the one" allied with the concepts of Tibetan Buddhism. Through exercises designed to strengthen and purify sexual parts of the body, tantra attempts to deliberately and irrevocably dissolve human identity.

As Brooks Alexander describes the practice: "Tantra unravels the normal world of perception and understanding and reweaves it into an intricate network of occult correspondences that ultimately vanishes into the One . . . Tantra is how the world looks as it disappears."[19]

Something like the line in the country and western song: "I thought happiness was Lubbock, Texas, in my rearview mirror." Or maybe reminiscent of the laws in Lewis Carroll's *Through the Looking Glass*, where people approach objects by walking away from them.

And the list of mass-marketed psychotechnologies goes on: est (Erhard Seminar Training, now called the Forum),

Lifespring, Actualizations, and a plethora of other short-term seminars compact the "One for all" into intensive meetings where old beliefs are torn down and values are restructured through a potpourri of Freudian theory, behavior-modification techniques, Eastern philosophy, and transpersonal psychology.[20]

Frances Adeney, whose analysis of the human potentials movement has been widely cited in Christian literature, says of est:

> [It] is geared toward stripping a person of values, mores and religious beliefs so that one may begin "freely" choosing values and creating one's own reality. The humanistic assumptions of the perfection of the individual and the potential for transcendence are crucial for est. . . . The world is illusion; you see whatever you choose to see. You may create anything you like around you, and in fact, all you see is your own creation. Everything in essence is one; you are perfect; you are God.[21]

Followers of Africa, a nationwide spiritual organization, search for the "essential self" through such techniques as Egyptian gymnastics and African dances. Its workshops and intensives also involve chanting mantras and meditating by concentrating on colorful wall symbols known as yantras. The goal is to achieve the divine life, somewhat akin to the *satori* sought by Buddhists.[22]

A key ingredient in all New Age psychotechnologies is evolution toward a consciousness that seeks to explain the meaning of everything through an amalgamation of mystical and scientific perceptions. Thus, New Age "science" and psychic phenomena merge in the psychology of the Self. The next step is to look at scientific support for this mystical worldview.

20

Science: Universal Mind Over Matter

"Bend! Bend! Bend!" forty seekers shout in unison. They hold up assorted knives and forks at the command of their instructor, Jack Houck, who says he is in charge of advanced research "at a major aerospace company."

Talking about the "field effect" and the "mind connection," PK (psychokinesis) party-giver Houck urges the attentive audience (each paid $20 to attend his workshop) to "realize your potential for applying your mind. Put your mind into that silverware and COMMAND it to bend. Then let it happen!"

Houck's theory is that under paranormal mind-control, metal becomes soft for a five-to-thirty-second "time window." During that interval, a person with good PK power can, with only light pressure, bend and shape the malleable silverware.

At least half of those attending the spoon-bending seminar were able to twist their silverware (which Houck provides and then retrieves after the workshop). Some spoons were only slightly bent. But the man next to me (a friend of Houck's and a PK-party veteran) wrapped his stainless steel fork around itself until it looked like a pretzel.

Unfortunately, my spoon—price sticker of fifteen cents from the St. Vincent de Paul Society still affixed—wouldn't cooperate. I didn't qualify for one of Houck's "Certified Warm Former" buttons, which he hands out to successful "graduates" at his PK parties. Interestingly, Houck won't demonstrate spoon-bending by doing it himself. And he refused to identify the aircraft company that employed him when I asked.[1]

About forty adepts hold PK parties, Tupperware style, all over the world, Houck said, adding that 85% of the 8000 persons who have attended his sessions since 1981 have bent silver. But he allowed that "very scientific and analytical" people may not be able to make PK do their bidding.

Not being sure I fit that category, I tried harder. More pressure. Both hands. A little more . . . more. Yeah! Steady as she bends.

I pocketed the evidence. (And even now as I write, St. Vincent's spoon, with its one right-angled bend in the narrowest part of the stem, hangs as a memento from the lamp above my computer.)

Houck talks about "buckling bowls," "time shifts"—sending information telepathically at one time and receiving it from another—remote viewing, psychic farming, and making soybean seeds sprout on command. (He has some along, moistened just this morning. Nobody has any luck, however, despite loud commands of "Sprout! Sprout! Sprout!")

The importance of it all, Houck intones, is "the shift I see in people regarding self-confidence. . . . They can see the power of positive thinking to change their lives through positive commands."

New Age parlor games? Or evidence that the mind can control physical objects? Or, maybe, that the material world is only an illusion; consciousness is all that's real.

"Mysticism is just tomorrow's science, dreamed today," Marshall McLuhan once said.[2]

Or put in the characteristically optimistic words of the chief Aquarian conspirator, Marilyn Ferguson: "Science is only now verifying what humankind has known intuitively since the dawn of history."[3]

Robert Ellwood believes New Age thinkers seek legitimization by linking parapsychology, right/left brain models, ESP, and the like to scientific respectability. At the same time, Ellwood noted during an interview in his cubbyhole office at the University of Southern California, New Agers make a "desperate attempt" to assert human autonomy in a world that seems to be totally dominated by science and technology.[4]

There also appears to be a similarity between PK party-goers shouting "Bend, Bend, Bend!" and firewalkers chanting "Yes, Yes, Yes! Cool moss, cool moss, cool moss!" as they cross beds of glowing embers in one of the hottest fads of the 1980s.

Cool Mind over Hot Coals?

"Just holding the thought in your mind that you're not going to injure your feet alters the chemistry of your body," insisted Tolly Burkan, once professionally known as Tolly the Clown and of late one of firewalking's most renowned gurus. "Indeed, at many firewalking rituals . . . belief is reportedly all that is needed."[5]

But Al Seckel, a physicist who heads the Southern California Skeptics society, said several Skeptics did the firewalk. One took the pre-walk training to still fear and instill "mind over matter"; the other just appeared at the proper time and hotfooted it through the embers. Neither was burned, Seckel said.[6]

"People can tolerate brief walks through coals. Wet feet also help," he added.

Debunkers aside, the workings of the mind often resist rational analysis. The jury is still out on whether there is a paranormal world exempt from generally known—or at least accepted—natural law.

"There are no unnatural or supernatural phenomena, only very large gaps in our knowledge of what is natural. . . . We should strive to fill those gaps of ignorance," says Edgar D. Mitchell, the *Apollo 14* astronaut.[7] In 1973, Mitchell founded the Institute of Noetic Sciences in Sausalito, California, to investigate PSI, which is shorthand for phenomena that escape traditional scientific definitions, including telepathy, clairvoyance (broadly referred to as ESP), precognition, and PK (psychokinesis).

Across the Golden Gate Bridge at the Center for Applied Intuition (CAI) in San Francisco, scientists say things like, "Tune in to your center and trust what you hear," and they describe intuition as "your direct knowledge without benefit of access to information or learning."

This New Age organization uses a team of channelers—"intuitives," or "expert acumen persons," CAI prefers to call them—to obtain a "consensus" about such things as the physics of earthquakes, the nonphysical aspects of pregnancy and childbirth, and where to dig for precious ore or archaeological treasure.

"We've done things that would make parapsychologists' hair stand on end," confided CAI director William Kautz, who for thirty-one years was a staff scientist at prestigious SRI International (formerly Stanford Research Institute) in Menlo Park, California. "It's hard to raise the money to validate [the findings] . . . but we've a tiger by the tail."[8]

Farther down the coast in Los Angeles, the Mobius Group, an unusual exploration and research organization, stirred up more than mud in Egypt's Alexandria Harbor several years ago when they uncovered ruins of what they claimed were the ancient palaces of Antony and Cleopatra. Through "psychic archaeology" the Mobius team of archaeologists and eleven psychics discovered what were believed to be the underwater buildings that had eluded searchers for more than 100 years. Two Egyptian archaeologists promptly disputed the findings, saying the pillars could have come from any harbor facilities.[9]

Parapsychology—which achieved some respectability in 1969 when the prestigious American Association for the Advancement of Science made the Parapsychological Association a full member organization—is still a marginal science. Problems of validation persist, while disclosures of deceptions, shoddy and ignorant research, and failed predictions have sidelined much of parapsychology in the eyes of the mainstream scientific community.

To those who already believe in the paranormal, scientific evidence is unnecessary; for the stubbornly resistant, no amount of proof is convincing.

But there is a second plank in the bridge New Agers seek to build between science and the mystical view of universal mind over matter: modern physics and quantum theory. To get a handle on that, we need to backtrack for a moment to Descartes, Newton, and Einstein.

René Descartes (1596–1650), the seventeenth-century French philosopher and mathematician, used an analytic method to break thoughts and problems into pieces which he then arranged into logical order and sequence. And Sir Isaac Newton (1642–1727) expanded the Cartesian concept of the universe into the "billiard" model. This has frequently been illustrated by depicting the atom as a nucleus surrounded by electrons, which orbit it like tiny billiard balls. Newton's three-dimensional geometric universe operated according to exact mathematical laws of motion in the context of absolute time and space—"an arena of perfectly coordinated cause and effect," said *New Age Journal* writer Doug Stewart.

"Those who shared his mechanistic worldview argued that everything, from weather to the movement of stars, could surely be predicted if only we had the tools and the time to measure the events leading up to them. Chaos was neither mysterious nor random, just complicated."[10]

Modern science orbited Newton's universe for nearly two centuries—until an unknown Swiss patent clerk published a "modest" little scientific treatise in 1905 called "The Special Theory of Relativity." And, as Alice and Stephen Lawhead suggest, Albert Einstein's E equals mc^2 collided with the old Newtonian physics in a way that has made *relative* a key word ever since—especially for the New Age.[11]

Einstein's famous equation stated that matter and energy are not strictly separate; all mass has energy, and matter may be turned into energy. Space and time are relative to each other and in relation to the fixed speed of light. Einstein's discovery set off explosions in the scientific world, both figuratively and literally.

Tucked away in the neat formula was the revolutionary concept that the universe as observed by the human senses was not necessarily the universe as it really existed. Newtonian notions of independent reality, order, and intelligibility crumbled. An ardent theist, Einstein (1879–1955) was deeply troubled by the implications of unpredictable behavior of atomic particles demanded by his theory. "God does not play dice with the universe," he insisted. Or, as he also expressed it: "God may be subtle, but He is not malicious."[12]

Science writer K. C. Cole neatly capsulized it: "In the realm of the very small, where quantum mechanics rule, every thing appears acausal, elusive. You cannot put your finger on a particular atomic particle as you would on a die. You cannot hit an electron with a known force and say at precisely what speed and direction it will fly off. You cannot follow its movements and say precisely where or how it will wind up. You can only say where it will probably be moving. Atomic particles do not obey the classic Newtonian laws of cause and effect; they are governed by the dictates of chance."[13]

Just five years before Einstein's relativity treatise was published, Max Planck (1858–1947) fathered quantum theory: the idea that "matter absorbed heat energy and emitted light energy discontinuously" in unexpected bursts called "energy packets." Einstein later called them "quanta."[14] Together, Einstein's relativity theories and quantum mechanics came to be referred to as the "new physics."

While quantum theory has prospered among scientists and solved some atomic mysteries, it has created others. One of the most perplexing is central to Werner Heisenberg's famous "uncertainty principle," which he enunciated around 1927. Simply stated, his theory describes limitations in our knowledge of subatomic particles, since observation at that level— such as bouncing particles off other particles—interferes with the phenomenon being observed. In other words, measuring one quantity renders impossible the simultaneous measurement of a related quantity. Thus, the more you know about momentum, the less you know about position, because by the very act of measurement you change the latter.

Heisenberg's principle has sometimes been compared with trying to fix the position of a tomato seed; the gelatinous blob is so slick that by attempting to pinpoint its location, you move it. But science writer Douglas R. Hofstadter warns that the uncertainty principle "is more than an epistemological restriction on human observers; it is a reflection of uncertainties in nature itself. Quantum-mechanical reality does not correspond to macroscopic reality. It's not just that we cannot *know* a particle's position and momentum simultaneously; it doesn't even *have* definite position and momentum simultaneously!"[15]

According to quantum thinkers, then, no one can predict a precise future by examining the present. The basic particles of the universe interact too mysteriously. "The deeper we penetrate," says physicist Max Born, "the more restless becomes the universe; all is rushing about and vibrating in a wild dance."[16]

David Bohm, another heavyweight theoretical physicist, says: "The primary emphasis is now on *undivided wholeness*, in which the observing instrument is not separated from what is observed."[17]

Although these brief explanations may oversimplify the complex theorems of modern physics, they should be sufficient for our purposes here: to gain an initial understanding of how all this relates to New Age.

The connection, in the New Age worldview, is the confluence of mysticism and quantum physics, intuitive meaning and spirituality. This construct is predicated upon a sense of the oneness of all existence and the cyclical rhythms of life and death. And to explicate these ideas, we turn to Austrian physicist Fritjof Capra and French Jesuit paleontologist Pierre Teilhard de Chardin.

Teilhard (1881–1955), whom Marilyn Ferguson found to be the single most influential individual in the thinking of 185 New Agers she surveyed, made major contributions to twentieth century scientific thought, primarily in his theory of evolution.[18] In his law of "complexity-consciousness," Teilhard stated that evolution moves toward increasing complexity. This increase is accompanied by a corresponding rise of consciousness, or awareness, culminating in human evolution; and, finally, a point of convergence, which he called "Omega," is reached. To Teilhard this was God, the Center of centers, and specifically, Christ.

In his writings—considered unorthodox and suppressed by the Roman Catholic church—Teilhard talked about multiplicity and unity; the one, the many. Matter and energy, said the priest, are a single principle, two aspects of one energy. And he considered spirit to be a function of matter.

So intimate was the relationship between matter and spirit for Teilhard, summarized Clarice Lolich, that "he described matter as 'the matrix of consciousness' and consciousness as being 'born from the womb of matter.' In fact, Teilhard was not even afraid to speak of matter becoming spirit: "There is in the world neither spirit nor matter: The 'stuff of the universe' is rather spirit-matter.' "[19]

With Teilhard's theories of progressive evolution and unification of world consciousness in place, along with the quantum physics view of fundamental reality as a shimmering web of vibrant pulsating energy, enter physicist Fritjof Capra, a leading New Age exponent.

Rushing in where the majority of contemporary scientists fear to tread, Capra has become a major mouthpiece for the New Age contention that modern science irrefutably supports mysticism and the "universal One." In his influential and much-quoted book, *The Tao of Physics*, the University of California, Berkeley, physicist declares:

> [T]he basic elements of the Eastern world view are also those of the world view emerging from modern physics. . . . Eastern thought and, more generally, mystical thought, provide a consistent and relevant philosophical background to the theories of contemporary science; a conception of the world in which man's scientific discoveries can be in perfect harmony with his spiritual aims and religious beliefs. . . . The further we penetrate into the submicroscopic world, the more we shall realize how the modern physicist, like the Eastern mystic, has come to see the world as a system of inseparable, interacting and ever-moving components with man being an integral part of this system.[20]

Capra's views stem at least in part from a "visionary experience" he had while he sat on a beach meditating—and which he acknowledged was primed by psychedelic herbs: "I suddenly became aware of my whole environment as being engaged in a gigantic cosmic dance. . . . I 'saw' cascades of energy coming down from outer space, in which particles were created and destroyed in rhythmic pulses: I 'saw' the atoms of the elements and those of my body participating in this cosmic dance of energy, I felt its rhythm and 'heard' its sound, and at that moment I *knew* that this was the Dance of Shiva, the Lord of Dancers worshipped by the Hindus."[21]

In his later book, *The Turning Point*, Capra elaborated on Heisenberg's theory that observation affects the object observed. The electron, Capra said, "does not *have* objective properties independent of my mind."[22]

Other scientists have taken Capra to task for overstating the uncertainty principle. It is the detection apparatus, *not* the observer as a human being, that influences the measurement, they maintain. Indeed, a distant star, observed now, has been behaving like a star for eons without human observation. Capra's assertion is rather like saying that trees only fall in the forest if someone is there to see and hear them topple.

In fact, authentic science itself is not possible without some form of objective reality. Illusion cannot be measured.

"I may give you the greatest description of my observation of molecules, but if my reality doesn't correspond to yours, it means nothing," explains Dean C. Halverson, a critic of world religions and the New Age. "We *do* change things by observing and measuring, but we don't create, or actualize, them" in process.[23]

In what their critics consider a quantum leap of logic, New Age scientists like Capra thrust consciousness into the metaphysical driver's seat. Rather than recording reality, they say, we determine it.[24]

New Age spokesman Michael Talbot avers: "The entire physical universe itself is nothing more than patterns of neuronal energy firing off inside our heads. . . . There is no physical world 'out there.' Consciousness creates all."[25]

New Age apologists are usually quick to appropriate scientific breakthroughs as props for their worldview. At the time of this writing, however, I was unaware of any material by New Age systematizers tying the "string" theory of eminent physicist Edward Witten of the Institute for Advanced Study in Princeton, New Jersey, to New Age assumptions about energy and matter.

K. C. Cole describes modern superstring theory as the hypothesis that "the universe started with 10 dimensions, six of which retracted after the 'Big Bang' into space far smaller than even that occupied by subatomic particles."[26]

Witten's string theory, Coles maintains, "could provide entirely new answers to fundamental questions asked by philosophers, poets and theologians since the beginning of human time: Why is the universe the way it is and what is the origin of matter?" Cole does point out that no evidence other than "mathematical consistency" supports the existence of six extra dimensions; but, he says, if the theory is correct, mathematical inconsistencies that have plagued scientists' previous efforts to reconcile quantum theory and gravity "wondrously disappear."[27]

Yet superstring theory remains just that—theory—and Witten's work can't be tested in a lab. It may be a hundred years before its value and applications, if any, can be known, Witten himself acknowledged.

String theory may be too arcane to unravel, but New Age science types have picked up on the holographic phenomenon to support the grandiose theory that every part of the universe contains every other piece.

The hologram, a three-dimensional photograph made from light (laser) beams, was invented by Dennis Gabor in 1947. Here's how Judith Hooper and Dick Teresi describe it in *The Three-Pound Universe*: "Unlike an ordinary two-dimensional photograph, a hologram is an eerily lifelike three-dimensional image. Its code, stored on the film, bears no resemblance to the object photographed, but is a record of the light waves scattered by the object. Suppose you drop two pebbles into a still pond and then immediately freeze the rippled surface. In the overlapping wavefronts is stored a complete record of the pebbles' passage through a moment of time. So it is with a hologram."[28]

The hologram can store almost infinite quantities of information in almost no space, and any part of the hologram contains information about the whole. "The 'message' in a hologram is paradoxically located everywhere and nowhere."[29]

In 1966, Stanford psychology professor Karl Pribram proposed that for these very reasons, the brain functions holographically. An organ the size of a grapefruit can contain a lifetime of memories, and brain functions do not seem to be located in specific parts of the brain. For example, stroke victims don't lose discrete parts of their memory "bank"— memories from 1975–80 or all words beginning with the letter "B."

Pribram went on to speculate that perhaps the entire cosmos is simply a gigantic hologram! In such a universe, New Age exponents suggest, information about the whole is available at its every point, and consciousness somehow contains a mechanism which psychically affects reality itself.[30]

Hooper and Teresi found little support for Pribram's holographic brain child among the scientists they interviewed,[31] but the concept is popular among New Age theorists. And the holographic paradigm lights up significant ramifications:

(1) If the whole is contained in each of its parts, God is sheer light waves and mathematics. The supernatural is part of nature.

(2) The New Age slogan, "You create your own reality" becomes a reality.

(3) The paranormal becomes possible. We can all become psychics because we have equal access to the "One."

Shades of Jung's collective unconscious!

Suggests Marilyn Ferguson: "In this framework, psychic phenomena are only by-products of the simultaneous-everywhere matrix. Individual brains are bits of the greater hologram. They have access under certain circumstances to all the information in the total cybernetic system.

"In a nutshell, the holographic supertheory says that *our brains mathematically construct 'hard' reality by interpreting frequencies from a dimension transcending time and space. The brain is a hologram, interpreting a holographic universe.*"[32]

During an interview in her spacious hilltop home in Los Angeles, I asked Ferguson if her thinking has changed since 1980 when she wrote *The Aquarian Conspiracy.* Does she still believe science supports mysticism?

"Even more so!" she exclaimed without hesitation. "Astrophysicists may be the ones to discover God. Or, maybe . . . molecular biologists."

I find it interesting that Ken Wilber, another New Age writer and a scientist, has edited a book whose major thrust is that modern physics "offers no positive support (let alone proof) for a mystical worldview." Yet he takes pains to point out that every one of the eight physicists whose writings comprise the book—including Einstein, Planck, and Heisenberg—was a mystic.

"There *are* certain similarities between the worldview of the new physics and that of mysticism, the physicists believe," Wilber writes, "but these similarities, where they are not purely accidental, are trivial when compared with the vast and profound differences between them."

And then Wilber repeats this bit of wisdom: "To hitch a religious philosophy to a contemporary science is a sure route to its obsolescence."[33]

21

The Politics of Mysticism

Just as parapsychology blends with science in New Age thought, so science merges into politics. The New Age belief that the universe is evolving toward total unity is based on the optimistic assumption that, despite setbacks and forces that hinder, humans are becoming ever-better beings in an ever-higher and interconnected order. The old model of power and politics was based on the Newtonian view of a mechanistic, atomistic universe; the New Age paradigm is one of flux—politics' counterpart to modern physics.[1]

And just as they are key figures in the marriage of New Age science with mysticism, so Teilhard de Chardin and Fritjof Capra are paramount in the unfolding drama of "politicized mysticism."

David Horner, head of Christian Research Associates in Denver and an analyst of Teilhardian thought, sees the basis of human morality for Teilhard as "simply the recognition that man is born into the cosmic stream of evolution and must continue it. . . . Specifically, humans must cooperate in the task of racial perfection, or eugenics (which is the process of attempting to improve the human species, generally by controlling heredity through selective breeding and sterilization)."[2]

The goal of Capra's holistic paradigm, which roots in quantum physics, is to "restore creation and heal humanity's alienation. . . . [W]ith a nurturing goddess as the cultural

179

image of deity, decentralized power and egalitarian social organization will emerge," says New Age critic Robert Burrows.[3]

Or, to quote New Age interpreter Beverly Rubik: "An emerging worldview of the cosmos is that of a supreme work of divine art, alive and continuously evolving toward richer complexity and intimately dependent on us."[4]

But how do we know a political paradigm shift when we see one? Heed New Age theorist Marilyn Ferguson: "A political paradigm shift might be said to occur when the new values are assimilated by the dominant society. These values then become social dogma to the members of a new generation, who marvel that anyone could ever have believed otherwise."[5]

That there is a New Age political agenda, then, should surprise no one. Its influence on the overall political climate of the nation has so far been modest, and its aims are diverse and diffuse. But there are clear signs of growing power and consolidation as the decade moves to a close.

Several observers of the New Age scene, including Brooks Alexander of the Spiritual Counterfeits Project, see "organized activism" in the ecological or environmental realm as a primary vehicle for New Age ideas and concepts to merge into mainline political thinking and to shape public policy.

Carl Raschke, the witty religious studies professor at the University of Denver, says that "closet Aquarian conspirators" are beginning to identify with the movement as it snowballs in a way comparable to the Reaganism of the early 1980s. It is, he said, as we chatted in a small Arabian restaurant a block off campus, "a politicizing, like the new Christian Right."

Then he added: "But there are few Reaganite Republicans or Texas Baptists joining up. . . . New Age political tenets appeal to oldline liberals and militants of the 1960s, peace advocates, those who espouse the unity of all religions, et cetera. Now we are being told this is part of New Age."

Although Raschke doesn't see much impact by openly New Age political candidates, he *does* see "a lot of political enthusiasms . . . co-opted and incorporated into a kind of mystical social agenda." For example, he says, the Hands

Across America event of Memorial Day weekend in 1986 was orchestrated by New Age opinion-makers.

Another example, the December 31, 1986, World Instant of Cooperation—also called World Healing Day—was observed on seven continents and involved more than 500 spiritual and peace-oriented groups. The event was one of the first efforts to visibly mobilize an international political constituency for New Age projects and goals.

According to Raschke, the political themes of New Age are becoming more and more visible: critical rhetoric against the establishment political system . . . bringing in the ideological "heavy cannons" from the past twenty years—New World Order, Planetary Society, global politics. "The ultimate objective of the New Age push is to create a new political set of values and standards—the shaping of a new political global social vision."[6]

The predominant themes of transformational politics include ecology, feminism, and global order. The latter, says Robert Muller, retired assistant secretary-general of the United Nations, is "planetary civilization . . . [the] Planet of God."[7]

The New Age ecological consciousness springs from a perception of "universal oneness" and the interconnected web of biological life. It shares many goals of the environmental movement as a whole, and plugs into the heightened national appreciation for Native American culture and its reverence for Nature. Further, New Age participation in peace concerns and opposition to nuclear weapons go hand in hand with causes generally associated with liberal politics and liberal religion. Indeed, the Roman Catholic bishops of the United States have endorsed similar positions in their policy pronouncements.

Other political fallout from New Age ecology includes advocacy of zero population growth, sexual freedom, abortion, and the use of solar, rather than fossil, fuels. However, while New Age advocates typically identify with these positions, obviously not all those who support such causes are associated with the New Age movement or its philosophy. And, as we have noted earlier, there is no litany of commitments one must recite to qualify as a card-carrying New Ager.

What is distinctive about New Age ecology goes deeper. In fact, Capra calls it "deep ecology."

> It is rooted in a perception of reality that goes beyond the scientific framework to an intuitive awareness of all life, the interdependence of its multiple manifestations and its cycles of changes and transformation. When the concept of the human spirit is understood in this sense, as the mode of consciousness in which the individual feels connected to the cosmos as a whole, it becomes clear that ecological awareness is truly spiritual.[8]

To many New Agers, ecology contains the basic religious truth from which all religions spring. Another way of saying that is, "I *am* the Earth."

Bob Hunter, writing in *Greenpeace Chronicles*, described ecology as New Age religion: "Nature is quite obviously the physical totality of God's work. Within it, as part of it, viewing what is Our Self from the individual compartments of our little selves, we become aware that Nature is, in fact, *us*. The world is Our Body . . . Mother Earth is *not* passive. To align oneself with Her energies is to liberate at the same time the true animal within."[9]

Deep ecology asserts that all forms of life have "intrinsic value" apart from any human considerations. It assumes humans have no right to control or reduce the populations of other life forms except to satisfy vital needs. By rejecting the view that nature and its species exist to serve humans, deep ecology gives a clear message that all life has equal value; humans have no superior rights over any other life.[10]

Taoism, Capra says, forms a good base for the mystical dimensions of deep ecology. The best expression, however, is found in the goddess worship of radical feminism, which Capra and Charlene Spretnak spell out in their book *Green Politics: The Global Promise*.

To Capra and Spretnak, only a female goddess from the East can deliver humanity from the authoritarianism of an oppressive patriarchal style of religion that has dominated in the West. As we saw in the earlier chapter on goddess worship, a powerful strand of New Age philosophy blames men for the evils of human history, including wars and the suppression of women.

Petra K. Kelly, cofounder of West Germany's Green Party, expressed the values and commitment of this radical and rapidly growing worldwide political group in a first-person account called "Growing Up Green."

Kelly, a native of Bavaria, said she broke with her childhood Roman Catholic faith "because I am deeply religious and feel whole and equal to men and feel a need for feminist spirituality. I do not need an authoritarian male institution to help me look for my own inner truth or search for gods and goddesses of cosmic energy and love-light."[11]

There is subtle but sexually potent clout in Kelly's call for women to love only men who are willing to speak out against violence. She also urges women to unite "in changing the world" by being elected to political and economic offices.

We must think in global terms, say New Age political activists. National boundaries are obsolete, yet to most New Agers the notions of top-down bureaucratic government or a one-world global ruler are repugnant because these models shift power from grass-roots individuals. A minority of New Agers, however—particularly those influenced by the writings of Theosophy disciple Alice Bailey—buy into the concept of an elite, ruling hierarchy such as her "New Group of World Servers."[12] Carl Raschke calls this "the tradition of genteel occult politics in America."

Major New Age strategists Ferguson, Barbara Marx Hubbard, Mark Satin (pronounced like the fabric), and others promote a unified world order and planetary unity while at the same time favoring decentralized civil government—a difficult balancing act.

"Fully local in uniqueness and integrity" but "interconnected with all others in the world community," is the way Earl D. Brewer, director of the Center for Religious Research at Emory University in Atlanta, holds the two together in creative tension.[13]

Satin has proposed a planetary guidance system, complete with planetary taxation to help redistribute wealth to poorer nations. In his political paradigm, there is neither socialism nor capitalism—"that kind of question would be decided on by the individual communities"—but rather "an economy of life-oriented, mostly human-scale enterprises."[14]

Satin is editor of a slick monthly political newsletter called

New Options, which has an advisory board of 100 premier "thinkers and activists" who broadly reflect the New Age movement. This publication covers *"post-*liberal, *post-*conservative, *post-*socialist options in labor, business, economics, feminism, the peace movement, global development, religious and minority activism" for $25 a year—"less if you're poor."[15]

Declaring that *New Options* regularly covers the activities of 200 "innovative national groups," Satin boasts an insider's touch: "We know who the 'appropriate technology' sympathizers are at the World Bank. Which foreign service officers are globally responsible. Who spends time at the Congressional Clearinghouse on the Future."[16]

Planetary Citizens, a group founded in 1972 by Donald Keys, a consultant to the United Nations, has attracted New Age heavies such as David Spangler and Peter Caddy (both formerly of the Findhorn community in Scotland), historian William Irwin Thompson, futurist Willis Harman, former astronaut Edgar Mitchell, and Michael Murphy of Esalen Institute. Distinguished members listed by Douglas Groothuis in 1987 included Isaac Asimov, Rene Dubois, and honorary chairman Norman Cousins.[17]

To Keys and a flotilla of other New Age architects, the United Nations represents the epitome of planetization.

Robert Muller, veteran of nearly forty years of UN service and an ardent admirer of Teilhard's philosophy of global evolution, puts stock in the UN as "the first universal, global instrument humanity has ever had." Survival and further progress will depend largely "on the advent of global vision," he has written.

"The supreme unity of the human family, universal and interdependent, as seen by all great religions must now become a political reality; the hour has struck for the implementation of a spiritual vision of world affairs; the next great task of humanity will be to determine the divine or cosmic laws which must rule our behavior on this planet."[18]

Muller's mystical and lyrical tones sound low key when compared with adulation reserved for the UN by Hindu meditator Sri Chinmoy, the marathon runner/weight lifter who is also a United Nations chaplain.

The United Nations . . . is the way, the way of oneness, that leads us to the Supreme Oneness. It is like a river flowing toward the source, the Ultimate Source," Chinmoy wrote. "[T]he United Nations becomes for us the answer to world suffering, world darkness and world ignorance. The inner vision of the United Nations is the gift supreme. This vision the world can deny for 10, 20, 30, 40, 100 years. But a day will dawn when the vision of the United Nations will save the world. And when the reality of the United Nations starts bearing fruit, then the breath of immortality will be a living reality on Earth.[19]

Planetary Citizens and World Goodwill—both New Age political lobbying groups—are headquartered at the United Nations Plaza. World Goodwill was founded to unfold Alice Bailey's "plan" for a new world government and world religion. The material for the plan, Bailey said, was revealed to her telepathically by Djwhal Khul, a mysterious Tibetan master.

Other New Age notables espousing political activism include Benjamin Creme, who has widely announced the coming of Bailey's Christ figure, or Maitreya. Creme's newspaper ads have indicated that the Maitreya would end world hunger and war, and usher in a one-world socialist government that would redistribute wealth through the United Nations.[20]

Singer John Denver's nonprofit organization, Windstar, whose slogan is "In peace there is power," promotes his New Age concepts. And M. Scott Peck, author of runaway bestsellers, selectively endorses the New Age political agenda.

In his 1987 book, *The Different Drum*, Peck proclaims that his call for a "new American Revolution" of community building would facilitate gradual disarmament and the creation of a world government. Such goals are articulated best, he says, by people in a final, advanced stage of spiritual development. This stage is typified by being part of caring communities, a commitment to more than oneself, and "the ability to relish and cope with paradoxical situations."[21]

New Age ideology has many organizers, but no central political machinery. Several politicians exemplify or promote New Age values, however, and some transformational "planks" were written into the 1982 California Democratic platform.[22] Jerry Brown, former California governor and erstwhile Democratic presidential hopeful, has New Age leanings, as does Barbara Marx Hubbard, who was active in the 1984 Democratic vice-presidential campaign.

California Assemblyman John Vasconcellos of Santa Clara was instrumental in the 1976 founding of a statewide organization called Self-Determination, designed to promote interaction and empowerment between persons and institutions. Called the "touchy-feely" politician by detractors because of his legislation dealing with human potentials causes, Vasconcellos was treated to headline attention—and a few snickers—when he created a state-supported commission on self-esteem.

"Hold onto your hot-tubs, the California Task Force to Promote Self-Esteem and Personal and Social Responsibility is going local. In fact, it may be coming to your county soon," Beth Ann Krier gibed in the lead of her *Los Angeles Times* article in September 1987. Even before the task force was launched, Krier noted, citizen interest boomed: A full 350 applicants sought the group's 25 slots—more than had ever applied for any task force in state history.[23] And after cartoonist Gary Trudeau ribbed the group—along with Harmonic Convergence—in his "Doonesbury" strip, *thousands* of Californians volunteered to sign up.

New Age agendas seem to spread more effectively by networking than by overarching structure, however.

"Simply stated," said New Age activist John Naisbitt in his popular *Megatrends*, "networks are people talking to each other, sharing ideas, information, and resources. . . . The important part is not the network, the finished product, but the process of getting there—the communication that creates the linkages between people and clusters of people. . . . They are structured to transmit information in a way that is quicker, more high touch, and more energy-efficient than any other process we know.[24]

Marilyn Ferguson says the network is the tool capable of producing transformation, "poised for reordering . . . plastic, flexible. In effect, each member is the center." The shared assumptions of these New Age networks," she adds, "*are* the conclusion." And, "Those of like mind can join forces as quickly as you can photocopy a letter, quick-print a flyer, dial a telephone, design a bumper sticker, drive across town, form a coalition, paint a poster, fly to a meeting . . . or simply live openly in accordance with your change of heart."[25]

During an interview early in 1988, I asked Ferguson whether the paradigm shift was on schedule.

"Things are happening in many ways more quickly than I ever expected," she answered, ever the optimist.

"For example?"

"The thaw in U.S.-Soviet relationships. . . . In a way, there is no turning back. . . . We are now moving towards the place where our interdependence is being sealed."[26]

J. Gordon Melton, veteran analyst of American religious movements, is skeptical about whether networking can catalyze the broad support for New Age shifts that Ferguson blithely projects.

"Networking builds marketing, not movements," he says tersely.[27]

Carl Raschke responded differently when I interviewed him at the University of Denver: "Conglomerates market thousands of products to give the impression of diversity. Just because the New Age movement appears to be spontaneous, loose and diverse doesn't mean that it is. Madison Avenue has created that illusion for years. Why can't we package ideas?"[28]

Is the New Age movement a conspiracy, then?

"A conspiracy?" Raschke repeated the question, mulling it over as he finished his coffee, fast growing cold in the mile-high city's December air. "We're not talking about men in black robes in a huddle with secret computers . . . or in corporate boardrooms. But take the analogy of the drug cartel or an underground organization with a public front of anonymity yet coherent. There are no Mafia headquarters in Chicago, for example, but there is power and influence. It's decentralized but organized."[29]

Finally, Robert Burrows had this to say:

> The New Age movement's collusion may not be tightly organized, sharply focused, or bent on apocalyptic totalitarianism. . . . Its premises are not readily apparent and thus not easily critiqued. It is the New Age movement's unobtrusiveness, its ability to conceal and not offend, that has consolidated its grip and assured its spread. Without formal organization, it is difficult to net. Not bound by any tradition, it freely spins its mystical web in endless variations. Chameleon-like, it

adapts to its environment and is not easily seen. Vibrantly positive, it is quickly embraced.[30]

Later we'll return to the conspiratorial aspects of New Age, as well as the overreactions of some Christians who are triggering alarm bells in steeples across the land. But right now let's look at how New Age thought is penetrating religious organizations and churches.

22

Religion and Churches

The 2,738-seat Avery Fisher Hall at Lincoln Center in New York City is all but filled—as usual—for the eleven o'clock Sunday service. A well-dressed crowd, ranging from miniskirted teens to elegantly frocked grandmothers, has gathered expectantly to hear the Reverend Eric Butterworth, the slim, white-haired minister of this low-key Unity Church. He begins to speak in gentle and reassuring tones.

"It is our purpose to let people discover their divine depths, to challenge you to break down barriers and be rid of worry and fear." Then, paraphrasing Shakespeare: "There's nothing good or ill but thinking makes it so."[1]

Thus described in *Forbes* magazine, Butterworth, who hosts a daily radio show and is author of ten books, including *Life Is for Living* and *Discover the Power Within You*, sells a hot product these days: self-help through spiritual awareness.

The message is simple: "We alone have the power within us to solve our problems, relieve our anxieties and pain, heal our illnesses, improve our golf game or get a promotion."[2]

So what's New Age or even new about that? Butterworth's message is duplicated in thousands of houses of worship each week.

It is closely akin to the teachings of the Church of Christ, Scientist, founded by Mary Baker Eddy in 1879, and bears striking resemblance to the self-esteem theme of Reformed Church in America minister Norman Vincent Peale, whose

189

Power of Positive Thinking was an immediate smash in 1952 and remains so to this day.

It is also echoed in some of the preachments and writings of another Reformed Church minister, Robert Schuller, whose giant Crystal Cathedral in Garden Grove, California, has become synonymous with "Possibility Thinking." Ever since the ebullient prophet of happiness mounted the tar-paper roof of a drive-in theater snack shack in 1955 and launched the nation's first year-round drive-in church, Schuller has pronounced that a lack of self-esteem separates the average believer from fully understanding God.

After reading the first edition of this book, Schuller telephoned me, objecting strongly to being classed as "a fellow traveler" with New Agers. "I don't deserve that," he chided. "And I categorically deny that I believe in pantheism, reincarnation, channeling, astrology or crystals." Schuller added that he was "frustrated with the New Age movement" although, in his opinion, too much of the "anti-New Age work today is simply condemning it." Schuller went on to defend his concepts of "self-esteem" and "self-potential" theology, saying they are biblical ideas taught by Jesus.

Step back 125 years and you can find "positive thinking" in the writings of American Transcendentalists like Henry David Thoreau (1817–62), and in the indigenous religious movements such as Spiritualism, Unity, and New Thought.

The "self" of Whitman's *Leaves of Grass* "becomes a tireless, divine presence in all things, a ganglion of creative power which carves myriad experiences into a scintillating, personal vision."[3] Emerson, influenced by Hindu religious literature, spoke of the "Over-Soul," the "mystic force within all nature and human personality" governed and brought into existence by Mind.

The Transcendentalists sought God in nature. And both Transcendentalism and Unitarianism exalted the human potentialities—the transcending impulse for self-realization that has come to be the sine qua non of modern pop psychology.

Transcendentalism took the Eastern holy books, the *Bhagavad Gita* and the *Upanishads*, which had recently been translated into English, and created what religious historian Gordon Melton has called "a uniquely American form of mysticism ... the first substantial religious movement in North America with a prominent Asian component."[4]

In religious terms, "mind-cure" theology "frequently links the finite, personal mind with the divine or transcendental Mind to which ordinary consciousness must be assimilated," writes Carl Raschke.[5]

New Thought, dipping into Hindu Vedanta wisdom as well as Emersonian philosophy, popped up in denominations like the Divine Science Church, the Church of Religious Science, and the Unity School of Christianity.

Then add the fad of Spiritualism, the occult preoccupation with communication between the living and the dead that swept the nation like an uncontrolled brush fire in the 1850s. Together with the eclectic New Thought, Spiritualism contributed a major stalk to an emerging variety of American Gnosticism that some historians see coming to full flower now in the New Age movement of the 1980s.

Now stir in the arcane Oriental and occult notions of the volatile Russian mystic Helena Blavatsky, whose 1877 book, *Isis Unveiled*, divulged "secret doctrines" that laid the foundation for Theosophy. Madame Blavatsky's "unveiled truth" declared the soul's capacity to become God through increasingly refined inner knowledge" until engulfed in the great cosmic vision of reality."[6] Ancient "ascended masters" guided the destiny of humanity, she taught.

Theosophy, Spiritualism, and New Thought all splintered into factions when Blavatsky died in 1891. And Alice Bailey, an influential and prolific writer, left the Theosophical Society to form the Arcane School (School for Esoteric Studies) early this century. She may have been the first to use the words "New Age" to describe the gestating forces of the "movement"; it appears on page nine in her 1948 book, *Reappearance of the Christ*. Meanwhile, Blavatsky's appointed heir, Annie Besant—who taught that a person is the result of his or her own act of "self-creation"—nominated Indian master Krishnamurti Jeddu as the embodiment of the Theosophists' vision of a new world religious teacher. A disillusioned Krishnamurti later rejected the role.

Then in the 1930s, Guy Ballard founded the "I AM" movement, model for Elizabeth Clare Prophet's Church Universal and Triumphant of 1960s origin.

This compressed history highlights the precursors of the New Age movement, and reminds that a diversity of organizations such as neopagan, metaphysical, and spiritualist churches as well as the Theosophical Society—which is currently enjoying a renaissance of sorts—and Unitarian-Universalism have both molded mainstream American religion and been shaped by it themselves over a comparatively long period of time.

On the one hand, New Age motifs are being openly embraced by some arms of liberal Christianity; on the other, the New Age movement "is sucking up like a black hole many of the more familiar doctrines and orthodoxies, religious and political, of the liberal churches of the last twenty years," according to Carl Raschke.[7]

At the same time, New Age metaphysical groups often co-opt the language and trappings of the traditional Christian churches, thereby making newcomers feel more comfortable in their transition to alternate forms of belief and practice.

For example, the Institute of Metaphysics in Los Angeles, founded in 1976 by James Thomas, can advertise itself as a New Age Center and at the same time hold a fund-raising jamboree with "the rousing music of oldtime Gospel . . . featuring Rev. Ketina Brown and Bishop James Davis."[8]

Meanwhile, the four-times married former Mrs. California, Terry Cole-Whittaker, who was ordained by the Los Angeles Church of Religious Science, can bid farewell to her super-size San Diego congregation, dump "the Reverend" from her title, and proclaim a health and wealth individualism ("Be your own guru") through her Adventures in Enlightenment Foundation—and never miss a beat nor lose her following. Just-plain Cole-Whittaker insists that, despite shedding the mantle of religions, her work is still "spiritual."[9]

The self-improvement, visualization, and guided imagery techniques—including meditational yoga—have percolated into many liberal Protestant denominations, some Roman Catholic circles, and not a few conservative and Pentecostal/charismatic Christian churches. (We'll take a deeper look at the trends of visualized prayer, "inner healing," and "healing of memories" in chapter 27.)

The Reconstructionist wing of Judaism has also been receptive to New Age ideas. And Baha'i, an independent world religion that teaches the spiritual evolution of human society and the oneness of God and all religions, has picked up on New Age thought in the realm of mystical science, promoting it at conferences and in dialogues between scientists and Baha'i scholars.[10] Through the years the Unitarian-Universalist Association, a creedless denomination, has exerted a powerful influence in American politics, science, arts, and letters while maintaining a veritable "Who's Who" list of UU notables. Recently it has also become enamored with the "new physics." Unitarian-Universalist president William F. Schulz has said that the recognition of parallelism between Eastern mysticism and Western physics is growing in UU circles. Increasingly, he and other UUs share much of the monistic worldview of physicist Fritjof Capra that all things are related in a "deep ecology" of "the divine One."[11]

The Roman Catholic Church has also been a fertile soil for New Age-associated theology and suppositions.

Jewish psychotherapist Ira Progoff—who has been touted by his organization as "the Freud of the age" and "the Einstein of psychology"—has made deep inroads through his "Intensive Journaling" seminars. About 35% of them are held under Catholic auspices, including sessions in monasteries and retreat centers. Another 35% of the 400 that he and his corps of 125 leaders conduct around the country each year are sponsored by other religious groups and churches.

Based on prayer, meditation, and writing exercises (journaling), Progoff's intensive seminars involve getting in touch with "a quality of wisdom that is in us but beyond us . . . an expression of touching a depth level where we sense truths that are larger than personal in their significance." Participants are told to meditate on a self-chosen "mantra crystal," a short phrase intended to create a "pendulum rhythm" and to express "the crystallized essence of your life and experience."[12]

In an interview, Progoff insisted that the technique is theologically neutral and not limited to any particular doctrine or religious concepts. But there is, he said, a supernatural dimension: A "Person of wisdom" has touched the meditator with truth in the "underground stream" of his or her being.[13]

Wabun, an associate of Native American mystic teacher

Sun Bear, brings ecofeminist concerns of New Age to Catholics and other church groups. She said she had addressed a group of 3000 Catholic women in 1987 "who are challenging the patriarchy of the church."[14]

One of the most controversial links between Eastern mysticism and Christianity is "creation spirituality," developed by former Dominican priest Matthew Fox of Oakland, California. In addition to similarities to New Age views on the sacredness of nature, creation spirituality posits the New Age mystic-science worldview and the evolution of consciousness projected by Jesuit Pierre Teilhard de Chardin.

Popular and casual in style, Fox speaks widely at church conferences and teaches at his Institute in Culture and Creation Spirituality at Holy Name College in Oakland, although he was suspended from his order in 1992 because of possible heresies in his copious writings. Fox has denied his works are unorthodox.

The faculty at Fox's Oakland institute includes a self-described witch named Starhawk, who teaches classes on ritual making and sexuality and on spirituality in native religions; a Bible scholar; a physicist; a masseuse; a gestalt therapist; and an African dance teacher.

Fox, who says "98% of Bible scholars agree with me . . . that we need to go back to 'original blessing'—not 'original sin,'" frequently refers to God as "She" and affirms a belief in *panentheism*, the view that "everything is in God and God is in everything." (He rejects *pantheism*, which holds that "everything is God and God is everything.")[15]

"Religion could be playing such a fundamental role in healing and announcing good news instead of being preoccupied with control and anthropomorphic agendas," the soft-spoken priest said with a hint of puckishness as we chatted by a crackling log fire in the lounge of All Saints Episcopal Church in Beverly Hills, where he was about to begin a weekend seminar.[16]

One indication that New Age-related theology is strongly influential in the world of organized religion is the fact that half the students who had attended Fox's institute were from Catholic religious communities; the rest were predominantly middle-class "religious seekers" of all faiths, ranging from housewives to Episcopal clergy (1986 figures).

But the biggest camel's nose to slip into the churches' tent could well be the 1,200-page, three-volume compendium of New Age thought called *A Course in Miracles*. Within a dozen years, what began as an obscure manuscript has been quietly transformed into a teaching phenomenon sparking sales of more than a half-million copies and spawning hundreds of study groups in churches, institutions, and homes across America. In Southern California alone, 153 separate ongoing classes in "A Course in Miracles" were offered in September 1987. Fourteen were listed just in San Diego! Sets of the blue-bound text, workbook, and teacher's manual line the shelves of major bookstore chains (now in softcover for $25, down from $40), and the teachings are firmly established in New Age circles.

My wife, Marjorie Lee, and I drove to Tiburon, a Marin County community in a jewel-like setting just north of the Golden Gate Bridge, on a glistening day in late November 1987 to meet several of the principal actors in the unfolding drama. Tiburon is an artsy and affluent little bedroom community a short ferry ride across the bay from the glimmering skyscrapers of downtown San Francisco. It's the kind of place where the locals understand and appreciate New Age humor, such as the sign posted in a main-street gift shop: "Shoplifting raises hell with your karma."

First we stopped in at Dr. Gerald G. Jampolsky's Center for Attitudinal Healing, which the psychiatrist—also author of the best-selling *Love Is Letting Go of Fear*—founded in 1975 in response to a vision he received from studying "A Course in Miracles." (It was officially published by others a year later.) Now forty-five of his centers dot the world, helping children and adults cope with life-threatening diseases and other crises, without charge.

A onetime militant atheist of Jewish background, Jampolsky himself has recovered from a life shattered by divorce and alcoholism. The principles of his healing therapies include "love, forgiveness and ways to achieve oneness with God and one another. . . . We can't feel God's peace until we let go of negative feelings and fear," he said as we sat in his office at the center's compact, wharf-front headquarters.

Behind Jampolsky's desk was a large poster that sums up "attitudinal healing": "[T]rue friendship is a state of bliss where we see only the God self in each other; it is a state of inner knowing that we are always connected by love with each other and God forever."

Jampolsky, who has been on *The Phil Donahue Show*, *Today*, *60 Minutes*, Robert Schuller's *Hour of Power*, and has spoken to a variety of denominational religious groups, said his centers don't use "Course in Miracles" materials in treatment programs. And he added: "New Age is not a term I would use, myself."

But "The Course," as it is commonly referred to, is clearly "a perfect summary of attitudinal healing," Jampolsky has written. "A single Source unites all minds."[17]

I had read that Jesus speaks in the first person in the text of the Course, and that it "introduces man to his God-nature."[18] I also knew that in 1965, Jewish psychologist Helen Schucman, an employee in the Psychiatry Department at Columbia University in New York, began "hearing" that inaudible voice in her head and started dictating a comprehensive message that was to continue for seven years. Declaring herself an atheist and a reluctant scribe, Schucman nonetheless took down the revelations that detailed a metaphysical "New Thought" kind of salvation attained through a person's own efforts.

"You know that inner Voice—it won't leave me alone! It keeps saying, 'This is a course in miracles. Please take notes,'" she told colleague William Thetford, then a professor of medical psychology at Columbia and late a collaborator and editor of the Course materials.[19] Next morning, she showed Thetford her shorthand, which became the introduction to the text.

> This is a course in miracles. It is a required course.
>
> Only the time you take it is voluntary. . . .
>
> This course can be summed up very simply in this way:
>
> Nothing real can be threatened,
>
> Nothing unreal exists.
>
> Herein lies the peace of God.

While the Course's teachings are complex, arcane, and couched in Christian terminology with a psychological application, the nub of Schucman's channeled revelation is that

each person is God; the universe is one; and evil is illusion—
a spirituality that squares nicely with the ancient non-dualis-
tic Vedanta of Hinduism as well as with modern New Age
fundamentals.

Kenneth Wapnick, a onetime Catholic monk with a Jewish
upbringing, has become a chief interpreter of the Course. In
addition to several books expounding its teachings, he has
established a foundation to disseminate the Course's message. Wapnick, a resident of Westchester, New York, is
candid in saying that the Course is incompatible with biblical
Christianity—though he has also asserted that there are many
paths to Do, including Christianity, and that "in the end, all
theologies will drop away and what's left is only the love of
God."[20]

In a lengthy interview with Dean Halverson, who at the
time was a researcher for the Spiritual Counterfeits Project,
Wapnick explained why biblical Christianity is antithetical to
the teachings enunciated by the Jesus of the Course:

> There are three basic reasons. One is the Course's idea that
> God did not create the world. The second is the Course's
> teaching that Jesus was not the only Son of God. The third
> involves the Course's assertion that Jesus did not suffer and die
> for our sins . . . because once you see his death in that way,
> then you make sin real. You make sin real and then you have to
> atone for it. The whole idea of the Course is that sin is an
> illusion:
> The Bible teaches that God created the world and pro-
> nounced it very good. The Course teaches that God did not
> create this world, but the ego did, and that it's an illusion.
> The Course says that you forgive your brother for what he
> has *not* done to you, not for what he *has* done. . . .
> What I do with my guilt is project it onto you. And I attack
> you for it. When I forgive you and I correct my misperception of
> you, which means that I now see you as guiltless, I am really
> doing the same thing for myself. That forgives me of my
> guilt. . . . So forgiveness is basically seeing our true selves as
> sinless and guiltless as well. . . .
> The Course teaches that we are all equally Christ. The only
> difference is that Jesus was the first to remember who he
> was. . . .

The crux of the whole thing is that our relationship with God has never been impaired. It's only in our thinking that it was. For the Course, sin never really happened. . . .

The Course's definition of resurrection is much different from that of traditional Christianity. It's not the body that resurrects. Resurrection is defined as the awakening from the dream of death. . . .

[S]ome parts of the Bible have the Holy Spirit as their source. Other parts are from the ego.[21]

Summing it up, this is Halverson's side of the interview: "While superficial similarities between the Course and Christianity exist, the two belief systems could not be more opposed to one another. The Bible speaks of a sinful humanity that is separated from God and in need of reconciliation through the atoning work of Jesus Christ. The Course would dismiss such teaching by saying that its source is not God, but the guilt-ridden, separatist ego.

"Anyone who believes the Course is compatible with Christianity either does not understand the Course or Christianity, or both."[22]

Our next stop that November afternoon was the beautiful Tiburon cliffside home of Robert and Judith Skutch, whose nonprofit Foundation for Inner Peace publishes *A Course in Miracles*. Dressed in sweats and loafers, Bob Skutch showed us to his picturesque living room, where a huge clear crystal catches beams of sunlight streaming in from the picture window looking across Marin Bay.

Bob, a former television copyrighter, and Judy, long interested in the study of the paranormal, remote viewing, and Kirilian photography, have become official custodians of Schucman's legacy and "inner Voice" (she died in 1981). The Skutches promote the Course in a low-key way, overseeing its translation into multiple languages and coordinating distribution to a burgeoning informal worldwide network of teachers and study groups. Church groups—particularly Unity and Religious Science, and some Episcopal, Methodist, and Presbyterian—are among them, Bob said.

Judy sometimes lectures about the Course, but the Skutches do not head a cult-like operation. Neither are they pushing a high-profile marketing campaign nor a high-

powered organizational scheme. They think that's the way
Helen Schucman would have wanted it.

"The administration work and mail comes through here,"
Bob said, waving his arm toward a small back room. Decisions, he added, are made "through praying," which he
defined as "listening to the inner Spirit, your Teacher, the
Holy Spirit, or whatever."

I remarked that we had noticed San Quentin prison
crouched on a jutting point of land just around the bay from
their home. Oh, yes, Bob said, four groups of prisoners within
the maximum security facility were currently studying the
Course.

"How did that mesh with the Course's insistence that evil
and the physical world are illusion?" I asked. "How would
the inmates feel?"

"They have made the world they have chosen," he
answered. "Everything is an illusion except love. God didn't
create matter—nothing, nothing. It's an illusion.

PART IV

———

DISCERNING
THE NEW AGE

23

Positive Images

A watering hole for the soul . . .
An ongoing reunion of self-help junkies . . .
The next evolutionary step in networking . . .
The New Age's answer to the Kiwanis Club . . .

That's what more than 500 Southern California aficionados of the Inside Edge, an organization formed in 1985 by cookbook authors Paul and Diana von Welanetz, say about their weekly meetings, which typically begin at 6:00 A.M. Local chapters of the Inside Edge gather for live music, a hot breakfast—and a shot of optimism from upbeat New Age and metaphysical thinkers like author Marilyn Ferguson, cancer specialist Dr. Carl Simonton, or California Assemblyman John Vasconcellos (creator of the state's Task Force on Self-Esteem and Personal and Social Responsibility).

The close and powerful support system, dubbed "a breakfast club for New Age thinkers," is composed largely of upscale professionals, who pay from $1,200 to $1,600 a year in dues.

"The people who are involved with this organization are not lightweights by any means," says Wayne Dyer, author of best-selling *Your Erroneous Zones* and other self-help books. "They are highly public, highly visible people who believe in what they're doing and make a major difference in the world. They're part of what Marilyn Ferguson calls 'the network of good guys.'. . . If you can get a collective of human beings who are on the side of order rather than disorder . . . you can bring some order to the planet, and God knows we need it."[1]

Beverly Hills chapter member Frances Heussenstam, a college professor turned psychotherapist turned painter, told *Los Angeles Times* reporter Beth Ann Krier that what happens at Inside Edge meetings is "a genuine effort to help build a spiritual family."

Indeed, the New Age movement appeals to many because of what David Hinds, publisher of Celestial Arts, calls their "ongoing need for some sort of spiritual grounding." Adds Hedda Lark of DeVorss publishing: "I think people are searching for a sense of security in a world that's gone pretty mad, and they have the feeling that there must be more to life than this craziness."[2]

And Clayton Carlson of Harper & Row believes the sixties generation, now "grown up," is "questioning the meaning of it all. They're finding that the traditional systems aren't working, and are taking alternative perspectives more seriously."[3]

Says the Reverend Richard Spencer, a perceptive pastor of a large suburban church: "The New Age subculture is seeking to make sense in a vacuum of meaning where traditional options no longer make sense."[4]

This sentiment about the breakdown of traditional institutions was echoed by Chris Majer of Sportsmind during my interview with him, which I discussed earlier in chapter 16. New Age is of interest to persons in their thirties because there is "no [other] outlet for [our] version of spirituality," says Majer, who was baptized Episcopalian. "[We] believe in God but don't like churches. [We] feel displaced somehow. Traditional answers don't fit the bill so where do I turn? What do I do? . . . In New Age, many find answers that are a lot better than the ones we've been given so far. It makes more sense to some people. It holds together a lot tighter."[5]

Western society has periodically experienced intense spiritual hunger "accompanied by denunciations of the church as dead, formal, and spiritually bankrupt," according to new religions expert J. Gordon Melton. He contends that the New Age movement "was and is the attempt to find the social, religious, political and cultural convergence between the

new Eastern and mystical religions and the religious disenchantment of many Westerners."[6]

New Age, in the opinion of Alan Dundes, a professor of
anthropology and folklore at the University of California,
Berkeley, is "people latching onto a belief system to get
certainty where there is no certainty."[7]

Well, then, who *does* feel comfortable with the daily
uncertainties of life? Asked the late author Isaac Asimov:
"Can you blame anyone for convincing himself that he can
forearm himself against those uncertainties by seeing the
future clearly through the configuration of planetary positions, or the fall of cards, or the pattern of tea-leaves, or the
events in dreams?"[8]

Although there is a dark side, which we'll examine in
successive chapters, New Age may appear to meet basic
human needs. And that much seems positive.

Karen Hoyt, former executive director of the Spiritual
Counterfeits Projects, an evangelical Christian organization
dedicated to exposing unorthodox and aberrant religious
groups, concurs.

> New Age is addressing the horrible dilemma we're in that the
> church is *not* addressing. . . . New Age is trying to put together
> a way of coping with the overwhelming nature of life. . . .
>
> The church is convinced the answer is in the 'old' [tradition],
> which is true doctrinally—but it is not true in the practical
> aspects of life.
>
> Christians, too, are desperate [for answers], but they don't
> know how to tell church leaders that without feeling defeated
> or inadequate.[9]

In the introduction to the book, *The New Age Rage*, a
critical analysis of the New Age movement assembled by
Spiritual Counterfeits personnel, Hoyt identified ten areas in
which Christians might agree with the New Age, broadly
defined:

1. Their emphasis on cooperation instead of competition
   (in a personal, not economic, sense).
2. Their desire to protect creation, instead of exploiting
   and destroying the Earth's resources.
3. Their interest in creativity. (Christians often find

themselves defending mediocrity and rigidity, instead of encouraging spontaneity and creativity.)

4. Their promotion of the cause of peace in the world.

5. Their call for radical transformation—a total change of mind (although the Christian idea of the needed change is very different from the New Age movement's).

6. Their emphasis on the importance of the body and its care through proper exercise, healthy food, and good habits.

7. Their support of human potential and a positive self-image. (Christians believe people are created in God's image and therefore support human potential and the need for a positive self-image; however, they do not believe in unlimited human potential and in an unflawed self.)

8. Their position on the global village. One of the most radical changes in the last twenty years is the realization that we can no longer function as an isolated nation, politically and economically—a crisis in one country affects the whole world.

9. Their desire to work for a nontoxic environment.

10. Their use of networking. (When New Agers talk about this, some Christians get nervous and visualize world conspiracy, but the truth is that the most powerful and effective network ever is the Christian church.)

Perhaps here one could echo Protestant Reformer John Calvin, who said, "All truth is God's truth."

One of the few remarks by heavy-handed cult critic Dave Hunt that even comes close to being a semi-kind word about the New Age was his recognition that "The call to realize our full potential, to act out our destiny, to rise to new heights in the face of threatened ecological collapse and nuclear destruction and save our world and our race by setting up a new world government of love and equality has a universal appeal."[10]

When the sifting of the wheat and the chaff is done with discernment, my assessment is that there *is* some wheat in the New Age movement.

For example, modern medicine could be vastly improved if

physicians would adopt some of the philosophy—but not all the techniques—of holistic health care in their practices. Patients should be treated as whole persons, and the spiritual dimensions of well-being should play a vital role in medical intervention.

Much of today's health care is fragmented and frustrating. As I write this chapter, one of our married daughters (a registered nurse) has had just such an experience. She had her infant son treated by one physician at the pediatrician's office. The baby had to be hospitalized, but she never saw that doctor again after the baby was sent to the hospital—nor did she see any one doctor at the hospital more than once during her son's confinement. Specialists attended to half a dozen different tests, but no *one* caretaker was concerned about the overall condition of her child or how treatment might be coordinated!

This makes one realize how near the mark social critic Ivan Illich was when he said "the medical establishment has become a major threat to health."[11]

Nor should we assume that only the medical "elite" are qualified—or able—to heal. There is much to commend the growing "wellness" and sickness-prevention programs sponsored by schools and industry. The commensurate emphasis upon taking our own responsibility for maintaining personal health and making lifestyle changes congruent with physical fitness is praiseworthy and beneficial.

The New Age also has an apt analogy in its linking of human oppression and nature's oppression in the realm of ecology. Economic justice and ecological responsibility go hand in hand, as J. Ronald Engel, professor of social ethics at Meadville/Lombard Theological School in Chicago, has pointed out.[12] The paradigm of the struggle of the Earth and humanity as one united struggle surfaces in the Old Testament prophetical books of Hosea and Amos, as well as in Paul's New Testament letter to the Romans.

New Agers are also correct in their assessment of the fallacies in reductionist thinking about science and society. Cultural assumptions and structures need to be evaluated in light of "wholes."

French philosopher-mathematician Blaise Pascal (1623–62) said long ago: "All is held together by a natural though imperceptible chain that binds together things most distant and different; [therefore] I hold it equally impossible to know the parts without the whole and to know the whole without knowing the parts in detail."[13]

New Age physicist Fritjof Capra is on target in denouncing "the belief in the scientific method as the only valid approach to knowledge; the view of the universe as a mechanical system composed of elementary material building blocks; the view of life in society as a competitive struggle for existence; and the belief in unlimited material progress to be achieved through economic and technological growth."[14]

Ronald J. Sider, professor of theology at Eastern Baptist Seminary in Philadelphia, approvingly notes that Capra and Charlene Spretnak (co-authors of *Green Politics*):

> speak for millions in the West who rightly sense the failure of Western naturalism and materialism grounded in the 18th-century Enlightenment. They are groping for a recovery of meaning and spiritual depth. They know more and more material gadgetry is not the answer to human longing. . . . Evangelical Christians have been making the same points. We too reject modern philosophical naturalism's claim that reality is only material and scientific knowledge is the only avenue to truth. We know that supernatural revelation also provides knowledge.[15]

On the human potentials front, many New Age psychotechnologies are useful and have contributed some helpful tips and insights on handling anger, stress, fear, hurt, and pain. Biofeedback, hypnosis, assertiveness training, meditation, visualization, and dream analysis—among other therapies—can be helpful. A word of caution, however: This is a vast, gray, borderline area where careful discernment is essential to avoid pitfalls. And some techniques, as we shall see in chapter 25, are downright deceptive, utterly worthless—and even dangerous and life threatening.

On the other hand, New Age educational philosophy that encourages "whole-seeing," fresh perception, focused awareness, and a sense of flow is a positive contribution. Some of the techniques that teach athletes to set and net peak performance goals also seem both creative and healthy.

Along with these, we can chalk up penetrating inquiry,

questing for truth, and exploring imaginative, intuitive solutions to human and scientific problems on the plus side of the New Age evaluation.

"The [New Agers] are raising questions in new ways, making things salient, and . . . contributing to the climate of opinion," declared preeminent sociologist-author Robert Bellah during an interview in his book-lined office on the fourth floor of Barrows Hall at UC, Berkeley. "But they are not able to form strong groups; they're just too evanescent."[16]

And Robert Ellwood declares: "Don't overlook the possibility that at least some of the New Age people may be discovering important things about life. It's not all psychological reductionism and nonsense. Important things are emerging about people and reality."[17]

Gordon Melton says that while he thinks the New Age movement is "shallow" and "has to give way to a religion that can hold people for a lifetime," there is also a positive twist. "New Age can bring people into a religious awakening," the bearded professor from Santa Barbara comments wryly. "Insofar as it reaches people who would otherwise be unreachable, it's good."[18]

And noted evangelical Christian theologian Carl F. H. Henry paid a backhanded compliment to the power—if not the content—of New Age religion when he said it is "confirming evidence that the communists and others who would try to extirpate religion are engaged in a fruitless task. Man is by nature religious; human history is by nature religious history."[19]

To the extent that New Age, amorphous and multifaceted as it is, challenges us to critically examine our worldviews— what is real, what is right, what is true, metaphysically and ontologically—it performs a valuable service. Thus, it is crucial not only to understand this movement, but to discern its tenets wisely and well.

24

Conspiracy Theories

Militant New Age critic Constance E. Cumbey, a semire-
tired trial lawyer from Detroit, was in her element.

Talking nonstop all the while, she sifted frenetically
through a thick sheaf of file folders and page after page of
yellow legal-size notepaper that she had extracted in stacks
from her behemoth briefcase. Cumbey, whose 1983 book,
Hidden Dangers of the Rainbow, set off shock waves throughout the evangelical Christian community, was looking up
evidence to support her points in a spirited public debate.
Her opponents were other conservative Christian cult
watchers attending an annual anti-cult convention.[1]

Cumbey's basic contention was—and is—that the New
Age movement is a sinister conspiracy led by Satan to take
over the world, stamp out Christians and Jews, and force
universal worship of the Antichrist.

By 1988 Cumbey's sensationalist influence had waned
somewhat, but others had taken up the cudgel, churning out
similar dire conspiracy theories about New Age and the end
times. In the process, several prominent Christian leaders
had been fingered as collaborators in New Age diabolism—
according to Cumbey, exposé writer Dave Hunt, and others
of that ilk.

Most of the New Age conspiracy books have sold extremely
well in the Christian market, attesting to an ongoing fascina-

tion with end-time prophecies. The Spiritual Counterfeits staff calls the genre "Conspiracy Apocalyptic."[2]

Texe Marrs, a retired U.S. Air Force officer, wrote *Dark Secrets of the New Age: Satan's Plan for a One World Religion*, relying heavily on his interpretation of Bible prophecy, particularly the book of Daniel, to link "evil" New Age objectives with the "rush to Armageddon."

> The New Age appears to be the instrument that Satan will use to catapult his Antichrist to power. Once he is firmly entrenched, he will unite all cults and religions into one: the New Age World Religion. When Christians refuse to be initiated into this satanic religious system, they will be dealt with very harshly. Many will be put to death. The New Age is working hard today to set up an environment of hatred towards Christians and what they stand for, so the public mood will be ready when the Antichrist begins his brutal anti-Christian programs.
>
> A New Age propaganda campaign is already at full-throttle to brand *us* as warmongers and separatists. *We* are described as the Beast, the Antichrist, a racially inferior species unfit for the New Age kingdom. Discerning Christians see the signs and know what is happening (emphasis added).[3]

And Elissa Lindsey McClain, a former New Ager turned fundamentalist Christian, cites "the World 'Plan' by New Age 'Wise Persons'" as being "practically identical to Adolph Hitler's SS Occult Bureau in Germany on which Nazism was founded."[4]

She attributes this information to Cumbey (who wrote the introduction to McClain's book, *Rest from the Quest*) and Hunt, who laid out his conspiracy theories in *The Seduction of Christianity* and *Peace, Prosperity and the Coming Holocaust*, as well as other books.

The trouble with these books, from a journalistic perspective, is that the research, while extensive, lacks support from incontrovertible evidence. Facts are mishandled, claims are undocumented, conclusions are biased, and logic is flawed at vital connection points. That is not to say that all—or even nearly all—of the assertions are untrue. But they are often tied to unprovable assumptions as well as careless inferences.

So what about it? Is the New Age conspiracy fact or fiction? For starters, we need to examine what New Agers mean—

or at least *say* they mean—by conspiracy, and then compare that with the way conspiracy is projected by Christian critics of New Age.

Marilyn Ferguson, whose flagship New Age book, *The Aquarian Conspiracy*, roiled the waters and stirred much of the debate, talks about "a leaderless but powerful network . . . working to bring about radical change in the United States." This network "is a conspiracy without a political doctrine. Without a manifesto. With conspirators who seek power only to disperse it, and whose strategies are pragmatic, even scientific, but whose perspective sounds so mystical that they hesitate to discuss it."[5]

These "little clusters" and "loose networks" are everywhere, Ferguson believes: "tens of thousands of entry points"—all spreading the "new options" of the New Age in a kind of self-generating, self-organizing collective process.

A conspiracy? Yes, indeed, she proclaims. A collusion of shared assumptions: "A series of resounding clicks and the networks become the long-prophesied conspiracy."[6]

Hugely overstated, no doubt. Even wishful thinking. Like Hunt and Cumbey, Ferguson (to whom Cumbey, oddly, is a confidante) also sees conspiracies at the end of every New Age rainbow.

As Cumbey represented it in *Hidden Dangers of the Rainbow*, the leadership of the *entire* New Age movement has been united for decades in following the instructions of Alice Bailey (1880–1949), the onetime Theosophist and arcane spiritualist whose followers typically meditate together at every full moon. Her writings, averred Cumbey, are "followed meticulously by the New Age movement. . . . She is literally followed like a recipe."[7] And, Cumbey added, the overall direction of the conspiracy, called "the Plan," was strategized in H. G. Wells's book, *The Open Conspiracy*.

Elliot Miller, editor of the *Christian Research Journal*, a conservative anti-cult publication, rather neatly disposes of Cumbey's theory:

> [T]he NAM [New Age Movement] cannot be as Cumbey portrayed it in *Hidden Dangers* and at the same time be the loosely structured, uncentralized meta-network (network of networks) that both New Agers like Marilyn Ferguson . . . and

Christian observers like myself have claimed. For the entire movement to be following one detailed Plan "like a recipe" it would have to be tightly organized and hierarchical. Such perfectly coordinated activity is unheard of (among occultists, Christians, or anyone else) where such controls do not exist. . . .

For the NAM to be coldly orchestrating major developments on every level of society and capable of an imminent world takeover, it would have to be almost omnipotent and omnipresent. In short, we would no longer be talking about *movement* but a conspiracy in the most subversive and menacing senses of the word, similar to the all-pervasive, monolithic conspiracies attributed by some to the Illuminati, Jesuits, international bankers, etc.[8]

Miller also demolishes Cumbey's argument that H. G. Wells's world-state dovetails with the New Age "planetary guidance system." In fact, he says, Wells's plan left no room for mysticism.[9]

Alice Bailey *does* outline a "Plan" for preparing the world for the New Age and a New Age Christ, and some important New Age leaders *are* working to put it in place. The Bailey-related School for Esoteric Studies in New York advertises materials about the New Group of World Servers, which is the network of individuals Bailey predicted would channel the energy of the reappeared Christ, the eclectic Avatar of the New Age.[10]

But those who see the Bailey Plan as a present, organized conspiracy are naive. It is as if they believe a giant Dungeons and Dragons fantasy game is laid out, with rules and esoteric characters all in place, and that the players exist and are already interacting on some great "game board" of the world. Proof of this cannot be convincingly demonstrated.

Dave Hunt, an intrepid researcher and cogent lecturer, also overreacts to the dangers of New Age, in my opinion. He uses a mile-wide brush to paint into the same corner everyone who even faintly entertains notions compatible with New Age thinking. Thus, in defining "sorcery" he lumps in visualization and "positive/possibility thinking" with "any attempt to manipulate reality (internal, external, past, present, or future) by various mind-over-matter techniques that run the gamut from alchemy and astrology."[11]

That is not too surprising, perhaps, in light of Hunt's denial that psychology can be "Christian." So in Hunt's frame of reference, Christians who employ any of the psychotechnologies are in bed with the New Age, even if innocently.

Hunt's error, according to H. Newton Malony, director of programs integrating psychology and theology at Fuller Theological Seminary in Pasadena, California, is that Hunt "idealizes rationalism and correct dogma," turning it into a "hyper-rational religion."[12]

Interestingly enough, some consider Hunt a wimp and have taken him to task for presenting a "truncated vision" (in *Section of Christianity*) that doesn't assert the biblical worldview strongly enough.

"This shrunken faith cannot stand before the New Age . . . thinking [that] has swept over the modern church in a tidal wave of heresy, error and seduction," thump Gary DeMar and Peter J. Leithart in *The Reduction of Christianity: Dave Hunt's Theology of Cultural Surrender*.

But there is danger of overreaction from the other side, as well.

In response to a statement by Gordon Melton that he didn't see New Age as a threat, *TIME* magazine pontificated: "Even that, though, is perhaps too harsh a condemnation to serve as the final word on an essentially harmless anthology of illusions."[13]

The famous historian Will Durant predicted in the 1950s that the last major confrontation of Western history would not be between democracy and communism but between the Western Christian mind-set and Eastern religions. Such a clash of worldviews, occidentally or accidentally, is hardly harmless or, in today's world, an illusion.

A moderate—and correct, in my opinion—view of New Age as conspiracy is set forth in Douglas Groothuis's *Unmasking the New Age*: "[T]he New Age movement is better viewed as a worldview shift than a unified global conspiracy. This is not to minimize its influence but to recognize it as an intellectual, spiritual and cultural force to be reckoned with in all sobriety."[14]

In an interview in the basement office of the Probe Study Center in Seattle, Groothuis added this about overreacting to the New Age agenda: "The philosophy that if New Agers can do it, then we Christians can't do it, is a process that eventually quarantines off areas of life that God intended we should enjoy."[15]

Nor should distinctive New Age vocabulary be fenced off simply because it's in vogue. It would be "as erroneous to conclude that these words always indicate New Age spiritual commitments as it would be to conclude that biblical terminology always indicates Christian commitment," points out New Age researcher-critic Robert Burrows.[16]

The Cumbey guilt-by-association trip taints perfectly good words like "holistic," "peace," "global village," "global thread," "spaceship Earth," "Mother Earth," "rainbow," "interdependent," "paradigm," "vision," "self-realization," "consciousness," "personal growth," "positive mental attitude" (PMA), "human potential," "energy," "unity," "oneness," and "awakening," along with such phrases as "Do your own thing," "I'm feeling good vibes [vibrations]," and "That blows my mind."

For example, the New Age use of the rainbow symbol apparently began a number of years ago with small rainbow decals on car windows and license plates. The exact connection with the occult and which group or groups first used the symbol is unclear. Some observers point to the Tibetan teaching that the rainbow symbolizes man's ultimate perfect state of divinity and the fusion of good and evil, shadow and light. Others cite New Age references to the "rainbow bridge," "rainbow energies," and the colors of the "seven rays" of the chakras. In any case, the symbol's association with the New Age movement became firmly fixed in the minds of many with the publication of Cumbey's book, *Hidden Dangers of the Rainbow*.

Yet in the Bible the rainbow is God's first heavenly sign of promise; it has had great meaning for Jewish and Christian believers through the ages. Thus it seems an unnecessary capitulation on the part of these believers to veer away from a cherished symbol imbued with prior significance!

The meaning behind these expressions depends on who is using them and the context. Only from this deeper interpretation can the speaker's worldview be discerned.

The Southern Baptist Convention, the nation's largest Protestant denomination, issued a statement about the New

Age movement in 1985 that contains sound advice: "Be particularly careful that you are not inclined toward a kind of uninformed hysteria characterized by oversimplification and indiscriminate fear that you are threatened by conspiracies of all sorts. While New Age thinking and New Age-oriented activities are serious and dangerous, do not allow their presence and influence to drive you to indiscriminate distrust of fellow Christians and blanket disenchantment with authentic Christian institutions."[17]

Speaking colorfully about New Age conspiracy theories, Carl Raschke cautioned against falling for either of "two myths we live by."

One, he said, is the presumption that the New Age movement is "grassroots, unstructured, efflorescent, the deeply repressed longings and sensibilities that are popping up like mushrooms all over the dank soil of the Judeo-Christian culture.

"The other myth is that this is some gigantic, centralized conspiracy against the Christian church headed by Lucifer himself."[18]

Robert Ellwood, expert on New Age religions, had his own parting thought about putting it all in perspective as we closed an hour of discussion and he prepared to dash off to teach a class:

"[D]on't get carried away by seeing New Age as the only or most important thing going on in American society, or as a turning point in American history. Conventional religion is still big and probably will be all during the decade.

"There are always an awful lot of people living ordinary lives more or less untouched by what's being picked up by the media and appears to be prominent."[19]

25

Fakes, Frauds, and Placebos

Comedian-actor-iconoclast Woody Allen seems to love the "absurdities" of life. One he likes to tell is his version of the Abraham and Isaac story from Genesis 22.

According to Allen, Abraham believed God commanded him to sacrifice his son, Isaac, because "it was a deep, resonant voice, well-modulated, and nobody in the desert can get a rumble like that." Later, when Abraham was embarrassed that he did not get God's "little joke" about Isaac, God said to him, "It just proves that some men will follow any order no matter how asinine as long as it comes from a resonant, well-modulated voice."[1]

Although Allen takes the story out of context—God was testing Abraham, not teasing him—he cleverly points up the need for discernment. Some people will believe anything, especially when it comes through the voice of religion.

That seems particularly true for New Age "easy believism," where some outrageous, off-the-wall, and snake-oily assumptions and programs are swallowed whole by persons desperate to find health, wealth, happiness, or just plain answers and meaning to life in a largely inscrutable world.

Some psychic arts turn out, upon close examination, to be well-intentioned fakes; other fringy New Age products and protocols are thinly veiled scams and frauds; still others produce results—but for reasons different from those advanced by their practitioners. (We have already considered the "placebo effect" in chapter 18.)

In the field of mystical medicine, techniques such as acupressure, kinesiology, and "Touch Therapy" are all based on the assumption that an invisible energy flow (Chi) surrounds the human body and affects muscle strength. By pulling on "indicator muscles," this energy field can be "read" to diagnose widespread ailments and food intolerances, or so the theory goes.

Dr. Paul C. Reisser recounts an example of this method: A therapist pulls downward on the arm of a patient who holds various foods in the other hand. "If the arm seems weak, the food held will be deemed undesirable for that person, regardless of its nutritional value. Such practices are said to reveal the 'wisdom of the body' in determining what it needs or what is wrong.

"Unfortunately," Reisser adds, "they have no basis whatsoever in physiology, and require the therapist (and, if possible, the patient) to accept the idea of an invisible energy flow."[2]

I saw this method of "testing" at the Celebration of Innovation in San Francisco.[3] A young man wearing an array of rainbow pins was trying to decide which one of five styles of wire pyramids was right for him. The salesgirl at the pyramid booth told him to place the pyramid, an open-framed affair, over his head and press his thumb and third finger firmly together.

She then pulled on his fingers until they separated. The pyramid offering the greatest resistance (purportedly producing the strongest finger bond) was the one he should buy, she said.

As it turned out, he plunked down $34.95 for the second-most expensive model and went merrily on his way. The next customer was a man looking for a pyramid to reduce stress while driving on freeways and "going into places like Seven-Elevens" (the jiffy convenience stores). I smiled, picturing the reactions of other freeway drivers as he tooled along in the fast lane with a wire pyramid over his head!

Meanwhile, Brett Bravo—psychic counselor, teacher, healer, jewelry designer, and organizer of "Emerald City spiritual spa"—was delivering a lecture on how to use crystal mystique for health.

Sit on the floor, she said, and hold a crystal in your left hand. Look at it for several minutes. "It will begin to balance your energies." Next, lie on your back, put the crystal on your solar plexus, and place one hand over it. "Cosmic rays will penetrate, and physical rays will stimulate your emotional body."

How to be sure your crystal has been properly cleansed? Bravo, who said she'd had a relationship with rocks since she was five, and who once analyzed drilling cores for Shell Oil Company, allowed that we could choose from (a) burying our crystal for a week, (b) washing it in sea water, (c) giving it a smoke treatment (a sage smudge is a favorite of Native Americans), (d) running a demagnetizer over it, or (e) putting it on our forehead and adjuring, "Clear!"

"The myth is for you to decipher; you do with this what your heart tells you to do," she said with a shrug.

While Bravo extolled the curing effects of crystals, however, she declared belief in the power of birthstones to be without merit—"they don't have anything to do with anything."

And nobody in the room challenged any of her assumptions. At times I thought, somebody oughta just stand up and shout, "Bah, humbug!" or words to that effect.

As social psychologist Theodore Roszak has observed, "It is the myth that we accept without question as truth that holds influence over us."[4]

The call for discernment regarding New Age technologies and claims should be especially loud and clear when these are processes involving the human body.

Responsible New Age opinion makers like Marilyn Ferguson and Ken Wilber concede that a field like holistic health offers numerous opportunities for fraud and deception. Ferguson has suggested that ground rules should include "making sure that the unorthodox procedures are used only to complement proven conventional treatments rather than subjecting consumers to needless risk."[5]

In this area, psychic surgery has been exposed for its prevalent use of sleight-of-hand procedures, such as folding the fingers to simulate their actually penetrating human flesh. Another is storing blood and phony tumors in a fake thumb made of plastic.[6]

The *Rocky Mountain Skeptic* newsletter reported that Bela Scheiber had palmed on a gauze concealed in his hand some of the material a psychic surgeon named "Brother Joe" had ostensively pulled out of his uncut body. When he had the blood sample on the gauze analyzed by the Chematox Laboratory in Boulder, Colorado, it turned out to be "non-human cells consistent with fowl [chicken] blood."[7]

Those who have debunked the psychic side of firewalking found that the secret lies in knowing the distinction between temperature and heat, and between the concept of pain and the concept of being burned. A metal skillet, heated to 400 degrees in an oven, for example, contains much more "burnable" heat than a cake baked at the same temperature. While the stunt may help participants overcome fear and develop self-confidence, the claim that firewalking involves paranormal powers is specious.

Still, it seems no one is immune to false beliefs. Peter Glick, a social psychologist at Lawrence University in Appleton, Wisconsin, reported on psychological testing that showed that all of us are susceptible to a belief in astrology. Those who believe in horoscopes are more likely to distort the evidence they receive so that it doesn't challenge their prior beliefs. But even skeptics, though they tend to view information more objectively, may fall prey to faulty reasoning when the description of the horoscope is flattering, as most horoscopes are.

Glick writes: "It is known that people tend to be inordinately impressed with the accuracy of descriptions containing such vague statements as 'though you are a friendly person, at times you are rather shy'—even though such statements can apply to almost anybody."[8]

When in May 1988 the media spotlight shone on the Reagans' use of astrology forecasts, the president did not deny that he read horoscopes. And Nancy Reagan's press secretary confirmed that ever since the 1981 attempt on the president's life, the first lady had often consulted "a friend that does astrology" in San Francisco to seek reassurance of the president's safety.[9]

The *Philadelphia Inquirer* said that Nancy Reagan, after consulting an astrologer, insisted that her husband sign the U.S.-Soviet nuclear missile treaty at 1:33 P.M. on December 8,

1987.[10] Reagan, who signed the treaty with Soviet leader Mikhail Gorbachev at exactly that time, denied making policy decisions based on astrology.

Astrology assumes that the position of the stars and planets influences human events, and it categorizes people according to the astrological alignments prevailing at the time they were born. There is no evidence that these claims are true, and amid the White House astrology flap, scientists expressed dismay over "the apparent return to medieval superstition" in the guidance of international affairs.

The Committee for the Scientific Investigation of the Claims of the Paranormal issued a statement which said that dozens of rigorous tests in recent years by scientists have found that horoscopes "fail completely in predicting future events." In one test, said Andrew Fraknoi, an astronomy professor at San Francisco State University, two scientists examined more than 3000 predictions by astrologers and found them to be correct less than 10% of the time.[11]

"Scientists have been warning for years that the uncritical prominence given to astrology may have a deleterious effect on the public," the statement continued. "The intrusion of astrology into the highest levels of national security thinking now is a cause for further concern. . . . [I]t is vital that the public have a clear understanding between science and pseudoscience."[12]

The astrological system was established in ancient times, Fraknoi added; and since then the Earth's position has shifted slightly relative to the constellations so that the signs of the zodiac viewed now are not those seen by the ancients.

Another claim of astrology is that the gravitational and tidal effects of the heavenly bodies can influence the life of a child. But scientists have calculated that the gravitational influence of the obstetrician who delivers a baby is six times greater than that of, for example, the planet Mars. And the tidal effect of the obstetrician is greater by a factor of two trillion!

The same fuzzy mechanism of wishful thinking and uncritical reasoning is at work in channeling.

Persons seeking news from departed loved ones want to hear reassuring things from "the other side." And the most popular mediums seem to be the most adept at psychology, watching the expressions of the seekers for clues, drawing them out, following up on vague information tentatively advanced, making it more specific if they receive confirmation.

Science writer Karl Sabbagh offers an explanation:

> I believe that the human brain has a ratchet, and it is one that swings into place whenever people are confronted with something they really want to believe in. Whenever they come across an example of a phenomenon that reinforces the belief they are interested in preserving, the mainspring of their belief tightens a little bit. But, if a little later they come across something that doesn't reinforce the belief, something that even contradicts the hypothesis they are fondly nurturing, the wheel rotates in the opposite direction but the spring doesn't loosen—it's still as tight as it was, and their faith is unshaken.[13]

While we already dealt with the modus operandi of channelers in an earlier chapter, it is important to again mention it, stressing that this is an area where deception and fraud are rampant. Says Patricia-Rochelle Diegel, a Ph.D. psychologist and trance medium in Sedona, Arizona, who gives "immortality consultations": When a channeler claims to be the "exclusive channel or energy [for an entity] . . . a little light should go on that says 'Greed'!"[14]

Diegel, a cheerful, plump woman who likes to wear large strings of pink and blue beads over a matching blouse, notes that Jane Roberts, the famous channeler of "Seth," "was walking around smoking while giving [Seth's] messages" in a casual manner. Seth, speaking through Roberts, claimed that he spoke *only* through her. But an estimated 300 mediums claim to have channeled Seth, and Roberts is now dead. Which presents an interesting dilemma: Either 299 mediums are deceived, or else they are liars. Or Seth lies. Or Roberts lied. At the very least, mediumship is suspect.

In their book, *The Fakers*, magician-investigative journalist Danny Korem and psychiatrist Paul Meier describe a broad range of ways the mind and senses can be fooled: through sleight of hand; use of principles of psychology, mathematics, and physics; hidden mechanical devices; physical and mechanical deception; optical illusion; misdirected attention; use of a stooge; and luck and probability.[15]

These techniques—the stock in trade of magicians and

illusionists—have been used as well by unscrupulous evangelists and faith healers. The Pentecostal, or charismatic, wing of the Christian church particularly needs to clean up its act in this area. The "miracle mongering" of many television evangelists and the slick purveyors of the "health and wealth gospel" should be called to account by responsible churchmen or denominational leaders. Unfortunately, little control exists over many of the most blatant charlatans because they are not responsible to any denomination and answer to no one other than themselves—or to figurehead boards who rubberstamp anything they do.

That psychics and mediums have been guilty of fakery and fraud is well documented. Some have admitted it; others— like psychic surgeon—"Brother Joe"—have been exposed.

When *San Francisco Chronicle* reporter Ben Fong-Torres and a photographer visited trance-channel Kathy Reardon, she introduced them to the spirit of a fifteenth-century Irish barmaid. Reardon lapsed into a trance, her face twitched and her shoulders hunched, but the spirit of "Moira" could not provide answers to specific questions. In fact, Moira gave several incorrect answers, Fong-Torres reported.

He added that when Reardon "came to," she seemed unfazed by Moira's performance. "If you feel it made a little sense, fine," she said. "If part of it was bunk, fine, too. I tell people, 'don't take anyone's word over your own.'"[16] (For a comprehensive description of exposés of several well-known earlier psychics and mediums, see the *TIME* cover story of March, 4, 1974.)

After a two-year study, the National Academy of Sciences concluded emphatically that 130 years of research had produced "no scientific justification" to support widespread belief in the existence of extrasensory perception (ESP), mental telepathy, or similar phenomena.[17]

The committee reserved its sharpest criticism, however, for the realm of parapsychology and claims of evidence for such things as "the putative use of mental power to bend spoons and jam computers." The committee chairman was quoted as saying that the quality of research in the field was surprisingly poor.[18]

Only when we learn to discriminate will we be able to "reject the bizarre and avoid being mesmerized by its novelty," observed Irving Hexham, a religious studies professor at the University of Calgary in Alberta, Canada.[19]

Richard Ofshe, a University of California, Berkeley, professor who won a Pulitzer prize for his research on the Synanon cult, suggests reality testing that asks: What is the theory behind a program or technique; how do the procedures relate to the theory; and are there objective criteria for evaluation?[20]

Truth matters, says Timothy Philibosian, who runs a small organization in Englewood, Colorado, called Rivendell. Named after the city of sanctuary and wisdom in J. R. R. Tolkien's *The Lord of the Rings*, Rivendell is dedicated to discerning conflicting worldviews and evaluating claims of truth.

"We always ask people to define their terms," explained Philibosian's former partner, Daniel Davis, as the three of us lingered over dinner at Poppie's on Denver's south side. "I usually ask, 'What do you mean by that?' If they define vague terms by other vague terms, alarm bells should go off in your head that the person literally doesn't know what he's talking about."

"'How do you know that?' and 'So what?' are other stoppers," chimed in Philibosian, an attorney who now devotes all his time to Rivendell.

For example, he continued, Shirley MacLaine tells a woman who has been raped that in a previous life she most likely had been a man who had raped a woman and now she's working off her karma.

"We ought to simply ask, 'How do you *know* that?'"[21]

When a therapist talks about "balancing your energies through psychic powers," the response should be, "What do you mean by 'energies'? What do you mean by 'psychic power'? Define your terms." Ask a medium who purportedly is in touch with an ancient Egyptian to identify a simple word, like the Egyptian word for "air." And if the entity comes up with a word, check it out.

Don't let others do your thinking for you. Children must understand not only *what* is true, but *why* something is true. They should begin to learn to analyze what they read, see on television, and hear in class. What assumptions are being made? What train of logic (if any) is being followed? Are propaganda techniques being used? Is there a hidden agenda? Are facts differentiated from feelings?

Asking the "right" questions, looking for evidence, weighing it, separating essentials from nonessentials, and assigning probability—these are important ways to decipher New Age pseudoscience.

I differ heartily with the hard-core rationalistic worldview of the late author Isaac Asimov. But in my opinion he hits the nail on the head when he says: "Inspect every piece of pseudoscience and you will find a security blanket, a thumb to suck, a skirt to hold. What have we to offer in exchange? Uncertainty! Insecurity!"[22]

Daniel Davis says he sees an increasing self-centeredness in New Age thinking, corresponding to a disinterest in "difficult things. . . . Wanting to be rich without working, smart without studying, and holy without giving up any vices."[23]

The New Age movement, both Davis and Philibosian say, works rather like a giant placebo: New Agers don't want to deal with pain. So they seek relief through crystals, acupuncture, channelers, and other hoped-for panaceas and utopias.

"A fantasy world leads to disappointment in the future," says Philibosian. His observation was echoed in different words by Karen Hoyt of the Spiritual Counterfeits Project: New Age is "a culture stuck in adolescence . . . in great intensity. It's a way of escaping reality because people can't keep up with the changes in culture; the change is too rapid to process."[24]

New Agers, like everyone else, want answers. They seek transcendence. But all too often, their manufactured mysteries are promoted by hoax and hype rather than truth. And sometimes truth must wait.

As Al Seckel, director of the Southern California Skeptics society, remarked: "People must be able to live without the answers to some things rather than to have answers that are wrong. . . . There are *real* mysteries out there. The adventure is finding them."[25]

To which we would add the wisdom of the Old Testament Book of Job, as interpreted by a noted Jewish scholar, the late Robert Gordis:

[T]he author of Job is more than simply a philosopher. By the alchemy of beauty he is able to get us to feel and appreciate and participate in the joys and glories of the world, recognizing that . . . after we have given all the explanations which human ingenuity and human insight can offer, there will remain a core of mystery. But it isn't only a mystery, it is also a miracle. It is not only something unknown; it is also something beautiful, and in that beauty, we can find what is required to face those aspects of life which personally we find painful, agonizing and even ugly.[26]

26

Unproven Hypotheses and Non Sequiturs

apodictic: logic (of a proposition); necessarily true or logically certain.

non sequitur: an inference or statement that does not follow logically from the premises or anything previously said.

Now that we have outlined a few discernment skills for evaluating New Age assumptions and technologies, we can also apply these tools to hypotheses advanced by New Age thinkers and practitioners. Unlike techniques and beliefs that turn out, under scrutiny, to be bogus, however, we are looking now at theories that are illogical, that are by their very nature impossible to verify, and that have failed so far to win acceptance by mainstream science.

Hypotheses are just that: *hypotheses*. They are not apodictic but are a kind of philosophical non sequitur. Thus, to hitch one's moral beliefs and worldview philosophy to such unproven theories can be at best misleading, and at worst fatal.

This New Age science-mysticism link needs careful examination.

Remember the Heisenberg "uncertainty principle"? This is the principle which says that our knowledge of subatomic particles is limited by the very fact that observation at that level affects the phenomenon being observed. From this,

New Age physicist Fritjof Capra concludes that quantum theory "thus reveals the basic oneness of the universe. . . . The human observer constitutes the final link in the chain of the observational processes."[1]

The Heisenberg principle is accordingly cited as evidence for the monistic unity of experimenter and experiment and—by extension—all of reality.[2]

Capra, Marilyn Ferguson, Gary Zukav (author of *The Dancing Wu Li Masters*), and other New Age headliners adduce that when physical reality is broken down to its most elemental parts, there are no parts; all is One. Separate, individualized entities are ultimately illusions of our own creation.

Whatever scientific evidence there is for the unity of the physical universe could fit the biblical view of God as a transcendent Creator just as well as the Eastern mystical view of a "seamless web of divinity at the heart of the universe," say Mark Albrecht and Brooks Alexander in their analysis of "The Sellout of Science."[3] Neither science itself nor any scientific evidence can ever settle the question.

The New Age interpretation is an overextrapolation, forcing a legitimate scientific principle to an unjustified metaphysical conclusion.[4]

In that connection, it is enlightening to recall that in Capra's visionary experience in which he "*saw*" the atoms of his body "participating in the cosmic dance of energy," he said he "*knew* that this was the Dance of Shiva, the Lord of Dancers worshiped by the Hindus."[5]

This is the type of conclusion that should be questioned: "Dr. Capra, how did you know that? Would you have drawn the same conclusion if you had not been familiar with the *Bhagavad Gita*, which describes Shiva's dance?"

As Albrecht and Alexander astutely point out, Capra was not proposing a theory, or reasoning from premise to conclusion; he was announcing a revelation.[6]

Or, consider the concept of *synchronicity*, popularized by psychiatrist Carl Jung and cited by New Age exponents as an evidence of interconnectedness—that everything is related as an indivisible whole. Jung used the term to describe the occurrence of two events in close proximity of time which appear to have no causal relationship yet nevertheless seem related. A simple example: You are thinking about someone you haven't heard from in years and just then he phones you. "Must be mental telepathy," you exclaim to the friend, only partly in jest.

The synchronicity principle allegedly receives strong "scientific" support from a theorem first proposed in 1964 by J. S. Bell in Switzerland. This derived from experiments which showed that if paired and identically charged particles fly apart and the polarity of one is changed by an experimenter, the polarity of the other particle changes instantaneously, as though each particle "knows" what the other is doing."[7]

But this is a far cry from the mystic's monistic vision. "All is related" does not require or even imply that "We are all One."

"The theoretical electrical effect of an electron on another particle anywhere else in the universe does not indicate that the particles are a singular unity. Here the New Age leap from physics to metaphysics assumes [that] monistic unity necessarily follows from intricate interconnectedness. The biblicist could argue the opposite: the interconnectedness evidences God's creation of wide variety exhibiting harmony and interrelated patterns."[8]

Tim Stafford, a perceptive staff writer for *Christianity Today* magazine, conducted numerous interviews for an article on the relationship between science and religion. "The physicists I talked to work daily with quantum physics, yet all thought that 'Zen physics' was sheer bunk," Stafford reported. "Scientists are cautious about drawing conclusions that reach beyond their data."[9]

Yet New Age practitioners are peddling a host of occult elixirs and psychotechnologies based on scientific non sequiturs. In their comprehensive *Wellness Workbook*, Regina Sara Ryan and John W. Travis, M.D., piggyback on Jung's synchronicity and Bell's theorem to "prove" ESP, psychokinesis, remote viewing, and psychic healing:

> If, despite their distance, or lack of apparent logical relationship, event A is connected to event B at the subatomic level— is it too difficult to make the leap in saying that ESP,

psychokinesis, distant viewing and psychic healing are merely everyday manifestations of an underlying connectedness? . . .

If you accept this relatedness you are immediately presented with alternatives that may significantly affect your life and health. In his popular book, *Occult Medicine Can Save Your Life*, neurosurgeon Norman Shealy, M.D., documents numerous cases in which psychic healing methods succeeded in both diagnosis and treatment where traditional medical practice had failed.

Irving Oyle, D.O., in his book, *The Healing Mind*, describes methods of helping his patients achieve an altered state of consciousness. In this state they "talk" with their "inner guides" to aid in diagnosing and treating a health-related problem.

At Quimby College in Alamagordo, New Mexico, a group of psychologists train students in moving their hands through the "aura," or energy field, that surrounds a patient's body. Called aura-balancing, this technique has provided new insights, increased energy, and even *healing* to those who have experienced it.[10]

Call this occultic but not scientific!

As quantum theorist Alastair Rae of Birmingham University in England has observed, quantum physics has made it easier for some people to believe in such claims "only on the basis that if quantum physics conflicts with everyday logic, then why shouldn't other things that conflict with everyday logic also be real? That is hardly a scientific reason for belief in the occult."[11]

New Age thinking also co-opts such scientific theories as dissipative structures, entropy, syntropy, and evolution for its monistic worldview.

Marilyn Ferguson claims that Belgian physical chemist Ilya Prigogine, who won a Nobel prize in chemistry for his theory of dissipative structures, may have found "the missing link between living systems and the apparently lifeless universe in which they arose."[12]

In essence, Prigogine's hypothesis is that the natural law of entropy (the Second Law of Thermodynamics), which states that all systems inherently run down or tend toward disorganization, is counteracted by another law. This higher law, called syntropy, accounts for the evolution of higher, more intricate levels of organization and design.

Prigogine claims there is a natural organizing force behind the universe bringing assorted parts into increasingly complex relationships. This occurs by the dissipation of energy, which creates the potential for sudden reordering.

> The continuous movement of energy through the system results in fluctuations; if they are minor, the system damps them and they do not alter its structural integrity. But if the fluctuations reach a critical size, they "perturb" the system. They increase the number of novel interactions within it. They shake it up. The elements of the old pattern come into contact with each other in new ways and make new connections. *The parts reorganize into a new whole. The system escapes into a higher order.* . . . Life "eats" entropy. It has the potential to create new forms by allowing a shake-up of old forms.[13]

From Prigogine's flowing mathematical formulations, Prigogine, Ferguson, Ken Wilber (author of *Up from Eden*), and others extrapolate a leap from the scientific model to a ladder of social evolution that applies to the transformation of society. This is the "paradigm shift" New Agers are so wont to describe in which cultures are the culmination of dissipative structures, the apex of "human physics."

M. Scott Peck also picks up on this social evolution model and applies it to the spiritual evolution of humankind.[14] Spiritual development is in a process of ascension, he says, just like physical evolution.

Ferguson takes it even further. In altered states of consciousness, she postulates, brain wave fluctuations may reach a critical level "large enough to provoke the shift into a higher level of organization. . . . They set off ripples throughout the system, creating sudden new connections. Thus, old patterns are likeliest to change when maximally perturbed or shaken—activated in states of consciousness in which there is sufficient energy flow."[15]

Ergo, Prigogine's theory is stretched to account for the effects of the New Age psychotechnologies.

The bogus "Hundredth Monkey" theory that we considered in the chapter on harmonic convergence, and the idea behind harmonic convergence itself, are based on the notion that modern science has verified the process of "wholemaking, the characteristic of nature to put things together in an ever-more synergistic, meaningful pattern," as Ferguson has described it.[16] In New Age parlance, social evolution has a ratchet. When enough meditators in a given area concentrate, there will be a threshold breakthrough—the "Maharishi effect"—ushering in peace and prosperity: a paradigm shift. When enough people—a "critical mass"—believe in or do something, it will become true or a reality for everyone: a paradigm shift.

The idea behind the Werner Erhard Hunger Project was that if 100,000 persons really believed world hunger could be ended by the close of the century, that "thought form" would catalyze the needed technical, political, and economic changes to make it happen.[17]

Such non sequiturs permeate much of New Age thinking. This is mystical thought masquerading as science. Bad science at that.

In the *Whole Earth Review*, a New Age publication, writer Maureen O'Hara fires off a blistering broadside at New Age's apparent infatuation with science. She considers the attachment shallow and "easily swayed by the tricks of the pseudoscience trade such as theorizing wildly in scientific-sounding language, sprinkling speculative discussion with isolated fragments of real data regardless of relevance, confusing analogy with homology, breaking conventional rules of evidence at will, and extrapolating from one level of reality into others wherein different principles operate."[18] The New Age variety of social evolution assumes that human nature is innately good—the precise opposite of the view held by the Judeo-Christian Scriptures. The Prigogine hypothesis, when applied to belief in inherent and ever-ascending social improvement, is also contradicted by the record of history.

India is a good case in point. One would think that a land dominated for thousands of years by a holistic worldview (the same worldview that New Agers now say science has verified) would have long ago synergistically eliminated hunger, violence, overpopulation, and the institutionalized racism of its caste system. This has not happened, of course.

New Age theorists would have us believe their unproven hypotheses and non sequiturs are the underpinning for a mystical vision of deliverance. But these theories seem to thrive best "in cultures that are in a perpetual state of disarray, where misery is rampant and corruption rife," observes Robert Burrows. "The problem is human perversity, not human perception. The pivotal issue is holiness, not holism; the only antidote is God's redemptive and re-creative grace in Christ."[19]

Paradigm shifts, if they occur, do not change human nature; they only change values and perceptions. There is no essential connection between social evolution and biological evolution. Neither a holistic worldview nor mystic enlightenment can erase the stubborn stain of individual and corporate sin and bring personal salvation.

27

Cautions and Dangers

Jeremy Tarcher, head of a major New Age publishing house in Los Angeles, has roundly castigated the media for concentrating on the "carnival sideshow" of the New Age movement rather than the main events in the "big tent." Instead of the fringe stuff—by which he means reincarnation, extraterrestrial contact, crystals, psychic phenomena, channeling, and turning big bucks—Tarcher has pleaded for the press to zero in on the efforts toward personal and social transformation which he feels are the core of New Age.[1]

His point is not without merit. There is an "up" side to New Age that deserves attention and responsible treatment. We media types are prone to pick up on bizarre and anomalous ideas and behaviors because, as Tarcher correctly acknowledged, they make "good copy."

But there is also a dark side to New Age thinking and practice. This wide zone of twilight—in which weirdness, fakery, loose assumptions, and non sequiturs abound—quickly wedges into darkness. There the universal vision of the divine "Higher Self" fades and blurs into the void.

This descent into darkness can occur subtly, almost imperceptibly, as the helpful and creatively positive give way to the questionable, and the questionable yields to the fallacious, and the fallacious to the dangerous. This too is part of the New Age story. Discernment is essential.

Take the case of the *Wellness Workbook*, a practical "self-

help" book about "creating vibrant health" and "alternatives
to illness and burnout" that contains many sound principles
and exercises that would benefit nearly everyone. The
authors warn against destructive habits and analyze good
nutrition; they tell the reader how to relax and how to breathe
and sit properly. They present insights about dealing with
anger and fear; emphasize the importance of play, laughter,
and listening skills; discuss how to prevent burnout and,
ultimately, prepare for death.

So far, so good. But by page 69, consider this advice on
"making medicine": "Fill a glass or bottle with water and
place it on a window sill of your house where it will receive
the first rays of the rising sun. Before you retire for bed, sit
with the water, telling it what you need for your increased
health and well-being. In the morning, drink the whole glass.
Believe it!"

Harmless, no doubt, although possibly misleading if substi-
tuted for needed medication. But notice the progression in
the next "exercise," which is titled "baptize yourself."

"This is one of the most beautiful and effective ways of
loving yourself. Compose a ceremony in which you use water
to symbolically cleanse your body (or the body of a loved
one), and your mind and soul from illness, darkness, 'sin,' and
painful memories. Make it a beautiful occasion. Take a new or
additional name to signify your new life. Be at peace."[2]

At this point in the book the line has been crossed from
health to religion—the religion of self. The New Age
universal Oneness assumption has been slipped into place.
The individual's Higher Self is "God," so "God" is the agent
as well as the recipient of the act. No omnipotent "Other,"
able to forgive sins, is needed.

This intrusion should be resisted regardless of one's
personal religious views because it degrades and cheapens
the sacrament of a major religion (Christianity) even as would
a "private marriage." Christian baptism is a public, outward
affirmation of commitment, the external and visible symbol of
an inner reality of God's grace.

Later chapters in the book state a belief in reincarnation
and suggest using pendulums, Ouija boards, and crystals for
diagnosis or treatment of ailments—"obtain[ing] information
directly from a deeper part of yourself that knows what's

really true for you. . . . [I]f you believe laetrile (or a crystal pendulum, or whatever) will work, then it will. . . . And if it works, go ahead and use it!"[3]

Sound familiar? You create your own reality. You are "God."

New Age worldviews also underlie the "wellness index" used in the workbook to construct a personal "wellness wheel," or profile of health. In the section on "wellness and transcending," the reader is to answer questions that include, "I am aware of that part of me which is greater than my mind, body and emotions," and "I experience a merging of my consciousness with a larger sense of consciousness (universal mind)."

Straight New Age worldview!

To be sure, authors Regina Sara Ryan and John W. Travis post a disclaimer at the beginning of the transcendence section, conceding that it "goes beyond the scope of most generally accepted 'scientific' principles and expresses the values and beliefs of the authors." Readers are told that it's okay to skip over questions that strongly grate against their beliefs, but the wellness index scores are weighted in favor of New Age answers and against the responses of biblical theism.

Another testing instrument called MindMaker6 (a registered trademark) has been developed by Brain Technologies Corporation of Fort Collins, Colorado, to "track . . . the power and opportunities of your world view." The survey measures values and beliefs, and a profile is constructed in which the person tested falls into "systems" defined as kinsperson, loner, loyalist, achiever, involver, and choice seeker. According to David Horner, director of Christian Research Associates in Denver, the theist comes out a loyalist, while persons with a New Age worldview score highest in the choice-seeker category.

Gregg Piburn, public relations manager for the Loveland, Colorado, plant of giant Hewlett-Packard Company (82,000 employees in 78 countries), said personnel management groups within the firm use MindMaker6 "as a tool . . . to understand each other and become more effective and productive."[4]

Both Horner and Piburn expressed concern about an

apparent "religious test" being used for company team building.

There truly is a danger if Eastern philosophical views of pantheism are part of a consulting firm's agenda to spread and foster the New Age vision. Worse, in some of the corporate management training programs that we looked at in chapter 16, there is an intent not to simply measure an individual's beliefs and values, but to restructure them. This is hardly "value neutral," as New Age consultants defend and advertise.

"Techniques that depend on protocols that command the learners to project themselves into some 'other' reality and then to experience themselves as being one with all things, including God, are hardly neutral," observed senior editor Ron Zemke in *Training* magazine. "They are certainly not neutral to Christians whose faith rests on the concept of God as an entity outside themselves.

"In other words, there can be no such thing as a centered, self-hypnotizing, yoga-practicing meditator who is also a Bible-believing Christian. You're one or the other."[5]

Zemke, also critical of New Age techniques being "slipped" into training programs, makes the point that if New Age is based on respect for the rights and dignity of individuals, the right to be told the truth should be paramount.

Adds Richard Watring, the former personnel director for Budget Rent-a-Car Systems in Chicago: "Private corporations that are not church-related should neither attempt to change the basic belief systems of their employees nor should they promote the use of techniques (i.e., altered consciousness) that accelerate such change; and while spiritual growth is important, corporations should not prescribe the methods whereby employees grow spiritually."[6]

Tom Brandon of the Christian Legal Society has advised workers who object to such job-related seminars to ask their employers to substitute nonobjectionable programs that do not violate the employee's religious convictions. Failing this, Brandon said, legal recourse is open because employers are prohibited from discriminating against employees' religious principles and are required to make reasonable accommodations.[7]

Surely not all techniques used by New Age advocates are objectionable, some might say. What about yoga, hypnosis, visualization, and positive imaging, among others?

My advice is: cautious discernment—for several reasons.

First, there is no conclusive proof that biofeedback and other exotic methods for alleviating stress, improving memory, and accelerating learning work any better than conventional techniques, according to a recent $425,000 study by the National Academy of Sciences.[8] There is, however, some indication that the *mental practice* of physical skills and athletic events may reinforce learning and enhance performance. So some "unconventional" methods, if not tied to an unacceptable worldview, may be appropriate, even helpful.

Second, visualization could be defined simply as the use of imagination and the formation of pictures in the mind. Indeed, thinking is almost impossible without visualization. (Try describing a tree without mentally picturing one.) On the other hand, visualization—which is common to meditation, inner healing (also known as the healing of memories), dream analysis, and other therapies (such as "journaling") used by both New Age and Christian practitioners—can be described as the intention to "manipulate realty or evoke the appearance and help of Deity."[9]

There's an important distinction between thinking or remembering, which involves mental images, points out Eric Pement of *Cornerstone* magazine, "and dwelling on those images for their own sake, believing that thought forms by themselves will bring things into being. . . . New Agers have co-opted visualization because they believe the universe is a form of consciousness, and reality exists by common consent."[10]

Pement goes on to say that, for Christians, a problem with using visualizations for inner healing may be the idea that thought or the power of suggestion does the healing, rather than a transcendent God.

I agree with Dave Hunt's and T. A. McMahon's assessment at this point: "If reality can actually be created or manipulated by visualization, this would allow everyone to play God with the universe. What would happen when competing realities were being visualized by different persons? If visualization taps into some power inherent within the universe and available to anyone, it would be the ultimate weapon to hand over to human egos; and the result would not be paradise, but hell on earth."[11]

A third practice requiring discernment is yoga. It is frequently claimed that yoga, or meditative practices derived from it, involves no religious beliefs. Yoga, in this view, is simply a "neutral" and healthy way of relaxing. Maharishi Mahesh Yogi, the Beatles' erstwhile guru whom we met in earlier pages, is the leading advocate of this position. Yet, observes Professor Irving Hexham, it seems certain yoga cannot be practiced in isolation from other Indian beliefs.

"The whole concept of yoga is based upon a carefully worked out theory of beliefs about the human condition. The terminology used to explain the practice itself involves acceptance of presuppositions with religious origins.

"This is not to deny that many people practice yoga because they honestly believe it to be healthy and value free. But as time passes, such people very gradually and imperceptibly begin to accept other concepts which involve definite religious convictions."[12]

With so many excellent physical fitness and relaxation practices available, why risk one aligned with Hinduism and altered consciousness?

A warning label must also be attached to psychedelic drugs, which are approved by many New Agers as the "entry level" for altered states.

Even Marilyn Ferguson, who could hardly be considered a wild-eyed New Age radical, noted (in 1980) that "It is impossible to overestimate the historic role of psychedelics as an entry point drawing people into other transformational technologies. For tens of thousands of 'left-brained' engineers, chemists, psychologists, and medical students who never before understood their more spontaneous, imaginative right-brained brethren, the drugs were a pass to Xanadu."[13]

Or a pass to a mental hospital for the "fried-brained."

By the late 1980s, there was growing experimentation and "research" with "high-tech . . . designer" psychedelic drugs among the "accelerated information and quantum reality culture," called Yummies—young upwardly mobile mutants—according to *OMNI WholeMind Newsletter.*[14]

That's part of the story about New Age transformational technologies, too, Mr. Tarcher.

Warnings about opening up the mind to hallucinations and "sinister entities" are regularly sounded by critics of the New Age. The alarms include the dangers of fantasy role-playing and imagination games like Dungeons & Dragons™, which swept through the youth culture several years ago.

Dungeons & Dragons is a doorway to the occult, charge critics. Don't be silly, counter advocates. It's only a game.

Although fantasy itself can be used positively as escapism, games like Dungeons & Dragons are laced with references to magic, occult wisdom, violence, and power.

Declares critic Stanley Dokupil, a former researcher with the Spiritual Counterfeits Project: "Mediumship or occultic powers may be acquired [in Dungeons & Dragons] through a process of visualization in which the individual imagines himself or herself in actual possession of such powers. At some point in the process the dividing line between the purely imagined and the real disintegrates; the process completes itself and the individual enters the world of unseen occultic forces."[15]

Not everyone who plays gets hung up in a morbid fantasy land, of course, and D & D isn't "the catechism of the New Age" as maintained by Peter Leithart and George Grant.[16]

Cautions are in order, however, just as they are for trance channeling, where there is always the danger of getting so caught up in mediumship that one begins to adopt the understanding of God, humanity, and reality that one's "entity" teaches.

Artist Joe Szimhart of Santa Fe, New Mexico, tells of "deprogramming" six followers of Ramtha who lost their ability to question because of just such a channeling lifestyle. They shifted their worldview to themselves, Szimhart said, attached to their past instead of present lives, and let go of committed relationships when they hit hard times.[17]

Outspoken as always, Carl Raschke calls channeling "a form of pseudo-religion that performs the same function as drugs.

"What we're seeing," he says, "is an attempt to harness a segment of society that's never had much religion to create an alternate religious worldview. In my view, it is a kind of pathology, and the more fascinated a person gets with it, the more likely it is that they can become mentally imbalanced by the process itself. Autohypnosis is a powerful tool not totally understood. It can lead to manipulation."[18]

The dangers lurk in all forms of what Aldous Huxley called "the Perennial Philosophy": the worldview that Nature—the Ultimate All—is all that is and all there is.

Beware! Whether it is a Scott Peck enthralling readers with his belief that they only need to look within themselves to find wisdom greater than their own and "become the ego of God";[19] a channeled entity informing distraught parents that they chose to have their child die; or a "Jesus" of the Course in Miracles admonishing telepathically that as one develops "true perception" he or she saves the world—from sin, "for sin does not exist."[20]

Be suspicious! Especially if a therapy, course, or teaching:

(a) is explained in terms of manipulating, balancing, or polarizing energies;
(b) deprecates the value of the mind or critical thinking;
(c) is supported only by testimonial anecdotes of the committed rather than by solid evidence and outside evaluation; or
(d) is based on "secret" esoteric knowledge revealed only to an inner elite.

As the Jesus of history exhorts us: "discern the signs of the times" (Matt. 16:3).

28

Reincarnation or Resurrection?

"If a man dies, shall he live again?" This question, asked by the Bible character Job (Job 14:14), has intrigued humankind since the dawn of history. The answer remains shrouded in faith and philosophy rather than in scientific proof.

Basically, there are three beliefs about what happens after death: annihilation, which holds that nothing happens because there is no reality outside the world of matter; resurrection, the Christian belief that a person's mortal body is transformed into an immortal one; and reincarnation, which theorizes that death is a passage to cyclical but unending rebirth. This last view permeates New Age thinking.

Until well into this century, reincarnation wasn't popular in either Europe or the United States. But now, according to several surveys including a 1982 Gallup Poll, about one-fourth of all Americans believe in some form of reincarnation. The proportion rises to 30% among persons under age 30. Gallup's Princeton Religion Research Center found the findings "particularly surprising in light of the fact that nine in ten Americans give their religious preference broadly as Christian and reincarnation is anathema to traditional New Testament doctrine."[1]

In a 1985 Roper organization poll, 44% of the adults sampled said they either believed (15%) in reincarnation or were not sure (29%) if they did.[2]

The wide U.S. acceptance of reincarnation, or transmigration of souls, has received a major assist from screen and entertainment celebrities as well as New Age personalities. Superstar Tina Turner reflects her reincarnation beliefs in the record "I Might Have Been Queen" with lines like "I'm a new pair or eyes, an original mind." Shirley MacLaine, whom F. LaGard Smith calls "the Pied Piper of today's reincarnation tune,"[3] claims that under the influence of psychic acupuncture she is able to talk to animals, trees, and an entity she calls "Higher Self."

The doctrine of reincarnation and its accompanying Law of Karma are present in the teachings of Buddhism and Hinduism. Some scholars trace their origin to the Indo-Aryans of Punjab and Sind, India, about 1800 B.C.[4] Others place it no earlier than 800 or 600 B.C.[5]

According to Norman Geisler and J. Yutaka Amano, there are ten versions of the reincarnation afterlife doctrine available in the world's marketplace of ideas.[6] Within the Eastern Yogic tradition, Hindus believe that when humans die, their souls pass, or transmigrate, into a new body with each incarnation. Buddhists, on the other hand, deny the existence of the soul but refer to a journey toward *nirvana*—a final release from the wheel of existence and the countless cycles of birth, life, and death. Nirvana also brings freedom from the bondage of karma, which has been defined as the cosmic law of cause and effect. Karma is the sum total of one's good and bad actions, a kind of ledger of credits and debits which together determine the circumstances of the individual's next rebirth.

Madame Helena Blavatsky, the founder of Theosophy, was a major shaper of an eclectic Western theory of reincarnation whose purpose and goal is to merge with God and end the painful rebirth cycle. Said Blavatsky: "It is owing to this law of spiritual development that mankind will become freed from its false gods and find itself finally—SELF REDEEMED."[7]

Alice Bailey's Arcane School—a Theosophy offshoot—and the copious writings of the late Edgar Cayce, the past-life psychic king whose convoluted incarnation theories included belief that Jesus had previously been the biblical Adam, also molded and influenced current reincarnation theories accepted by millions of Americans.

And under the New Age aegis, a hybrid form of reincarnation theory has developed on the American scene—one which "avoids the uncomfortable matters of guilt and responsibility before a personal and righteous God," according to evangelical Christian John Snyder, a reincarnation analyzer.[8]

Reincarnation American style meets psychological needs, attempting in the process to resolve the moral failures of life while hanging onto a hope for survival and salvation. At first glance, this seems to be a more just system than the Christian teaching of eternal judgment for finite transgressions. Under the reincarnation model, karma replaces sin and transgressors get additional go-rounds at life to make up for past errors and faults. Reincarnation is appealing also because it offers an explanation for the existence of pain and suffering: they are the result of wrong choices in previous lives.

Shirley MacLaine's Americanized version introduces "free agentry" into reincarnation and downplays the negative karmic buildup. Most, though not all, New Age reincarnationists reject the idea that the human soul can transmigrate backward to lower life forms once it has progressed upward from such lower incarnations as rocks, trees, and animals.

The notion of group reincarnation is also strong in the American version of working up the corporate cosmic ladder by working off bad karma. In his book, *Afterlife*, psychic investigator Colin Wilson tells the strange tale of a group of people who allegedly had been involved together in intertwined lives in thirteenth-century France and in Roman Britain in the fifth century, as well as in the Napoleonic era in France in the nineteenth century. According to Wilson, the "facts" as they emerge from the various cases "seem to support . . . [the] view of reincarnation as an evolutionary experience."[9]

In this connection, Lanny Buettner, analyzing the content of written trance communications by several modern psychic mediums, found them in essential agreement that reincarnation is not only a fact, but that "groups of souls may be working on a project over a period of lives, which could explain close cooperation during the past life."[10]

This "group soul," according to messages of channeled entities analyzed by Buettner (this type of scenario dovetails with the conceptions of many New Age reincarnationists, by the way), plans future incarnations based on the perceived state of the individual soul's karma from past lives:

> This is done in consultation with other souls, generally wiser, more advanced ones. The purpose or purposes for the next life are chosen and then what is often called a "blueprint" is drawn up which determines who the parents in the next life are to be (hence the place of birth and a certain social environment) and the physical characteristics (apparently through determining the combination of genetic materials which begins the fetus's growth). Michael [an entity who transmitted messages through an Ouija board] states that certain personality characteristics are also chosen. Finally, certain events are planned to facilitate circumstances appropriate to the goals or purposes of the incarnation (such as an accident at age 20 which will paralyze from the waist down, to help develop a goal of overcoming adversity). Blueprints are apparently coordinated with others, so that, for example, one would be born, knowing that a specific soul would incarnate a spirit as a younger sibling, or even that two souls would become incarnate intending to meet and marry and give birth to a third soul's incarnation.[11]

It is even possible, according to psychics who do "life readings," to be in touch with one's future incarnations. "Immortality consultant" Patricia-Rochelle Diegel outlined at a trance medium workshop how she had "been into" her own incarnations as far ahead as A.D. 5500![12]

Although reincarnationists insist that *choosing* to take on specific situations in future lives ensures free choice, it is hard to see—if Diegel's story is to be believed—how any element of free will in earthly life is preserved if the projected outcome of future karmic cycles can be known in advance.

The concept of justice is also dealt a fatal blow because personal responsibility for one's own actions vanishes. If I have no free will, then my uniqueness as a person is vitiated and I cannot be held accountable; if I am a truly unique individual with free will, it is unjust for me to bear the load of karma generated by someone else. As Mark Albrecht correctly points out:

"If reincarnation is true, Adolph Hitler will never have to pay for his crimes, for he has ceased to exist. Instead, completely new, unknowing and innocent personalities inherit Hitler's karma. Likewise the righteous also cease to exist, never reaping the benefits of their good lives and self-sacrifice. Others reap the reward."[13]

Since most of us cannot "remember" our past lives, how are we going to work off bad karma if we don't know what caused it? How then is reincarnation a learning experience to help one advance in the next life and eventually perfect the soul? Both the individual and society must suffer meaninglessly.

As proof of reincarnation, proponents cite alleged past-life recollections of people under hypnotic regression as well as case studies of persons who have described "near-death" and "out-of-body" experiences. Psychiatrist Helen Wambach, for example, has "regressed" more than 5000 patients into "prior lives," and her analysis of their "memories" appears convincing.[14] And thanatologist Elisabeth Kübler-Ross's study of the dying has led her to the conviction that they often "see" dead relatives. She has also accepted the spiritualist dictum that in the world beyond death there is no judgment of the dead; "they judge—and punish—themselves."[15]

But such "evidence" at most implies nothing more than a knowledge of the past; it does not prove that the person who "remembers" it was present in the past. And, under hypnosis, people will sometimes report events as being true when in fact they never happened. Further, even if these experiences support the case for ongoing life beyond physical death, they do not prove reincarnation—only immortality.

Past-life recall and instances of persons knowing information not available during their present lifetime could also be explained by spirit deception or even demon possession.

New Agers have often claimed that the Bible teaches reincarnation. What about this? Some have also stated that original references to reincarnation were deleted from the Scriptures and that—after previously teaching it—the Christian church suppressed the doctrine in the sixth century.

Biblical evidence for reincarnation, as Snyder shows, "is merely the product of wishful thinking and faulty literary criticism."[16]

Albrecht also lays to rest the false notion of biblical support for reincarnation.[17]

After examining four New Testament texts he considers "significant and deserving of exploration," Albrecht concluded: "While all the Eastern, gnostic and occult traditions enumerate karmic patterns and the destiny of rebirth with detail and precision, it is never mentioned in the Bible, which refers only to resurrection."[18]

The most-cited among a scattering of texts said to contain "vestiges" of reincarnationism is the passage in John's gospel where Jesus tells Nicodemus that he must be "born again" to enter the kingdom of God (John 3:3). Jesus' explanation shows that what is meant is not reincarnation but rather a spiritual birth. As James Sire points out in his book, *Scripture Twisting*, "[E]ach person who has been born physically must also be born spiritually in order to enter God's kingdom. There is no excuse of confusion, for the immediate context contains a definition."[19]

The New Testament book of Hebrews (9:27, RSV) clearly rules out reincarnation: "it is appointed for men to die once and after that comes judgment." Comments Gordon Lewis, a philosophy of religion professor at Denver Seminary: "The once-for-all death of Jesus is parallel to once-for-all death for all human beings. The Bible [texts] can't be wrenched out of context to defend reincarnation."[20]

Shirley MacLaine and other New Agers have rolled up mega-mileage on the claim that early church councils and dishonest Bible editors excised passages and stomped out reincarnation beliefs. But this horse never really gets out of the barn.

First of all, the New Testament canon was developed in the second and third centuries and received in final form by the fourth century, not in the sixth, as many New Age reincarnationists claim. The earliest versions of New Testament texts do not differ appreciably from those that the date *after* the sixth century.[21] Thus the "deletion" argument is stopped cold.

Further, the Council of Constantinople in A.D. 553 never considered reincarnation; it simply was not of great concern to the church fathers. The council *did* discuss—and reject— the idea of the preexistence of the soul, a view which had been held by church theologian Origen (c. 185–254). Origen believed human souls preexisted their physical bodies, but he did not believe in reincarnation. In fact, in his writings he specifically rejected reincarnation as contrary to the Christian faith.[22]

Why didn't the church suppress reincarnation? It didn't need to. The theory wasn't a serious option in Christian belief.

Finally, though New Agers cite some Bible passages to "prove" reincarnation, they at the same time fault Scripture for being unreliable and say the texts were "doctored." As several Christian apologists have noted, the reincarnationists can't have it both ways.

Resurrection is the Christian answer to Job's question, "If a man dies, shall he live again?" And reincarnation is incompatible with resurrection. They cannot both be true, despite efforts to synthesize or harmonize the two.

The historic evidences for the resurrection of Jesus are far superior to those advanced for the theory of reincarnation. As Snyder has observed, they rest upon a tripod of logic: "Jesus taught resurrection; He was raised from death, which among other things vindicated His teaching; and the sources that preserve the story of His life, death and resurrection are historically reliable and trustworthy."[23] Although we may not "prove" the accounts, their accuracy is "highly probably" and worthy of serious consideration.

The Christian claim, however, is not to be confused with the Platonic idea of immortality of the soul. The Christian concept is that the resurrection of the soul cannot be separated from the bodily resurrection. Thus, the integrity and unique personality of each individual are preserved at death.

Each resurrected person must face judgment. But instead of meeting a cold, relentless, and uncaring karma, the individual may depend upon the grace of a merciful, sovereign God who judges personally, justly, and with equanimity. And the ultimate state of those who stand before him depends upon their relationship to Jesus Christ: "For God so loved the world that He gave His only Son, that whoever believes in him should not perish but have eternal life. . . . Jesus said, . . . 'I am the resurrection and the life; he who believes in me, though he die, yet shall he live, and whoever lives and believes in me shall never die'" (John 3:16; 11:25, RSV).

Jesus taught that redemption comes through forgiveness of sin, not shuffling of karma.

In the final analysis, the doctrine of reincarnation does not solve the problem of suffering, injustice, and evil—it only pushes it ahead, perpetuating the endless turning of the karmic wheel.

29

Satan and the Problem
of Evil

The first Page-One story I ever wrote for the *Los Angeles Times* was about Satan.

It was January 1974, and *The Exorcist*, based on William Peter Blatty's novel about a demon-possessed girl, was drawing unprecedented crowds to movie theaters in twenty-four U.S. cities. An occult tumult had seemingly gripped the nation, and a beehive of debate and controversy swirled about the existence of demons and Satan—and ultimately about the nature of good and evil. Quoting French poet Charles Baudelaire, I pointed out that if the Devil's deepest wile is to persuade humanity he does not exist, then Satan was botching his job horribly.[1]

This was not the first nor the last time, of course, that there has been wholesale fascination with giving the Devil his due. In recent years a spate of popular books and films—including *Rosemary's Baby, Damien, Damien II, The Omen, Poltergeist*, and *The Amityville Horror*—has examined occult themes, evil spirits, haunted houses, and diabolical deeds. Satanic symbolism shows up frequently in heavy-metal rock lyrics. The much-publicized Church of Satan, founded in 1966 by Anton LaVey in San Francisco, is only one of a number of satanic groups claiming to worship or identify with the lord of darkness. The rites of some of these groups include heavy drug use, the "black mass," animal sacrifices, ritual sex, and mutilation. New Age neopagan groups may also evoke demons, but they are more oriented toward Wicca (witchcraft), magic, the powers of nature, and goddess worship.

Belief in demon possession dates back at least to the time of Jesus; the New Testament Gospels contain numerous references to his casting out devils from individuals. Accounts of the early church fathers in the second and third centuries speak of godly men requiring the disciplines of fasting and prayer in order to exorcise demons. In the Middle Ages in Europe, what was assumed to be demon possession often seemed epidemic. Starting with one hysterical nun, it rampaged through entire religious communities. Ancient exorcism rites in the Roman Catholic Church predate the Reformation, and a variation of the ritual has been preserved in the Anglican tradition. But the solemn ceremonies are rarely used today.

Views of Satan run the gamut—or gauntlet—from the vaudeville caricature of fiery "Mr. Redlegs" with pitchfork and tail, to seductive tempter and superforce of evil, to "a cool dude" who lets you "be on your own."[2]

"Interpretations of the meaning of Satan vary," declare Robert S. Ellwood and Harry B. Partin in their *Religious and Spiritual Groups in Modern America,* "from 'traditionalist' views of him as the antagonist of the Christian God to modern perspectives which see Satan as a symbol of the 'life-force,' creative evolution, or the affirmation of innocent pleasure. Proponents of the first see Satan more or less as the Miltonic Lucifer, a proud but heroic rebel with whom they identify. He is, contrary to lies told about him by the churches, able to reward his followers with an eternity of pleasure, and with opportunity for revenge, around his dark throne."[3]

New Age systematizers struggle with how to accommodate Satan and evil into their worldview.

"That's a tough one," Marilyn Ferguson admitted candidly as we sipped tea in her living room and chatted about the existence of evil. "I'm coming a little more toward an appreciation of this thing called evil but I think the jury is still out on what it is. The real perversity we have—the way we behave in a way that has evil consequences—it's because of the classical Luciferian attitude that we want to be God.

We don't understand our boundaries.... It's failure to understand our rightful place."

But, I pursued, in New Age aren't we all "God"?

"We *are* God, but not all of God.... People get overly carried away when they realize they create their reality.... There are other people out there and their needs and their realities have to interact with mine.... You can tap into this power, but you're not the sum total of it," Ferguson avowed.[4]

New Agers swing between explaining away evil as an illusion, or chalking it up to the "wages" of karma—the New Age equivalent of sin.

To Shirley MacLaine, there is no such thing as evil. Evil, she believes, is only what you *think* it is. This construct has roots in Transcendental thinking of the last century, as we have seen, as well as in Christian Science. Mary Baker Eddy taught that evil and sin, in league with error, sickness, death, and all forms of matter, are simply the products of false perception and do not exist in the all-good and all-knowing Mind of God.[5]

In MacLaine's view, evil is denied, change is always good, problems disappear, guilt evaporates, and potential is unlimited. The New Age way to eliminate evil is to eliminate everything finite because finite experience is itself evil.

In New Age thinking, observes Art Lindsley in *New Age Rage*, "the only way to transform this evil situation is to eliminate the illusion of the finite, the personal, and the social. Disease and suffering are illusory—a matter of consciousness. If we alter consciousness, we eliminate disease."[6]

And, apparently, even war.

New Age spokesman and physician Dr. Irving Oyle was once asked how America should deal with the Vietnam War. "If we all stop thinking about it," he replied, "if we all stop agreeing on its objective reality, it will cease to exist."[7]

Entities Seth and Michael, as channeled respectively by Jane Roberts and Jessica Lansing, stated that evil has only as much reality and power as people give it by their basic beliefs. The same applies to devils and demons.[8]

This view, according to researcher Lanny Buettner, gives demons alleged power through negative telepathic suggestion: "If a man believed his neighborhood was filled with muggers, he would telepathically attract a mugger, thus confirming his belief."[9]

This understanding of evil was affirmed to me by a New Ager who told me she "created" her own stabbing in an underground parking garage because she transmitted her fears that such an attack was likely to happen.

Beyond good and evil, in New Age thinking, is the monistic One, the God who is both good and evil. Stemming from this notion is the New Age belief in the essential goodness of humanity and in the upward spiral of social evolution. These assumptions root both in Hindu philosophy about the nature of God, and in Jung's theory of the "Collective Unconscious."

Jung was enamored with the impersonal deity of Gnosticism that is beyond good and evil or moral conscience, observes Carl Raschke: " 'Good' and 'evil' from the standpoint of the Collective Unconscious are complimentary and reciprocal elements. As archetypes they have equal worth in the economy of nature. There is no such thing as an absolute dichotomy between good and evil. Good and evil are what particular societies brand them."[10]

Even as an apple has a top and a bottom but both are parts of the apple, so God and the Devil, good and evil, are portions of a greater reality—a greater "good." The result of such New Age teaching is believing there is only what is "right" in the moment—there are no "rules" or sure prescriptions to steer one's life. This is moral relativism (a subject that demands our full attention in the next chapter).

Following up these implications for the area of sexual ethics, Buettner points out that "Presumably, then, no stigma need be attached to divorce, premarital, or extra-marital sex, or even incest, except when these acts do violence to another; the acts themselves are not intrinsically evil."[11]

Ferguson and other New Agers rely on the assumption of humanistic psychology that human beings have a natural bent toward goodness and growth; therefore, there is little room for "wrong"—even "poor"—choices. Ferguson believes that the "cure to evil is education. . . . We all want the same thing . . . a certain quality of life."

During the "evolution of intelligence," she explained in our interview, "we become prematurely crafty. We see that ignorance and greed work together to make a little mud, and we do dirty stuff and dumb stuff. It's only by developing our intelligence and our awareness that we see that doesn't work."[12]

Ken Wilber, a major architect of New Age thought, turns the biblical message of the Fall in the Garden of Eden upside down in his book, *Up from Eden*. Actually, he says, the "Fall" was an "evolutionary advance and perfect growth, but it was *experienced* as a Fall because it necessarily carried an increase in guilt, vulnerability, and knowledge of mortality and finitude."[13]

By eating from the Tree of Knowledge, Wilber continues, "not only did men and women realize their already mortal and finite state, they realized they had to leave Eden's subconsciousness and begin the actual life of true self-conscious responsibility (on the way to superconsciousness, or Actual Return [to godhead]). They did not get thrown out of the Garden of Eden; they grew up and walked out. (Incidentally, for this courageous act, we have Eve to thank, not blame)."[14]

The theological Fall, or original sin, Wilber contends, marked the "illusory separation of all things from Spirit." Creation itself was a fall because it was a centrifugal movement, the cutting off of all selves (even infants) from their remembering their ultimate inclusion in Spirit. Evolution, then, is a labored return toward Spirit, toward Source. Hence the title of Wilber's book, *Up from Eden*: Men and women "are up from the beasts and on their way to the gods."[15]

New Age karma theory appears to mesh here, for working off bad karma in successive lives supposedly would aid in the evolutionary return to godhead and negate the illusion of separate egos and paradise lost. The only sin would seem to be ignorance of wholeness and unity, the only evil belief in separation or distinction.[16]

Karma attempts to answer the problem of evil and suffering, as we touched upon in the preceding chapter. But if God is both good and evil, and no moral standards exist for an equitable distribution of karma in the next life, then capriciousness and nihilism are the bitter fruit of the Law of Return.

No religious system supplies a neat and easy solution to the paradoxes and problems of evil and suffering. But the One-Is-All philosophy that the One contains the eternal reconciliation of all opposites, including good and evil, leads to an attitude that one can do no wrong: Whatever one does is simply following his or her karma.

The deception lies in substituting our own images for reality, which is a virtual mirror image of the Big Lie of Satan that we can be as God himself.[17] Thus, Charles Baudelaire was right after all: The Devil vanishes behind his own image.

Yet our society of rewards and punishments is predicated upon the belief of biblical religion that human beings are able to choose between good and evil, right and wrong.

Said Judaism expert Robert Gordis: "The idea of freedom [of choice] is fundamental to the very nature of man and the universe. . . . Freedom means the right to be wrong."[18]

The suffering caused by Hitler's Holocaust—though we can never fully understand it—was the natural consequence of a monstrously wrong choice, Gordis said.

> The Nazis—Hitler, and his gang—chose the monstrous evil as against good. But that was necessarily part of the divine plan because God gave us all the right to choose. . . . The perspective is the goodness and glory of God revealed in the world. Also a fundamental idea that is basic: the concept of the moral freedom of man. . . .
>
> This approach helps us in our understanding—if not in our accepting and certainly not in our applauding—even the horrors of the Holocaust. There is only a quantitative difference between the murder of five people and six million. The death of one child, the suffering of a baby, is part of that great mystery of the world. But to the extent that we can understand it, it is part of the very nature of the universe and the constitution of man.[19]

The Bible, as opposed to the Eastern religious texts and the New Age worldview, speaks of a conspiracy of evil against God and his rule, and of Satan's influence (Job 2:6–7; Rev. 12:9–12). The New Testament is steeped in a dualistic view of human nature and abounds with descriptions of a cosmic struggle between the forces of good and evil (nineteen of the twenty-seven books of the New Testament speak of Satan). And, as we noted at the beginning of this chapter, Jesus and his disciples took the existence of demons and the "powers and instruments of darkness" very seriously.

A satanic explanation of evil may seem to be a quaint cultural myth that is passé in sophisticated, late twentieth-century society. Many prefer to speak about mental derangement and schizophrenia.

For others, the facetious remark, "The Devil made me do it," is a convenient cop-out to duck personal moral responsibility. But before we dismiss it altogether, shouldn't we at least consider the demonic as an alternative explanation for evil that seems to break in unbidden? Perhaps there *is* spirit possession. The existence of evil *incarnate* personalities is well established; why not *discarnate* evil personalities who interject themselves into our lives and institutions?

Many of us, however, may believe in *too many evils*: "We believe in a thousand evils, fear a thousand dangers, but have ceased to believe in Evil and to fear the true Dangers," wrote Denis de Rougemont. "To show the reality of the Devil in this world is . . . to cure ourselves. We are never in greater danger than in moments when we deceive ourselves as to the real nature of a threat, and when we summon our energies for defense against the void while the enemy approaches from behind."[20]

C. S. Lewis, the British author and common man's theologian, wrote advice in 1941 that stands well in this New Age: "There are two equal and opposite errors into which our race can fall about the devils. One is to disbelieve in their existence. The other is to believe, and to feel an excessive and unhealthy interest in them. They themselves are equally pleased by both errors, and hail a materialist or a magician with the same delight."[21]

30

Absolute Relativity

"Every age," intoned Pope John Paul II from the front of cavernous St. Mary's Cathedral in San Francisco, "poses new challenges and new temptations for the people of God on their pilgrimage, and our own is no exception."

The pontiff was speaking to 3000 delegates representing several hundred U.S. Roman Catholic lay groups, and he was sounding a note he repeated often during his ten-day pastoral visit to the United States in September 1987: America, with unprecedented material wealth and blessings, was all but suffocating in a secular materialism that threatened to snuff out spiritual development and stifle the joy of serving the less fortunate.

In his slow, accented English, the Polish pope continued his message:

> We face a growing secularism that tries to exclude God and religious truth from human affairs. We face an insidious relativism that undermines the absolute truth of Christ and the truths of faith, and tempts believers to think of them as merely one set of beliefs or opinions among others. We face a materialistic consumerism that offers superficially attractive but empty promises conferring material comfort at the price of inner emptiness. We face an alluring hedonism that offers a whole series of pleasures that will never satisfy the human heart. All these attitudes can influence our sense of good and evil at the very moment when social and scientific progress

requires strong ethical guidance. Once alienated from Christian faith and practice by these and other deceptions, people often commit themselves to passing fads, or to bizarre beliefs that are either shallow or fanatical.[1]

The high-vaulted cathedral resounded with applause when this warm and charismatic but most orthodox pope drove home his point: "Christ's message must live in you and in the way you live and in the way you *refuse* to live."

Meanwhile, Baptist Carl F. H. Henry, a foremost evangelical theologian, was sending out similar signals in a round of lectures during the summer and fall of 1987. The bottom line: Western civilization, nurtured by biblical notions of moral absolutes, purpose, and the ultimate triumph of good over evil, is now wallowing in a swamp of neopaganism.

"The West has lost its moral compass," Henry said. The culture thus sinks in a neopagan naturalism that says "nature alone is real, that man is essentially only a complex animal, that distinctions of truth and good are temporary and changing."[2]

Henry told gatherings of evangelical intellectuals that this reduction of reality to "impersonal, purposeless processes" and man to the "accidental product of a cosmic explosion" who himself "defines and redefines" good, left ethical standards in a shambles. And, he added, it sacrificed the metaphysical underpinnings that make sense of moral absolutes.

Orthodox religious leaders are not the only ones recoiling from the moral relativism that is eroding American values. Political and social scientists as well as secular educators have sounded similar alarms about collapsing moral standards and ethical disarray.

Pollster George Gallup has observed that the United States faces a "moral and ethical crisis of the first dimension."

During a July 1987 Prayer Breakfast in St. Paul, Minnesota, Gallup, an Episcopal layman, referred to a "deep spiritual malaise" and the "corrupting power of money and material success . . . at all levels of society." This was evident, he said, in widespread cheating on taxes, extra-marital affairs of "epidemic proportions," fraudulent telephone charges, pilfer-

age costing department stores $4 billion a year, and default-
ing on educational loans by many students.

People need to learn how to bring biblical principles into
their lives, admonished Gallup.[3]

Indeed, many Americans feel a need to reevaluate the basis
of morality and rebuild a structure of values. In a poll
conducted for *TIME* magazine by Yankelovich Clancy Shul-
man, "more than 90% of the respondents agreed that morals
have fallen because parents fail to take responsibility for their
children or to imbue them with decent moral standards; 76%
saw lack of ethics in businessmen as contributing to tumbling
moral standards; and 74% decried failure by political leaders
to set a good example."[4]

Michael Gelven, professor of philosophy at Northern
Illinois University, summarized beliefs underlying what he
calls a trendy kind of American cultural nihilism (which
denies meaning to everything): "Granting all opinions equal
status, the true one counts no more than the false one.
Indeed, the belief only in opinions admits of no truth at all.
And the fear of being wrong is replaced by the fear of being
right and appearing to be an ideologue."[5]

Gelven's analysis was made in the context of reviewing *The
Closing of the American Mind*, the landmark book by the late
Allan Bloom. This surprising best-seller outlines trends in
American higher education that have led to a breakdown of
discernible moral norms and a crumbling of the belief that
truth exists—or that it matters.

The students, said Bloom, come from a potpourri of
backgrounds and are unified only in their relativism and
allegiance to equality:

> And the two are related in a moral intention. The relativity of
> truth is not a theoretical insight but a moral postulate, the
> condition of a free society, or so they see it. They have all been
> equipped with this framework early on, and it is the modern
> replacement for the inalienable natural rights that used to be
> the traditional American grounds for a free society. That it is a
> moral issue for students is revealed by the character of their
> responses when challenged—a combination of disbelief and
> indignation: "Are you an absolutist?" the only alternative they
> know, uttered in the same tone as "Are you a monarchist?" or
> "Do you really believe in witches?". . . the danger they have

been taught to fear from absolutism is not error but intolerance. Relativism is necessary to openness; and this is the virtue, the only virtue, which all primary education for more than 50 years has dedicated itself to inculcating. . . . The true believer is the real danger.[6]

Arguing that few students wrestle with what is good, what it true, or what is right, Bloom said the self has displaced the soul, and "openness" and autonomy have usurped authority.

Openness, writes Bloom, "used to be the virtue that permitted us to seek the good by using reason. It now means accepting everything and denying reason's power. . . . True openness is the accompaniment of the desire to know, hence our awareness of ignorance. To deny the possibility of knowing good and bad is to suppress true openness. . . . [R]elativism has extinguished the real motive of education, the search for a good life."[7]

Bryn Mawr political scientist Stephen Salkever, quoted in *TIME* magazine's May 25, 1987, cover story, "What Ever Happened to Ethics," notes that once there *was* a traditional language of public discourse based partly on biblical sources and partly on republican sources. But that language, fallen into disuse, leaves American society with "no moral lingua franca."[8]

It is difficult to set a moral agenda in the prevailing American intellectual climate.

One lucid example: In November 1986, Cornell University president Frank Rhodes suggested to a Harvard audience that the nation's academic centers needed to pay serious attention to students' "intellectual and moral well-being." Catcalls from both faculty and students interrupted his address, and applause greeted a heckler who inquired just who would provide moral instruction for others and whose morality would be promoted.[9]

Bloom and others insist the problem of relativism is not inherent in democracy but stems from a misreading of our nation's forefathers.

The United States was founded upon a twin commitment to inalienable human rights and to the Calvinistic belief in an ultimate and divinely revealed moral right and the obligation of sinful beings to follow right conduct. These faith principles were incorporated into both the Declaration of Independence and the Constitution.

Charles Colson, well-known author who served as special counsel to President Richard Nixon before pleading guilty in 1974 to conspiracy charges related to the Watergate scandal, has observed that the "belief that law must be grounded in the transcendent truth that comes from God's revelation has been a cornerstone of American democracy for 200 years. Rooted in the Judeo-Christian tradition, it has been the principal bulwark to protect the weak and the powerless, and to preserve free institutions."[10]

And Bloom has noted that "The Constitution was not just a set of rules of government but implied a moral order that was to be enforced throughout the entire Union."[11] To Bloom, truth is the rationally discernible moral norms evident in natural law.

C. S. Lewis described natural law as that law beyond man which endures and is often contrary to humankind's desires and intent. Natural law must have some divine origin or it couldn't have survived, Lewis reasoned.

Things went wrong, said Bloom, in the poisonous subjectivism introduced by the German philosophers Friedrich Nietzsche (1844–1900), Max Weber (1864–1920), and Martin Heidegger (1889–1976). According to Bloom's analysis these Teutonic thinkers exported the seeds of modern nihilism to American shores at the same time that they pulled up the roots of truth.

Gelven summarizes Bloom's view in his insightful critique of *The Closing of the American Mind*:

> When "values" are substituted for "virtues," "commitments" for "morals," "life-styles" for "social behavior" and "alternatives" for "truth," not only is the English language weakened but the very foundation of all sensible action and thought is undermined.
>
> For then we may easily substitute things that are variable and temporary for that which is steady and constant: the truth. The loveliest, strongest plant in the world plucked from its soil and roots, no matter how splendid its blossoms, withers and dies. If any philosophical analysis is uprooted from the rich soil of truth, it too will die.[12]

These values are only a "cut-flower remnant" of the biblical heritage, asserts Henry, who believes that universal morality is not produced by natural law in itself but requires special divine revelation.[13]

Colson, in *Kingdoms in Conflict,* his "religious equivalent" of Bloom's book, adds the ideas of Freud and naturalist Charles Darwin (1809–82) to those of Nietzsche, proposing that together they formed a "destructive philosophic trend" that gripped American intellectuals and became the long fuse that finally set off an explosion of relativism: "All moral distinctions were equally valid and equally invalid since all were equally subjective," Colson says.[14]

"God remains dead," Nietzsche wrote. "How shall we, the murderers of all murderers, comfort ourselves? Must we not ourselves become gods simply to seem worthy of it?"[15]

That looks, sounds, feels, and tastes suspiciously like New Age philosophy!

Mix in the increasingly popular Eastern monistic thought that anything is permissible if God is everything and therefore beyond the distinctions of good and evil; there is no such thing as right or wrong, or coincidence, or guilt, or victimization—you choose your reality.

Add the barren existentialist writings of Albert Camus (1913–60) and Jean-Paul Sartre (1905–80), which captivated American college campuses during the 1950s and 1960s. And top it all off with the hard drugs, easy sex, and "do-your-own-thing" subculture of the 1960s.

The recipe's yield? A mind-set, a worldview, solidified. Notes Gelven: "The silliness has abated, the tear gas has long been dispersed by the winds, but the thinking is still nihilistic to the core and far more insidious because of its subtlety and quiet acceptability. The quiet victories won by the 60s are the most deadly, and they include confusing equality with egalitarianism, freedom with license, and truth with opinion."[16]

Three hundred years earlier, French scientist-philosopher Blaise Pascal (1623–62) had foreseen it. In a values vacuum, he said, humanity will pursue one of two goals: we will imagine that we ourselves are gods or we will seek gratification through our senses.

And thus we enter the reign of relativity! This is the appeal—and the Achilles' heel—of the New Age movement.

Relativism is appealing because, as Gelven, Bloom, and Henry point out, this is an age when "objective" truths are considered passé and "bad manners," if not divisive. Religion is supposed to traffic only in options: my karma is as good as your dogma (unless in the traffic my karma runs over your dogma!).

"To deny everyone else's gods violates public piety and its approval of the plural gods," remarks Carl Henry.[17] Or, in the words of New Age writer Margot Adler, "[D]iversity in the spiritual world will mark the health of the human community. The polytheistic vision doesn't preclude monotheism as an appropriate individual path, but it does insist that the larger vision is multiform—that the universe is too rich and large and varied to be captured so easily by a single prophet, system or holy book."[18]

That goes over well in a do-as-you-please society where suave politeness, tempering bigot zeal, changes "I believe," to "I think I feel." Like the ancient Romans, our culture adds one deity after another to its modern pantheon. As Henry says, "The issue [is] not whether religious sentiment is true, but whether religious feelings are useful."[19]

New Age relativism also appeals because of its optimistic view of human nature and concomitant rejection of guilt and the need of atonement for sin.

"Christianity is portrayed [by New Agers] as narrow-minded, unrealistic, negative," commented Douglas Groothuis, author of *Unmasking the New Age*, during our interview in Seattle. "The New Age movement has no God to sin against. . . . [It] is utopian, thinking we can create a utopia by our own efforts."[20]

That view remains fashionable on television, in newspaper editorials, even in some church pulpits. It is essentially a man-made religion, brimming with optimism about human capacities, but it flies in the face of a century filled with terror and depravity.[21]

Moral foundations crumble and chaos descends when everyone does "whatever is right in his own eyes" (Deut. 12:8, NASB; see also Judges 17:6; 21:25; and Prov. 21:2).

As we accelerate down the road where New Age moral

relativity takes us, there is, as F. LaGard Smith puts it, "no absolute truth, no center stripe down the highway of life."[22]

The Landscape of Relativity

"[T]he evolution of the race is for man to learn not how to obey the law but how to *be* the law," says David Spangler, one of New Age's major spokesmen and a founder of the New Age Findhorn Community in Scotland. "There is a vast, vast difference. If you *are* the law it means that you are at one with the whole. For divine law simply exists. . . . When a person understands this, when he begins to have that attunement, when he is the law, he is not going to act in any way that will disturb or distort the true balance of the true wholeness. . . . The New Age is an age where there is needed that group of people who through attunement can be self-governing, act as the law, as the divine, as the right, as the love."[23]

Unfortunately, Spangler's presumption of an intrinsically good human nature sets the stage for dictatorship or anarchy—or both. Like all Gnostic elitist corps, Spangler's enlightened "seers" would use their new self-knowledge to decide for the rest which patterns and relationships would benefit the whole, for only those crowned with cosmic consciousness are fit to lead the planet into the New Age.

But New Age philosophy is a morally unfit vehicle for political leadership because "it lacks any absolute standard that would tell us that the outcome of the great transformation would be more good than evil," Groothuis declares.[24]

Relativism—plugged into reincarnation theory—denigrates the value of human life by reducing all life to the lowest level. John F. DeVries, president of Bibles for India, graphically makes this point in the *Indian Journal*: "In India, human babies are no more important than rats! Rats may not be killed because they are expressions of the same universal energy that characterizes man. As a result, rodents and other animals eat 20% of India's grain crop every year—food that could be available for starving children."

With this mind-set that all life forms are equal, DeVries continues, "one can picture the ludicrous scene of an injured man and a wounded cat sharing the same hospital emergency room! The eventual results of such a belief are obvious."[25]

Applied to the politics of "deep ecology," the New Age assertion that all life has equal value produces "the ultimate consequence of relativity," one that is morally false and completely untrue, according to Kevin Kelly, a writer for the *Whole Earth Review.* "What *is* true is that a human counts more than a flea. Simple," Kelly declares (emphasis added).[26]

Relativism scores no higher when it comes to abortion, murder, and sexual ethics.

Reincarnation is the engine that drives much New Age opinion on such matters—the machine of moral relativism. For example, psychiatrist Helen Wambach uses reincarnationism logic to conclude there's nothing morally wrong about abortion: it's only the body, not the soul, that is killed, she declares; and if a fetus is aborted the soul can choose to enter another fetus.[27]

With this logic, suicide becomes simply a decision not to go ahead with a life plan but instead recycle to another to complete one's karma. J. Z. Knight, channel for Cro-Magnon entity Ramtha, says that murder isn't really wrong or evil. "If you believe in the continuation of life [reincarnation] it's a different story," she said on ABC's "20/20."[28]

Ritual murderer Charles Manson, while disowned by responsible New Agers, was involved with several pantheistic groups and studied occult literature. This apparently led him to believe that he had reached a mystical state of consciousness in which he transcended death and slipped beyond the confines of good and evil. If, in the All is One, good and evil are reconciled, then one can do nothing bad; thus Manson was only acting logically.[29] As Groothuis has noted, the fact that Manson's followers knew him as both Satan and Christ highlights the collapse of distinctions between good and evil under moral relativity.

Another prime example of moral relativity, propped up by monism and fed by notions that whatever one does is right, is the teaching of Indian mystic Bhagwan Shree Rajneesh. James S. Gordon of Georgetown University Medical School, who initially found much to admire in Rajneesh, came to this chilling assessment of the master manipulator on the final page of his book, *The Golden Guru:*

In the end, Rajneesh became the kind of man, the kind of religious leader, he had always derided. If indeed his ego had once dissolved and melted like a drop into the ocean, it seemed over the years to have renewed and enlarged, and in his isolation it grew gross with his attachment to power and luxury and position. . . .

On his ranch, surrounded by armed guards, dressed up and doped up, imperious and imperial, he resembled Jim Jones far more than Buddha or Krishna or Jesus. He was unwilling to learn or change, or to admit that there was anything to be learned or to change.[30]

Rajneesh, like many New Age leaders, lifts the limits on sexual expression. In New Age morality, monogamy is often seen as inhibiting needed "deep interpersonal relationships" with many persons.[31] If All is One, then—unless violence is used—no form of sexual activity violates another person's sanctity. Even the homosexual lifestyle is valid.

"So if love is as natural as breathing, and eating, and working, and playing," wrote Ryan and Travis in the *Wellness Workbook*, "it is as natural as 'sexing' besides. If love becomes our 'life-support system,' then every decision we make, sex included, will be guided by it. We will choose to have sex with one another if it enhances our experiences of unification with all that is."[32]

New Age relativism also decimates traditional categories of religion. As Carl Henry has remarked: "Naturalism grants Christianity no ontological credentials superior to the legendary and mythological gods of the Babylonians, Greeks, or Romans, and no more metaphysical legitimacy than Hinduism or Taoism. In whatever guise it appears, naturalism is the metaphysical nullification of the God of the Bible."[33]

Henry's observation is not just theoretical. New Age author Spangler has written: "We can take all the scriptures and all the teachings, and all the tablets, and all the laws, and all the marshmallows and have a jolly good bonfire and marshmallow roast, because that's all they are worth. Once you are the law, once you are the truth, you do not need it externally represented for you."[34]

And George Craig McMillan, describing Laya Yoga and enlightenment in the New Age magazine, *Life Times*, says "belief in God or non-belief in God means nothing because you are part of that process [of enlightenment], generating, organizing, destroying, continually."[35]

The United Nations meditation room, where New Ager Sri Chinmoy gives chapel services, is also a memorial to no god at all and a fitting symbol of New Age relativism. As Charles Colson describes it: "Lights in the ceiling create bright spots of illumination on the front wall. One focuses on a piece of modern art: steel squares and ovals. Beyond the abstract shapes, there is nothing in those bright circles of light. They are focused on a void. And it is in that void that the visitor suddenly sees the soul of the brave new world."[36]

Looking for God within the self makes truth personal, say trance channelers Verna Yater and Ellwood Babbit. What one person perceives is considered truth, even if it conflicts with another's perception. When a reporter asked them if there was any room for absolute truth, Babbitt said: "The absolute truth is that we are all gods in our own rights."[37]

Process theology, which views God as being incomplete in some respects and a companion of humanity in creative transition toward perfection, fits nicely with New Age relativism. Process theology headwaters spring from philosopher Alfred North Whitehead (1861–1947), who drew together the growing belief in evolution and the concept of relativity in his 1929 book, *Process and Reality*. God, say some process theologians, is "the inescapable energy that moves through all things."[38]

But the changing process is unworthy of worship, according to Neoorthodox theologian Emil Brunner: "Were God one who is 'becoming,' then everything would founder on the morass of relativism. We can measure nothing by changing standards: changeable norms are no norms at all; a God who is constantly changing is not a God whom we can worship. He is a mythological being for whom we can only feel sorry."[39]

In laying out the New Age ideal of an education curriculum that fosters autonomy, Marilyn Ferguson clearly shows the direction relativity can take. [I]f our children are to be free," she says, "they must be free even from us—from our limiting beliefs and our acquired tastes and habits. At times this means teaching for healthy, appropriate rebellion, not conformity. Maturity brings with it a morality that derives from the innermost self, not from mere obedience to the culture's mores."[40]

Freedom to think and seek truth, unfettered by sterile preconceptions—this much I accept. But morality derived from the inner *self*? In New Age thought the self is the One, which is the impersonal, relativized "Force." There are no standards of right and wrong; good and evil are interchangeable. What instructs the self, or, as Roman Catholic theologians would say, informs the conscience?

That was a question that gnawed away at Bill Coulson, who for nearly twenty-five years considered humanistic psychologist Carl Rogers his hero as well as his mentor. Coulson finally parted company with Rogerian concepts and the Center for Studies of the Person in La Jolla, California, which the two men had founded in the 1960s. As we saw in chapter 19 on the human potentials movement, Rogers started with the premise that human beings were essentially good and could act correctly without being told to do so—or *how* to do so.

But Coulson gradually came to the conclusion that Rogers had made a tragic mistake in generalizing beyond his therapeutic insights. "We went from the fine distinctions that can be made about therapy and the scientific evidence that supported it to something that was insupportable. We made it gross," Coulson said recently.[41]

Now Coulson is saying it's a grievous error to tell youngsters they must make up their own minds. In 1987 testimony before a Michigan legislative committee conducting hearings into juvenile delinquency prevention, Coulson declared: "Culturally, societally, we've got to tell children, 'Yeah, make up your own mind—*but by all means, make it up the right way!*' And there are some things we know that are right, and some things that are wrong."[42]

In an interview with Jeannette DeWyze for San Diego's *Reader* magazine, Coulson followed up on his crusade against allowing children unbridled free choice.

"I think we have to charm our children into doing the right thing," he said, "because otherwise, somebody else is going to try to charm them into doing the wrong thing." As an example, Coulson cited a booklet put out by the Tobacco Institute. Its underlying strategy, he concluded, was teaching parents to tell children, nonjudgmentally, that they must make up their own minds about cigarette smoking. But this leaves youngsters completely vulnerable to unabashed arguments that smoking is good—that is, it leaves them vulnerable to cigarette industry advertisements, Coulson fumed.[43]

Allan Bloom scanned the educational wasteland and perceived that what students lacked is so "simple and yet so elusive that only the more gifted teachers can spot its absence," observes Michael Gelven. "What these students lack is truth. I do not mean that their beliefs are false. I mean that the *idea* of truth is simply not there—that truth exists and can inform and even replace opinions. The belief that truth exists causes us to inquire after it in the first place: moreover, it is the true ground for our respect for others' opinions, recognizing the possibility that others have the truth that we may lack."[44]

The foundational error of the New Age worldview is the assumption that there is no absolute truth "out there" that need concern us. Sadly, this perception has spread widely in this land, as even the visiting pope from Rome could discern. The loss of objective authority and a transcendent morality has infected our national ethical foundations with a sickness nigh unto death.

New Agers, writes new religions critic Elliot Miller, hold that "there should be nothing absolute or fixed about any particular system—including their own."[45] But there is a joker in that deck: New Agers essentially contradict this very belief by tenaciously embracing monism as the only system that makes relativism possible. But absolute relativity is an absurdity!

Thus, New Age's most dangerous trait is also its most vulnerable flaw.

PART V

THE SEARCH FOR
TRANSCENDENCE IN
THE NEW AGE

31

Beyond the Self

God has set eternity in the hearts of men.
—Eccl. 3:11

The Tower of Babel, described in the Old Testament (Gen. 11:1–9), was probably a cosmic temple connected with the occult religion of astrology, as was the Babylonian ziggurat built later on the same site.[1]

This towering structure, symbolizing humanity's innate desire for transcendence and a groping toward heaven, drew God's attention. When he came down to check out the scene, however, the Lord was not pleased. He associated the effort with vain human imagination: the desire to be divine and worship the self.

The Almighty's reaction was to confound the people's language, and as he did so, he declared: "This is only the beginning of what they will do; and now nothing they have imagined they can do will be impossible to them" (Gen. 11:6, AMPLIFIED).

Thus, since the beginning humanity has sought to organize itself around an instrument of its own creation. This search for self-realization has ascended to the pinnacle of self-idolatry—and has been flattened beneath the righteous hammer blows of a Higher God.

The tower and the city, suggests William H. Willimon, were misguided efforts to achieve unity on human terms rather than God's terms, "trying to attain a spurious oneness derived from human self-sufficiency and autonomy. It didn't work then and it doesn't work now."[2]

Yet, as the wisdom of Ecclesiastes declares, "God has set eternity in the hearts of men"; and this yearning for transcendence has gripped humanity since our first parents "walked with God" (Gen. 3:8).

In our day, Allan Bloom found evidence of this longing for the transcendent dimension on our university campuses. Richard John Neuhaus bemoans the "naked public square," where the force of transcendent authority is absent from public life and "then there are no rules rooted in ultimacies that can protect the poor, the powerless and the marginal."[3] Charles Colson declares, "We desperately long to know the Power beyond us and discover a transcendent purpose for living."[4] And Anglican theologian John Stott proclaims that "without transcendence, the person shrivels. . . . Ecclesiastes demonstrates the meaninglessness of a life that is imprisoned within time and space."[5]

But there are vast differences between the "transcendent purpose" enlivened by the historic Judeo-Christian Scriptures and the spiritual awakening and God-vision of Eastern and New Age mysticism.

"Who is God?" asks United Nations meditation chaplain Sri Chinmoy. "God is man's eternal cry for the highest Transcendental Supreme," he answers. "And where is God? God is in man's soulful smile and our soul's smile. Where smiles loom large in our existence, there alone we see God's very presence."[6]

The closest place to look for grace, says New Age-allied psychiatrist Scott Peck, is within oneself: "If you desire wisdom greater than your own, you can find it inside you. . . . To put it plainly, our unconscious is God. . . . [T]he goal of spiritual growth [is] . . . the attainment of godhead by the conscious self. It is for the individual to become totally, wholly God."[7]

New Age luminary Marilyn Ferguson has lyric praise for the movement's desire for transcendence, new meaning, and hope. To her, "God is experienced as flow, wholeness, the infinite kaleidoscope of life and death, Ultimate Cause, the ground of being, what [New Age philosopher-guru] Alan

Watts called 'the silence out of which all sound comes.' God is the consciousness that manifests as *lila*, the play of the universe. God is the organizing matrix we can experience but not tell, that which enlivens matter."[8]

These ideas, she explains, "are part of all traditions of direct knowing: the glimpse of the true nature of reality . . . connection with the source that generates the world of appearances, reunion with all living things."[9]

In an early manuscript of a new book she and her husband, Ray Gottlieb, were writing, Ferguson described the "wiser Self":

> This is the fearless, ageless thread of awareness that seems to run through all our experiences. It functions even when the personality is in fugue state (amnesia). It even seems to be relatively independent of the physical body, judging from the growing body of near-death experiences. Indeed, it seems as if it cannot die because it was never born.
>
> In those rare instances when our hopes and fears and pretenses are pulled away, when time itself is not an issue, we [see] in others a nameless core of wisdom that bears a striking family resemblance to our own best self.[10]

That is New Age transcendence, and it bears a striking resemblance to the Taoist way to transcend the tangible. In *The Wandering Taoist*, Deng Ming-Dao describes his master, monk Kwan Saihung, doing "inner-gazing" meditation: "His body expanded in a silent explosion. His perfect mechanism unwound and shot itself in a thousand directions. The body was gone, but an intention still lingered. A memory, distant and shimmering—a strange streak of individualism still floating in space. The streak dissipated. Beyond stars, planets and dimensions, beyond any kaleidoscope of reality, piercing infinite layers. Gone. There was only Nothingness."[11]

To achieve a state of "void unity," the occult mystic in effect retraces the steps of God, "taking his creation apart brick by brick in order to first uncover, then vanish into, its foundation," comments new religions expert Brooks Alexander. The mystic merges with it "to the dissolution of identity and individuality."[12]

In New Age and Eastern worldviews, intuition and mystical experience become the supreme way of knowing God, or

Ultimate Reality, which is an immanent, impersonal Absolute—even Nothingness—rather than a personal Creator. Reason and observation "can be superseded by direct Knowing, of Reality itself and of our profound interrelatedness with all that is."[13]

Carl Raschke notes that while the ancient gnostics conceived of man as a spark of divine fire trapped in matter, these latter-day Gnostics "patter about the transcendental 'consciousness' that is blocked by man's robot-like actions."[14] The cure, in this view, is to unleash the mind's power and inject a megadose of infinite awareness. But this leads to a mindless indifference to the problems of society, Raschke avers. The "New Narcissism" invites a solipsistic worldview and flourishes wherever there is a death of common purpose, a dread of the future, and a mad rush for personal legitimacy in a psychic war of all against all. The Gnostic does not reach out, but tucks himself away like a mollusk against the battering tides of history. He finds happiness as he luxuriates in the glow of his own consciousness, which may however turn out to be reflected light from the fire that is burning his own house down."[15]

Long ago, the saying of Jesus that "the kingdom of God is within your midst," was erroneously translated "the kingdom of God is in you" (Luke 17:21), and this error still abounds. This interpretation is essentially a revolt against God, for it implies that if we truly understand who we are, we will realize that we are one with the soul of the universe, that each of us *is* God. That is pantheism. But Jesus was a theist, though he certainly taught that the immanent God—the Holy Spirit within—sustains us.

"I surely would not want to be God as Shirley MacLaine claims, if God is simply what I am," quips Raschke. And J. Gordon Melton paraphrases the title of the J. B. Phillips classic, "The New Age God is too small."

Paradoxically, the New Age attempts to reach *out* to God and finds Him *within*. But in this inward redirection, the seeker finds no ultimate transcendent reality. The God within is not the transcendent God of the universe who stands outside of—apart from—his creation and guides it, even intervening in human history. The God within is only my own shadow, and that is small indeed—even if my shadow is merged with the collective shadows of all other mortals, past and present.

True transcendence moves beyond the realm of creation to communion—not union—with the uncreated and living God. The Fall (sin) broke the relationship between God and humanity (we will return to this theme in the final two chapters); but the incarnation of Jesus restored communion between holy God and sinful man, mediated through Christ's atoning death on the cross and his resurrection from the grave.

Historic Christian theism emphatically denies any vision of self-bestowed divinity. Only the God of Abraham, Isaac, and Jacob, the God and Father of the Lord Jesus Christ, is big enough to deliver salvation and regeneration on a cosmic scale.

In an unpublished critique of the New Age movement, Melton gives further insight into how Christian faith differs from the mystical New Age search for transcendence:

> Christianity, in contrast, offers the God of the Scriptures, a very personal deity, whose basic characteristic is a loving relatedness, within Himself as Trinity and toward humanity through creative action. . . .
>
> As Christians, we invite people to a personal relationship with a loving, caring God, and that relationship takes precedence over any mystical appropriation of the unity of existence. Within the Christian tradition, mystical experience has an important place, but is always judged by its relation to the God of the Scriptures.[16]

God is the transcendent Creator of the cosmos, but separate from it. He "spoke" the world into existence by creating it *ex nihilo*—out of nothing—rather than by making it out of himself by extending his essence.[17]

"Man and the cosmos are in no sense parts of God," declares Carl F. H. Henry, author of the six-volume *God, Revelation and Authority*. "The whole creation is judged by the Creator. If deep down in my inner being I find God, then it is not possible to find that man is any sense a sinner."[18]

In other words, it is not possible to believe in our own godhood and at the same time accept God's forgiveness for our sin of pride.

Shedding light on the issue from a different angle, Mark Albrecht cites an essay by Tim Dailey that points out that karma, "the law of action and reaction, differs significantly from the biblical concept of sin. . . . [T]here is no Transcendent God of the universe (existing outside yourself) to transgress against. It has been written: 'Karma is the Master Law of the Universe but there is no Lawgiver.'"[19] There is no one to judge if there is no one at all. And if there is no objective revelation from a higher divine authority, then only human subjectivity—the divine within—is the matrix of truth and meaning.

Yet, in an odd sort of twist, many New Agers end up seeking counsel from mediums, gurus, and outside "spirit guides." That irony was not lost on F. LaGard Smith in his critique of Shirley MacLaine, *Out on a Broken Limb*: "It is an inconsistency that the Christian avoids by looking only to Jesus Christ for spiritual guidance. In looking for truth and meaning, Ms. MacLaine turned to the very source of her emptiness—herself."[20]

Christians look for the wisdom from above (James 3:17) rather than the wisdom within. God comes from the outside in, not the inside out. New Agers, however, "went inside, and like the rest of us, found themselves wanting. Divinity is a burden that humanity simply cannot bear."[21]

This sets off what Brooks Alexander calls a "spiral of error": "[A]ny quest for an integrating vision of reality that begins without access to the living God will likewise end without knowledge of Him. Any search for ultimates that refuses 'the God who is there' and takes humanity as its starting point will end with humanity as its ultimate. Any quest for unity that starts from just the data of consciousness will end with a rearrangement and reinterpretation of that same data."[22]

The apostle Paul, in his letter to the Romans, succinctly puts his finger on the problem: They "changed the truth of God into a lie, and worshiped and served the creature [the creation] more than the Creator" (Rom. 1:25, KJV).

The Judeo-Christian God is intensely personal. That is a major distinction from the impersonal, universal force that is the deity of the New Age. A personal God is necessary for transformation. Self-empowerment is not the same as per-

sonal transformation, and an impersonal force cannot transform persons any more than it can produce ethics or love.
Love and moral attributes are personal and do not derive from
impersonal matter or energy. Human beings, made in the
personal image of God the Creator, find that *imago dei* to be a
gift and not a hindrance to enlightenment. (You may want to
check the helpful chart comparing the secular humanist, New
Age, and Christian worldviews in *Unmasking the New Age*.[23]

Christianity—and Judaism, from which it sprang—is distinctive in its worship of a God who is a "self," according to
writers Alice and Stephen Lawhead. "The Christian God is
not a force of nature, not a state of mind, not a spiritual fog or
an energy ball loose in the universe, not a state of perfection
or unity to be obtained by any amount of personal discipline
or striving. God is not an 'it.' God is a person. God has a
personality. God has emotions. God has desires, perceptions
and will, and even needs."[24]

"We cannot live consistently with the implications of
ultimate truth being impersonal," notes Dean Halverson in
The New Age Rage, "because it is in personal relationships
that we naturally find value and fulfillment. How could this
be any less true when talking about our relationship with
God?"[25]

We can have a personal relationship with the God of the
Bible, Gordon Lewis observes, but not with an impersonal
organizing principle or "being" itself. "And God is not the
inner energy of people but is active with His believing
people in accord with His redemptive purposes for the
present age."[26]

Several pages later in *Integrative Theology*, his treatise on
God as an active, personal Spirit, Lewis speaks about the way
in which God takes personal initiative in carrying out his
purposes: "Those who imagine that God transcends the
personal in such a way that their deity is more like a vapor or
a gas diffused throughout the universe may seem philosophi-
cally profound, but unfortunately, they are profoundly wrong.
God is more like a faithful lifeguard or an all-wise personnel
manager than an impersonal 'Force.' "[27]

Since God is an unlimited personal being, neither mysticism nor science can pin down his mysteries nor can they
lead us into an intimate personal relationship with him; by

the same token, however, a personal transcendent God makes science possible. As Halverson says: "Through scientific techniques, we are able to discover laws in the universe—not because we mentally invent them, but because the Creator placed them there. They are a reflection of His coherence, not ours."[28]

The biblical perspective on the proper relationship between humanity (creature) and God (Creator) signifies "meaning as well as mechanism," Brooks Alexander and Mark Albrecht point out. "We are not bags of atoms buffeted about by cosmic currents that flow past in silent indifference to our transient existence."[29]

Only a Creator God can give meaning to life because only this God adds the missing dimensions—eternity to time and transcendence to space—says British Bible scholar John R. Stott of the London Institute for Contemporary Christianity. The Christian mind should resist the attempt to banish God from his own universe. "If you deny the reality of [a transcendent] God, you're dehumanizing human beings . . . who were made by God, like God, for God, to live in fellowship with Him; and without Him everything is meaningless."[30]

That was the lesson God meant to teach the world when he scattered the people from their vain imaginings and striving after an intimation of eternity at the Tower of Babel. Their speech became a babble of miscommunication, cutting them off from one another and from God.

The man-made building of a way to heaven is through technological achievement—whether by a lofty tower futilely straining toward transcendence, or by New Age psychotechnologies and states of altered consciousness. But these are doomed to failure. The proud tower rose only several hundred feet; the technologies extend only as far as the fallen human psyche.

The need of the hour is for real transcendence and for transcendent worth.

Bring the transcendent back into American life, Chuck Colson preaches as he travels across the land, challenging Christians to restore the objective truth of the living God in Christ. His message usually has four points:

(1) Restore orthodoxy. Live by the laws of God's kingdom

and Jesus' teachings of Christian truth. Fundamental, basic beliefs are necessary (2 Thess. 2:15). To preach that if you come to God he'll give you anything you want is to preach a false gospel. Lose orthodoxy and you lose the heart of the church.

(2) *Be* the church; it is the community of the redeemed. Be God's people. Make Jesus Lord.

(3) Think and, therefore, act like Christians. Apply the truth of Scripture in the marketplace. Argue every principle of life from this perspective: "current events in the eyes of God."

(4) Confess the faith. Be the salt and the light—take the Good News to others so they may understand the gospel and glorify God (Matt. 5:13–16).[31]

Yet despite such ringing calls to reassert transcendence, Christians sense a dichotomy between their noblest aspirations of goodness and the base selfishness that so easily intrudes upon even their best intentions and contaminates their choicest efforts. That is the curious mixture within humanity that is so profoundly and accurately chronicled in the early chapters of Genesis. And in the New Testament, where the apostle Paul moans: "I do not do the good I want, but the evil I do not want is what I do. . . . So I find it to be a law that when I want to do right, evil lies close at hand. For I delight in the law of God, in my inmost self, but I see in my members another law at war with the law of my mind and making me captive to the law of sin which dwells in my members. Wretched man that I am!" (Rom. 7:19, 21–24, RSV).

Blaise Pascal, the French theologian and scientist, spoke of the "wretchedness and the greatness" of man,[32] at once miserable and masterful. He remains dust, yet there is a "rumor of glory, a hint of transcendence, a whiff of dignity and destiny."[33] For we have been made in the image of God.

Our intrinsic worth is that we are *like* God. We are *not* God, not divine, but *like* him. Even after the Fall marred and defaced and spoiled the divine image. The *imago dei* is still present. That's our dignity, says Stott. But there is also the fact of our depravity. "And we must never affirm one in such a way as to deny the other." Christians should opt for the "radical realism that keeps together the depravity and the dignity," for man is both, the white-haired expounder of the faith said in his lecture in Santa Barbara, California.

> Human beings are capable of the loftiest nobility and the basest cruelty. We can behave like God, in whose image we were made, and like the animals from whom we were meant to be forever distinct. Human beings are able to think, choose, love, pray, worship; but human beings are also able to covet, to fight, to hate and to kill. Human beings are the inventors of churches for the worship of God, hospitals for the care of the sick, universities for the acquisition of wisdom. And human beings are also the inventors of torture chambers, concentration camps and nuclear arsenals. Strange, bewildering paradox. Noble, and ignoble; rational and irrational; moral and immoral; god-like and bestial.[34]

And then Stott quotes what Richard Holloway, the bishop of Edinburgh's Episcopal Church of Scotland, said at a recent conference:

> This is my dilemma: I am dust and ashes; frail, wayward, a set of predetermined behavioral responses, riddled with fears, beset with needs, the quintessence of dust, and unto dust I shall return.
> But there is something else in me. Dust I may be, but troubled dust. Dust that dreams. Dust that has strange premonitions of transfiguration, of a glory in store, a destiny prepared, an inheritance that will one day be my own. So my life is stretched out in a painful dialectic between ashes and glory, between weakness and transfiguration. I am a rebel to myself, an exasperating enigma, this strange duality of dust and glory.[35]

That's the human paradox: the glimmer of transcendence—the hope of glory—that shines through the shadow of our waywardness and rebellion.

New Age transcendence revels in innate human potential; Christian faith confesses the innate *inability* to please a righteous God but glories in the potential of his grace to transform human personality into the likeness of the face of Christ (2 Cor. 4:6).

32

The Broad Way and
the Narrow Way

Enter by the narrow gate; for the gate is wide, and the road that
leads to destruction is broad with plenty of room, and many go
that way; but the gate that leads to life is small and the road is
narrow, and those who find it are few.

—Matt. 7:13–14

Throughout this book, I have quoted a number of times
from Scott Peck, whose New Age-tinged books have topped
best-seller lists in recent years. I find it interesting that Peck
chose as one of his titles *The Road Less Traveled*, for these
are the very words Jesus used to warn his followers about the
dangers of sin. Take the road less traveled, the Son of God
admonished, for the road to spiritual death is wide and well-
traveled—a veritable superhighway (Matt. 7:13).

In fact, the third chapter in the first book of the Bible tells
of the four-lane highway to hell that detoured Adam and Eve
as they were on their way to God's garden party in Eden.

The first lane they traveled was *doubt.*

The serpent, the most subtle of God's wild creatures and
representative of Satan—whom the Bible presents as a
personal, wicked entity whose will opposes God—sowed
seeds of doubt in Eve's mind: "Did God say, 'You shall not
eat of any tree of the garden'?" (Gen. 3:1, RSV).

"Did God say?" Modern Eves—and Adams, too—have
been tricked by the seductive power of these words. Did God

283

really say, "You shall not commit adultery"? Did God really mean "love your neighbor as yourself"?

And so doubt casts an ominous shadow of suspicion over the authority and authenticity of God's Word.

Certainly a person who claims to have no doubts is either lying or else has stopped thinking. And doubt can be good if it is handled properly: when it either "worries weak ideas into exhaustion or exercises them into greater strength," as Carl Michalson notes in *Faith for Personal Crises*.[1]

But the kind of doubt referred to here, the first lane of hell's highway, is the doubt that causes a person to fall away from God in unbelief. Theologian Paul Tillich called it "total doubt" because it "constitutes a disastrous suspension of the answer to man's deepest need."[2] Jesus called it "doubt in the heart" (Mark 11:23).

To doubt God's biblical Word means that one questions the validity of revelation and whether there can be such things as absolute truth and transcendence.

"We are, whether we like it or not," wrote renowned sociologist Peter Berger in his celebrated book, *A Rumor of Angels*, "in a situation in which transcendence has been reduced to a rumor." The "theological surrender to the alleged demise of the supernatural defeats itself in precisely the measure of its success. . . . For most people, symbols whose content has been hollowed out lack conviction or even interest."[3]

So New Age relativist Kenneth Wapnick, in his interpretation of the channeled "Course in Miracles" material, candidly admits that he "picked and chose" which parts of the Bible he took as valid and which he considered invalid.

"Some parts of the Bible have the Holy Spirit as their source," Wapnick told Spiritual Counterfeits Project researcher Dean Halverson. "Other parts are from the ego. Any passage that speaks of punishment or of hell, I understood that as being from the ego. Any passage that speaks of forgiveness and love, the unreality of the body, etc., I took as an expression of the Holy Spirit. I did not take the Bible as being totally true or totally false."[4]

Halverson: "You reinterpreted it?"

Wapnick: "Yes. There's no question. That is what I did."

Did God say?

The central theme in the Genesis story of the Fall is distrust. Eve and Adam desired the "knowledge of good and evil" that would make them "like God"—that is, independent from him. And they sought a short-cut, suggest Irving Hexham and Karla Poewe: knowledge "gained by the ritual act of eating rather than through growth and thought. If this interpretation is correct, the story symbolizes the ever-present human desire for magical short-cuts to knowledge and power at the expense of trust and understanding. . . . The Bible presents the Fall as an act of unrestricted self-indulgence based on the impossible desire to be like God. Instead of leading to freedom, it results in bondage."[5]

Having once doubted the underlying authority of God, Eve was easy prey for the next onslaught of the serpent: *denial.* Lane number two of the superhighway to spiritual oblivion.

"You will not die," the serpent declared when Eve said that God had commanded them not to touch the tree in the middle of the garden, lest they die (Gen. 3:4).

Have you heard that one lately? I have.

"It doesn't matter . . ." "It's only human . . ." "It couldn't be very wrong . . ." "God will forgive me, after all, that's his business."

So the insidious whisper of Satan reaches our ears, too: "Go ahead, you will be like God! You won't die." And we find ourselves moving into the second lane: denying that sin has separated us from God; denying the broken relationship at the primary core of our being; denying death.

New Agers acknowledge the need for transformation. But the question is: What caused the rupture that requires transformation? Was it sin or "unawakened consciousness"? And what can bridge the gap: God or self?

The problem is perception, elaborated Halverson in our interview at Denver Seminary, and I was to see that more clearly as I chatted three weeks later with Sportsmind executive Chris Majer in Seattle:

> A question for all of us is what leap of faith are you prepared to take: One, he [Jesus] is the unique Son of God, the one guy created of the Virgin Birth; the other, he is absolutely unique as a master, but there have been lots of others like him. And what are the implications of each? Maybe it's safer to take the route that says he's the unique, only Son of God and I don't have to

worry about living this Christianity stuff because when I die I'll be forgiven and go to heaven anyway. The other way is to say, hey, if he was a guide and I can be just like him, then that creates a potential and I need to be working a whole lot harder to attain that same level of spiritual growth and development. . . .

It holds together a lot tighter to believe that Jesus was born just like you and me and he was fortunate to learn some of the secrets and the teachings . . . In the desert and [he] came in communion with God. But lots of people have been able to have that kind of mastery and experience throughout history. So, maybe there is a point of view that says we are all born with that same kind of ability. . . . When he said to "do works greater than I"—maybe Jesus meant it literally. We're all the sons of God.

See where I'm going with that?[6]

Yep, sure do.

Only a white line (or should I say a white lie?) away is the third lane: *disobedience*.

"So when the woman saw that the tree was to be desired . . . she took of its fruit and ate . . . and gave some to her husband, and he ate" (Gen. 3:6, RSV).

Basic doubts about God's moral laws and transcendence are raised; a benefit or pleasure is held out; and then, crunch! The "apple" is bitten again. In prideful self-assertion the misdeed is rationalized, justified, and the harmful part denied.

"Sin is essentially idolatry—giving something other than God the status of God," reminds Douglas Groothuis in *Unmasking the New Age*. "Idols are best unmasked and then shattered. The idol of the New Age is consciousness itself; cosmic humanism seeks to tap the divine within, to merge with the One. Yet in it all we see what Freud correctly called 'the will to death' . . . for man is not God, the creature is not the Creator."[7]

Spiritual blindness leads to a loss of ability to "see" God as a transcendent, personal Creator, and an inability to foresee the consequences of sin and the ultimate judgment that it brings, which is the fourth and final lane: *death*. "Then . . . they knew that they were naked; and . . . the man and his wife hid themselves from the presence of the Lord God" (Gen. 3:7–8, RSV).

And so the Fall of humanity is complete. The result of doubt, denial, and disobedience is not the rosy picture painted by the serpent. It is shame, guilt, and estrangement from God. The inside fast lane brings spiritual death, and the hell-bent victim dismembers bodies and shatters personalities as he or she collides with the hard-rock reality of God's order, dragging others into the twisted wreckage of mind and soul. The transcendent Creator God cannot be disregarded without serious consequences.

All who fail to grasp God's wisdom injure themselves, says Proverbs 8:36; "all who hate me are in love with death" (NEB).

The biblical worldview, according to Brooks Alexander and Robert Burrows, is that the rebellion of sin produces death. "Sin fragments, separates, and alienates. It divides us from God and deepens our spiritual blindness. . . . Continually avoiding God, we soon cannot see Him at all. Sin also divides people, internally, against themselves. And, of course, it divides human beings against one another. It is useless to talk of humanity solving its own problems as long as it is infected with sin; for it is sin's nature to divide people and turn them against one another."[8]

In the Sermon on the Mount, Jesus said there are but two roads: the Broad Way of destruction and the Narrow Way that leads to eternal life (Matt. 7:13–14).

But we doubt it. "Is the gate *really* narrow?" Then we deny it. We turn it around and make it read, "Broad is the way that leads to *life* and narrow is the way to *destruction*. Almost *everyone* will be saved." And then we justify it and disobey it until we find ourselves in the position of the motorist, who, when told that he was on the wrong highway, replied that he knew but that he was making such good time.

The wrong highway is broad and well marked and easy to find. One need only follow the crowd. And being universally accessible, this Broad Way appears in some form in virtually all religious traditions. Observed Elliot Miller, editor of the *Christian Research Journal*:

Those on the Broad Way usually assume that what is natural is also right: that the way we humans are now is essentially how we were originally intended to be. Therefore, to be "spiritual" all we have to do—indeed what we *must* do—is develop our own inherent spiritual potential. As this "natural spirituality" is cultivated, certain phenomena typically follow, including psychic powers, contacts with spirit entities, and ecstatic or mystical experiences. . . .

The very universality of these experiences convinces the advocates of mysticism that it is the one true religion of mankind, and the various religious traditions are merely the cultural packages which contain it.[9]

In contrast to the Broad Way, the Narrow Way of discipleship is difficult and costly, and it is sometimes lonely. It is no smooth four-lane superhighway, despite efforts of the "prosperity preachers" to feed us a sugar-coated "health and wealth" gospel.

Jesus said that he, himself, is the Narrow Way, the Way to salvation that must be entered through grace (John 10:7–9; Acts 4:12; 15:11; Eph. 2:8–9). But once inside, one enters a vast realm of spiritual experience and profound encounters with the infinite God of glory (1 Cor. 2:9).

The essence of the Narrow Way of discipleship is the life of faith. Yet it is not faith in faith itself but faith in a personal God who revealed himself in the person of his Son. Christian faith says, "I am a sinner, unworthy. I have fallen short of God's commandments. I am dust." Yet at the same time Christian faith says, "I can do all things through Christ who strengthens me" (Rom. 3:23; Phil. 4:13).

This paradox of faith found in the Scriptures and along the Narrow Way does not pit faith and reason against each other. "Faith is not a synonym for credulity or superstition. . . . Faith is a reasonable trust," declares John Stott. Knowledge is the foundation of faith: "Because we know that God is trustworthy, it is reasonable to put our trust in Him."[10]

Engraved on the inside of our wedding bands, Marjorie Lee and I have a verse from Psalm 32: "I will instruct you and teach you in the way which you should go; I will counsel you with My eye upon you" (verse 8, NASB). This kind of faith, say Hexham and Poewe, is "not a blind leap into the unknown but a confident step into enlightenment about the nature and love of God. Faith is the opposite of doubt and magical power. Faith is to redemption what magic and doubt are to the Fall. It frees us of anxiety because it entails our accepting our identity as creatures made in God's image."[11]

When people lack faith in a transcendent Creator God, they turn to the magic, rituals, and human devices of the Broad Way to find meaning and empowerment. Soon they deny even the existence of the Narrow Way, as does Shirley MacLaine when she says that it is blasphemous to worship anything higher than oneself, and not to worship the self is to think too little of oneself.[12]

But MacLaine may be too easy a target. "How did she get out on that limb?" asks Craig V. Anderson in the *Christian Century* magazine article, "Pruning Time for Shirley Mac-Laine?" More than 2,500 years ago, the prophet Isaiah scornfully predicted that in a time of calamity and confusion the Egyptians would dash around consulting a horde of "idols, sorcerers, mediums and wizards" (Isa. 19:3). "Have we a similar situation today?" continues Anderson. "Old certainties have come unglued; stable families are an exception; our economy is buffeted by worldwide forces; greater wealth has not brought greater happiness; the safety of the air we breathe, the food we eat and the water we drink is in question; existence itself is threatened by weapons our own technology provides. Conditions are indeed favorable for mediums and wizards; one can bank on people's anxieties, and many have."[13]

Ever since the Fall, humanity has been "marked by a magical understanding of the world and a desire to manipulate knowledge in a manner indistinguishable from sorcery."[14]

Yet both the Old and New Testaments abound in prohibitions against occult involvement and idolatry, along with such activities as astrology and fortunetelling, which confuse the creation with the Creator.[15] The apostle Paul links such activity directly to the work of Satan and the "spirit . . . of disobedience" (Eph. 2:2, RSV); and John exhorts us to "test the spirits to see whether they are from God. Every spirit which acknowledges that Jesus Christ has come in the flesh is from God, and every spirit which does not thus acknowledge Jesus is not from God" (1 John 3:1–3, NEB).

But how can one be sure that the Bible itself is trustworthy? Do we have to take it on faith?

Christians argue that the Bible contains the trustworthy divine revelation of an objective God. While the New Age worldview is that language and written revelation are inadequate and meaningless—and ultimately a barrier to experiencing enlightenment and truth—the biblical worldview is that the human language of the Bible is a valid and sufficient way to convey God's message to humanity.

Christians believe the Bible not because its message is easy to accept, but because there is strong evidence that it is *true*. Space here doesn't permit an in-depth look at the historical and manuscript evidence supporting the Bible's veracity, but many excellent books on the subject are available. Let it suffice to cite just a few examples:

- The time gap between the actual events mentioned in the Bible and the date of the first known existing documents describing them is far shorter than that of other ancient writings.
- Numerous eyewitnesses testified that the New Testament record was accurate, and more than five hundred people saw Jesus after his resurrection (1 Cor. 15:6).
- The New Testament manuscripts have proven to give an accurate historical picture of the first-century events they describe.
- Flavius Josephus, the learned Jewish historian and contemporary of Jesus—not a believer himself—wrote that "He was [the] Christ. And when Pilate, at the suggestion of the principal men amongst us, had condemned him to the cross, those that loved him at the first did not forsake him; for he appeared to them alive again the third day; as the divine prophets had foretold."[16]
- Noted experts in the fields of archaeology and textual criticism have firmly believed in the essential reliability of the New Testament.[17]

"[I]t appears that the documents enjoyed the distinct advantage of having the correcting influence not only of the community of faith, but also of hostile community, who would have been delighted to catch the Christian believers making assertions about Jesus that were untrue," theologian John Snyder points out. Citing biblical scholar F. F. Bruce, Snyder goes on to assert that "it is no exaggeration" to say that the New Testament text is "far better attested to" than any of the ancient writings by such prominent figures as Caesar, Livy, Herodotus, Thucydides, and Tacitus—as well as the Hindu *Vedas* and *Bhagavad Gita*, and the Muslim *Koran*.[18]

Virginia Stem Owens, writing in the *Reformed Journal*, noted that "the early Christians may not have been any brighter than the average person-in-the-pew today [but] they were, according to historical evidence, a frequently martyred minority who, by turning away from cultural norms of their time, risked both their lives and their religious identities."[19]

Biblical authority, then, is based on truth. But the Bible's authority is derived rather than absolute; its authority depends not only on the truth of its statements (where they can be tested) but also on the authority of its writers as men inspired by God," I. Howard Marshall sums up in his slim volume *Biblical Inspiration*.[20]

Many years ago the world's best-known living evangelist went on retreat at the Forest Home Christian Conference Center in the San Bernardino Mountains of Southern California. There, he wrestled with the question of whether he could wholeheartedly believe what the Bible said. As he pondered, he had a life-changing encounter with God. Just a short walk from Forest Falls, where I am now writing this chapter, a plaque is mounted at the foot of a wooden cross at the edge of spring-fed Lake Mears. It attests to Billy Graham's decision "to take the Bible by faith and preach it without reservation."

In the end, accepting the Bible as the authoritative Word of God is a matter of faith and trust. Our eternal destiny hinges on it.

Which highway will we travel?

33

The Man for All Ages

Who do people say the Son of Man is?

—Matt. 16:13

It was a precarious place. Treacherous, risky. So placid one moment, so wild and foreboding the next. With scant warning, squalls came howling out of the funnel-like gorges, where deep ravines furrowed the landscape like corrugated steel, dumping heavy rains and fierce winds on the Sea of Galilee.

That night, one of those sudden storms thundered out of the mountains ringing the sunken shoreline. Bursting from the heights, its shrieking winds whipped up waves that nearly swamped the small fishing vessel that heaved and pitched in the darkness.

The fishermen in the boat despaired of ever reaching shore. Caught in the peril and crisis, they cried out in panic to the man who was sleeping soundly in the stern.

"Master! Master! We're going to drown!... Don't you care?"

Exhausted from the day's preaching, teaching, and healing, Jesus of Nazareth had slept through it all. At their cry, however, he awoke, rebuked the wind, and commanded the sea: "Peace! Be Still!"

Then, out of the mystery of that man named Jesus, flowed an overwhelming calm and a question.

"Why are you afraid? Have you no faith?"

And the disciples, who such a short while before had been clinging to the tossing boat, were filled with awe. They said to one another, "Who then is this, that even wind and sea obey him?"[1]

At the moment of their distress it seemed to the disciples that this enigmatic, itinerant preacher they followed was an absent Lord. In their buffeting and helplessness, he appeared uninvolved, uncaring—a sleeping Christ.

But when they called out, he was there: accessible and responsive to their human insufficiencies and needs. At his command, turbulence gave way to calm, fear to assurance, and doubt to faith.

The savage sea subsided, lapping into a lull of strange, quiet serenity. The raging fury of the elements had been tamed by a Higher Force, a Greater Power.

Was it some Jesus Force? Was the Man from Galilee just one of many avatars, a periodic manifestation in the endless succession of God-gurus?

"Who do people say that I am?" Jesus asked his followers. And since the days he strode the dusty streets of the Holy Land, men and women have sought to answer his question.

The Jesus of history and faith has been coopted by nearly everyone wanting a towering figure from the past to confirm their own ideals of the present and vision of the future. "To Eastern-oriented religious groups, Jesus is an avatar—one of many incarnations of God; to Christian Scientists, he is the Great Healer; to political revolutionaries, he is the Great Liberator; to Spiritualists, he is a first-rate medium; to one new consciousness philosopher, he is the prototype of Carlos Castaneda's Don Juan, a sorcerer who can restructure events in the world by mental exercise. Everyone, it seems, wants Jesus for themselves."[2]

The Gospels, however, portray Jesus not as a man who attained "Christ consciousness," but as the incarnate Savior and Lord. He is "the Word made flesh" who "dwelt among us, full of grace and truth; we have beheld his glory, glory as of the only Son from the father" (John 1:14, RSV).

"But who do *you* say that I am?" Jesus asked his disciples.

To Christians, Jesus is absolutely unique. He is the one mediator between God and humanity. The Narrow Way.

The New Age is right, however, in perceiving that the scandal of Christianity is its exclusiveness, asserts Douglas Groothuis.

"Jesus Christ claimed to be 'the way and the truth and the life' and that no one could come to the Father apart from Him (John 14:6). The Apostle Peter proclaimed that 'salvation is found in no one else, for there is no other name under heaven given to men by which we must be saved' (Acts 4:12). Christ will not join the pantheistic pantheon of counterfeit gods but instead stands above it in judgment. Yet Christ's exclusivity is our liberation. There is but one way, and God calls everyone to go through that narrow door that leads to life."[3]

"He is not one avatar among many," declares Gordon Melton, who is a walking encyclopedia of knowledge about religious groups. "He is God present, and definitely so. He did not manifest a Christ Principle, a modern abstraction of New Age values, he fully incarnated God. He is not primarily a moral example (though he is certainly that as well), but *the* connecting link by which humanity, warped and unable to fulfill the Divine intention, is brought back into touch with God."[4]

In the New Testament, says theologian John Snyder, Jesus is depicted as " 'the one in whom is manifested' the Creator of the universe; the fullest disclosure of the character and person of God; the focal point of all that God had been doing in history; the chief personality in God's creation of the world; the ruler of natural forces; the watershed of human destiny, and the only path to the presence of God. Jesus is portrayed not simply as the greatest teacher, but as the foundation of all teaching—that is, truth itself."[5]

The Scriptures say Jesus has *power*: power to change things and to change people. And power to change the forces that dominate people's lives.

"Peace! Be still!" he said. And the storm was over.

The disciples marveled among themselves: "Who then is this, that even the wind and the sea obey him?"

And if it was difficult in Jesus' time—with his very presence as confirmation—to believe that he had all power and authority, what about today?

Is God in charge?

No, say many living in the New Age of the 1990s: Man is in charge.

And as far back as twenty-five years ago, science fiction writer Ray Bradbury penned this:

> [T]he living God is not out there. He is here. God did not create us. The blind rotation of dead Creator flint, in bombardment of radiation, in downfall of strange rain, seeded earth and from that birthed a living God-child-man who lurked in seas and shrank in caves, wild and insanely afraid of a universe he must someday test and own.
>
> Man, living too close to himself, could not see that he was the godhead, that he was the Lord and himself Christ, and all the other glorious and glorified names of saints and leaders under whatever name, in whatever age, who filled the skies with fire and the souls with holy dread.
>
> But now very late in the scroll of Earth, phoenix man, who lives by burning, a true furnace of energy, stoking himself with chemistries, must stand as God.
>
> Not *represent* Him, not *pretend* to be Him, not deny Him, but simply, nobly, and frighteningly *be* Him. . . .
>
> We are more than water, we are more than earth, we are more than sun. We are God giving Himself a reason for being.[6]

According to Bradbury, the biblical God is dead; man is God. Man has all glory and honor and power. And this is the insidious danger inherent in the New Age.

The December 7, 1987, *TIME* cover story portrayed New Age as a benign, if somewhat amusing, exercise in arcane arts and self-help technologies—an "essentially harmless anthology of illusions."[7] But the writers didn't deal seriously with the New Age worldview, which casts a long and ominous shadow over every aspect of human life. One's worldview determines what one believes, and what one believes has a great influence on individual behavior. The New Age worldview is that the self is all there is, that right and wrong are mere projections of whatever seems permissible to one at the time. From this perspective there are no rules or absolute moral imperatives, and therefore one is ultimately not responsible for one's actions.

Since there is no reality beyond that of one's own making, all is ultimately illusion and without transcendent meaning. Unfortunately, such major-media articles further engrave upon mainstream American culture the acceptability of uncritical, superficial thinking, and the imprint of a vacuous spirituality. The payload the New Age movement carries is no trivial cosmic joke or magic show; it is the heavy stuff that determines the destinies of men, women, and nations—even the eternal salvation of humanity.

Evangelical theologian Carl Henry puts it bluntly: "We must choose to cast our lot either with a society that admits only private faiths, and then simply add another idol to modernity's expanding God-shelf, or we must hoist a banner to a higher Sovereign, the Lord of Lord and King of kings."[8]

Gordon Melton is more conciliatory, but makes the same point: "While Christians can respect the beliefs of those who hold other faiths, and honor the contribution of members and leaders to culture and society, it must assert that in the long run, they have fallen short of the Divine for which the [New Age] movement seeks and that while they may be able to change society, they will fail in their goal of transforming it."[9]

Jesus himself gave an astounding commentary on God's power when he stood before the Roman procurator, Pontius Pilate, who held the power of physical life and death over those brought before him.

"Do you not know that I have power to release you, and power to crucify you?" Pilate asked Jesus.

"You would have no power over me unless it had been given you from above," Jesus replied (John 19:10–11, RSV).

What a startling thing for a beaten and condemned prisoner to say to a representative of Imperial Rome! To tell him that his only power came from God—not the emperor! God was in control and was *allowing this!*

Jesus' statement was incomprehensible to Pilate, who thought in terms of power politics, military might, and governmental law. And to the Jews looking on, it only confirmed their accusations that Jesus was not the Messiah, for he did not display earthly power to save himself. For them, it was blasphemous to think God could allow his chosen, anointed Messiah to be crucified. They did not foresee his resurrection.

And Jesus' claim is foolishness to those moderns who consider him a dead hero, not a risen Savior. Indeed, Jesus' words to Pilate would be vain and empty if the story ended with the crucifixion. For then the forces of evil would have triumphed and the power of man would have prevailed over the power of God. Without the resurrection, Easter morning would echo with the hollowness of deluded fools!

"The denial of eternal life . . . is not, as its adherents often claim, a nonegoistic, mature, realistic willingness to face the brutal limitations of finitude: rather, it amounts to a tragically unbelieving denial of God's honor—and thus of God's very existence. . . . Yet God's honor is at genuine risk. For the price of glory is high. God's own son must die to pay its price."[10]

Not only was God's honor satisfied, but the demand from the beginning that a blood sacrifice be made to requite man's original estrangement from his Creator, was uniquely satisfied in the crucifixion.

The Old Testament, through the prophet Isaiah, speaks of the vicarious sacrifice of Christ: "He was wounded for our transgressions, he was bruised for our iniquities; the chastisement of our peace was upon him; and with his stripes we are healed . . . because he hath poured out his soul unto death; and he was numbered with the transgressors; and he bare the sin of many, and made intercession for the transgressors" (Isa. 53:5, 12, KJV).

The veil separating holy God and finite man was forever parted when Jesus' blood was shed on the cross in a once-for-all atonement for sin.[11]

Pilate's question—and Jesus' answer—take on fresh meaning from the perspective of the Crucifixion and the Resurrection. The last word was not, "It is finished," but "He is risen!"

The resurrection of Jesus Christ became "of such finality and decisiveness" to the early Christian community that it immediately came to be the cornerstone of the believers' proclamation and defense.[12]

The disciples of Jesus were convinced—not because it is plausible for a dead man to live again—but because they saw, heard, talked to, and touched the risen Christ.

"Nothing less than *sight* convinced those who had the deepest desire to believe the tidings," notes Brooke Foss Westcott. "The resurrection was announced as a fact immediately after the Passion [three days after Christ's death].

Nothing else will explain the origin of the Christian Church. . . . Nothing can be more simply historic."[13]

And because he lives, we shall live also.

Jesus' resurrection means that the consequences of sin—humanity's attempt to "play God" in the garden of Eden—have been overcome. The chasm between a holy God and his creation has been spanned. It means evil does not have the final word. And it means there is a companion—a "Risen One"—who can be with us now. The Resurrection puts the stamp of authenticity on Jesus as the great comforter, sovereign Son of God, and royal King of Kings.

This "Risen One" left his followers with a commission: to announce to the world that through himself, others, too, could share the life of the Kingdom, the "real" New Age. "The New Age is not the Kingdom. But the Kingdom can be said to be the New Age."[14]

"When anyone is united to Christ," the apostle Paul taught, "there is a new act of creation; the old order has gone, and a new order has already begun" (2 Cor. 5:17, NEB).

The New Age of the Kingdom of God ultimately will be ushered in by the triumphant return of Jesus as the Redeemer-King (Rev. 22:20). Then there will be a new Heaven and a new Earth, and righteousness will reign supreme.

Meanwhile, says John Stott, "We are living in the in between time of what he [Christ] has done already and what he is going to do. . . . We live between Kingdom come and Kingdom coming."[15]

Charles Colson uses a familiar event from World War II history and an analogy for the two-stage process in the Kingdom of God strategy:

> Christ's death and resurrection—the D-Day of human history—assure his ultimate victory. But we are still on the beaches. The enemy has not yet been vanquished, and the fighting is still ugly. Christ's invasion has assured the ultimate outcome, however—victory for God and his people at some future date.
>
> The second stage, which will take place when Christ returns, will assert God's rule over all the universe. His Kingdom will be visible without imperfection. At that time there will be a final judgment of all people, peace on earth, and the restoration of harmony unknown since Eden.[16]

"Do you not know that I have power to crucify you?" Pilate asked Jesus.

What Pilate did *not* know was that Jesus Christ has all power, authority, and dominion over all humanity and all time, forever and ever. He frees the rejected from loneliness, the sinful from their depravity, the rich from the shackles of wealth, and the sick from pain. He is the resurrection and the life, and whoever believes in him "shall never die" (John 11:25–26).

*   *   *

The world still navigates that precarious sea between the hills of time. And out of the gorges comes the startling thunder of life's storms. As the tempest rages, we wayfarers huddle forlorn, unsure, quaking in the wind.

But even in the eye of the hurricane there is a friend willing to travel with us. He is the Man for All Ages.

"Where is your faith?" he asks when the wind howls and belief falters. "Be of good cheer."

"Surely I am with you always, to the very end of the [new] age" (Matt. 28:20, NIV).

Notes

Chapter 2: Prevalence of the New Age

1. Roland Mick, interview with author, San Francisco, Calif., 8 November 1987.

2. Cited in Carol McGraw, "Seekers of Self Now Herald the New Age," *Los Angeles Times*, 17 February 1987, pt. 1, 3.

3. Greely's research was conducted in 1973–74 by the University of Chicago's National Opinion Research Council; it was not published until 1987 (*American Health* [January–February 1987]: 47–49).

4. *Christian Herald* (February 1988): 51.

5. Cited in Marilyn Ferguson, *Aquarian Conspiracy: Personal and Social Transformation in the 1980s* (Los Angeles: J. P. Tarcher, 1980), 364.

6. Cited in a brochure of the Southern California Skeptics (Pasadena, Calif.).

7. Public Opinion Laboratory of Northern Illinois University; published in *American Demographics* and cited by EP News Service.

8. William A. Henry III and Denise Worrell, "Stranger in a Strange Land: Puppet or Alien, NBC's ALF Is an Intergalactic Star," *Time*, 21 March 1988, 71.

9. Celebration of Innovation Workshop, San Francisco, 7 November 1987.

10. Tal Brooke, interview with author, Redwood City, Calif., 23 November 1987.

11. John Leo et al., "A Holy Furor" (cover story), *TIME*, 15 August 1988, 36.

12. From *The Last Temptation of Christ*, viewed by the author, 10 August 1988.

13. American Family Association (Tupelo, Miss.), "Script Sheet on the Movie 'The Last Temptation of Christ,' A Sampling of Scenes and Quotes from the Script."

14. Nikos Kazantzakis, *The Last Temptation of Christ*, trans. P. A. Bien (New York: Simon & Schuster, 1960), 1–2.

15. Gordon Lewis, interview with author, Denver, Colo., 1 December 1987.

16. Nina Easton, "Shirley MacLaine's Mysticism for the Masses," *Los Angeles Times Magazine*, 6 September 1987, 8.

17. Carl A. Raschke, interview with author, Denver, Colo., 2 December 1987.

18. Cited in Ronald Enroth, "The New Age Movement," *Fundamentalist Journal* (February 1988): 49.

19. San Francisco Medical Research Foundation, *Human Ecology Catalog* (San Anselmo, Calif.: SFMRF, 1987), 14–15.

20. Beth Ann Krier, "In America, Yoga Finds Itself in Some Strange Positions," *Los Angeles Times*, 17 February 1988, pt. 5, 1.

21. Howard E. Goldfluss, "Courtroom Psychics," *OMNI* (July 1987): 12.

22. "Great Gifts from Waldenbooks" (advertisement), *New Age Journal* (November–December 1987): 24.

23. Meg Sullivan, "New Age Will Dawn in August, Seers Say, and Malibu Is Ready," *Wall Street Journal*, 23 June 1987.

24. Robert N. Bellah, interview with author, Berkeley, Calif., 25 November 1987.

25. Quoted in John Koffend, "The Gospel according to Helen," *Psychology Today* (September 1980): 77–78.

26. Maurice Smith, "Understanding and Responding to the New Age Movements," Interfaith Witness Department, Home Mission Board, Southern Baptist Convention, 1985, 6.

27. Ferguson, *Aquarian Conspiracy*, 363.

28. Maxine Negri, "Age-Old Problems of the New Age Movement," *Humanist* (March–April 1988): 23–24.

29. Karen Hoyt et al., *New Age Rage* (Old Tappan, N.J.: Fleming H. Revell Co., 1987), 44.

Chapter 3: Premises of the New Age

1. *Rivendell Times*, 1 September 1987.

2. Jeremy P. Tarcher, "New Age as Perennial Philosophy," *Los Angeles Times Book Review*, 7 February 1988, 15.

3. See "The Members Speak: What Does 'New Age' Mean to You?" *New Age Journal* (November–December 1987): 52.

4. J. Gordon Melton, *Encyclopedic Handbook of Cults in America* (New York and London: Garland Publishing, 1986), 113.

5. Marilyn Ferguson, *The Aquarian Conspiracy, Personal and Social Transformation in the 1980s* (Los Angeles: J. P. Tarcher, 1980), 380.

6. Fritjof Capra, *Turning Point: Science, Society and the Rising Culture* (New York: Simon & Schuster, 1982), 371.

7. Jack Underhill, "New Age Quiz," *Life Times Magazine*, no. 3, 6.

8. Douglas R. Groothuis, *Unmasking The New Age* (Downers Grove, Ill.: InterVarsity Press, 1986), 53.

9. Tarcher, "New Age as Perennial Philosophy."

10. Ferguson, *The Aquarian Conspiracy*, 100.

11. Underhill, "New Age Quiz," 6.

12. Cited in Joseph M. Hopkins, "New Age: What to Watch For," *Evangelical Newsletter*, 5 July 1985, 4.

13. Ronald S. Miller, "Marilyn Ferguson: Changes for a New Age," *Yoga Journal*, July–August 1981, 70.

14. Melton, *Encyclopedic Handbook of Cults in America*, 114.

15. Groothuis, *Unmasking the New Age*, 22.

16. Dean Halverson, interview with author, Denver, Colo., 1 December 1987.

17. Ferguson, *The Aquarian Conspiracy*, 26.

18. Ibid., 85.

19. Ibid., 23.

20. Ibid., 176.

21. Maxine Negri, "Age-Old Problems of the New Age Movement," *Humanist* (March–April 1988): 26.

Chapter 4: The Mind of the New Age

1. Kathleen Vande Kieft, *Innersource* (New York: Ballantine, 1988), 28.

2. Quoted in Marilyn Ferguson, *The Aquarian Conspiracy, Personal and Social Transformation in the 1980s* (Los Angeles: J. P. Tarcher, 1980), 156.

3. "A User's Manual to the Brain, Mind and Spirit," *OMNI Whole-Mind Newsletter* (October 1987): 130.

4. Herbert Benson and William Proctor, "Your Maximum Mind," *New Age Journal* (November–December 1987): 20.

5. Michael S. Gazzaniga, "The Social Brain," *Psychology Today* (November 1985): 38.

6. Quoted in Judith Hooper and Dick Teresi, *Three-Pound Universe: Revolutionary Discoveries about the Brain from the Chemistry of the Mind to the New Frontiers of the Soul* (New York: Macmillan, 1986), 378.

7. William H. Calvin, *Throwing Madonna: Essays on the Brain* (New York: McGraw-Hill Co., 1983), 105.

8. Jerre Levy, "Right Brain, Left Brain: Fact and Fiction," *Psychology Today* (May 1985): 43–44.

9. Shirley MacLaine, "MacLaine's Guide to the 'New Age,'" *Los Angeles Times*, 19 August 1987, pt. 5, 1.

10. Kieft, *Innersource*, 156.

11. Ferguson, *The Aquarian Conspiracy*, 297.

12. Marilyn Ferguson, interview with author, Los Angeles, Calif., 12 January 1988.

13. Quoted in Michael Brown, "Getting Serious about the Occult," *Atlantic Monthly* 242 (October 1978): 103.

14. Richard M. Restak, *The Brain* (New York: Bantam Books, 1984), 1.

15. Douglas R. Hofstadter, *Metamagical Themas: Questing for the Essence of Mind and Pattern* (New York: Basic Books 1985), 487.

16. Hooper and Teresi, *Three-Pound Universe*, 383.

17. Brooks Alexander, "The New Age Movement Is Nothing New," *Eternity Magazine* (February 1988): 34.

18. Quoted in Maxine Negri, "Age-Old Problems of the New Age Movement," *Humanist* (March–April 1988): 26.

19. Frank S. Mead, ed. and comp., *Encyclopedia of Religious Quotations* (Old Tappan, N.J.: Revell, 1965), 176.

Chapter 5: Historical Roots

1. Mark R. Mullins, "The Worldview of Zen," *Update: A Quarterly Journal of New Religious Movements* 7 (December 1983): 52–53.

2. Robert C. Lester, *Buddhism* (San Francisco: Harper & Row, 1987) 84.

3. Mullins, "The Worldview of Zen," 50.

4. Christopher Lasch, "Soul of a New Age," *OMNI* (October 1987), 84.

5. Carl A. Raschke, *Interruption of Eternity: Modern Gnosticism in the Origins of the New Religious Consciousness* (Chicago: Nelson-Hall, 1980), 24, 26.

6. Robert Anton Wilson, *The Cosmic Trigger: Final Secret of the Illuminati*, cited by Lasch, "Soul of a New Age," 85.

7. "New Age Movement and Anti-Semitism," 1987, a white paper prepared by Four Corners Associates, Denver, Colo., 4.

8. Jerry Isamu Yamamoto, "Footprints in the Sand" (reprint), *Spiritual Counterfeits Newsletter* (October–November 1978).

9. J. Gordon Melton, interview with author, Santa Barbara, Calif., 16 November 1987.

10. Martin Katchen, interview with author, Denver, Colo., 2 December 1987.

11. Colin Wilson, *Afterlife: An Investigation of the Evidence for Life after Death* (Garden City, N.Y.: Dolphin/Doubleday & Co., 1987), 88–89.

12. Nina Easton, "Shirley MacLaine's Mysticism for the Masses," *Los Angeles Times Magazine*, 6 September 1987, 10.

13. Brooks Alexander, interview with author, Berkeley, Calif., 23 November 1987).

14. Marilyn Ferguson, *The Aquarian Conspiracy, Personal and Social Transformation in the 1980s* (Los Angeles: J. P. Tarcher, 1980), 19.

15. Karen Hoyt et al., *New Age Rage* (Old Tappan, N.J.: Revell, 1987), 26.

16. Brooks Alexander, "The New Age Movement Is Nothing New," *Eternity Magazine* (February 1988): 34.

17. Raschke, *Interruption of Eternity*, 229–30.

18. Douglas R. Groothuis, *Unmasking the New Age* (Downers Grove, Ill.: InterVarsity Press, 1986), 39.

19. Cited in Ferguson, *The Aquarian Conspiracy*, 367.

20. Hoyt et al., *New Age Rage*, 31.

Chapter 6: Headliners and Honchos

1. Otto Friedrich et al., "New Age Harmonies" (cover story) *TIME*, 7 December 1987, 72.

2. "She's Having the Time of Her Lives," *People's Weekly*, 26 January 1987, 28.

3. Shirley MacLaine, *Out on a Limb* (New York: Bantam Books, 1983), 214.

4. Martin Gardner, *New Age: Notes of a Fringe-Watcher* (Buffalo, N.Y.: Prometheus Books, 1988), 36.

5. Shirley MacLaine, *Dancing in the Light* (New York: Bantam Books, 1985), 133.

6. Terry Clifford, "Shirley MacLaine's Spiritual Dance," *American Health Magazine* (January–February 1987): 50–53.

7. Cited in ibid., 54.

8. *Rivendell Times*, 1 September 1987.

9. Universal Press Syndicate, 1987.

10. Gardner, *New Age*, 188.

11. Dennis Livingston, "Taking on Shirley MacLaine," *New Age Journal* (November–December 1987): 79.

12. Clifford, "Shirley MacLaine's Spiritual Dance," 53.

13. Charles Colson, interview with author, Los Angeles, Calif., 19 November 1987.

14. "Phil Donahue Show," 2 November 1987.

15. Hilary Abramson, "Altered States," *Sacramento Bee Magazine*, 25 October 1987, 10.

16. "Ramtha Movement Spreading Rapidly," *Cult Awareness Network News* (September–October 1986): 5.

17. Katharine Lowry, "Channelers," *OMNI* (October 1987): 48.

18. "Air Talk," KPCC-FM, Pasadena, Calif., 21 October 1987.

19. Ibid.

20. Karen Hoyt et al., *New Age Rage* (Old Tappan, N.J.: Revell, 1987), 43.

21. Video clip presented at Trinity United Presbyterian Church, Santa Ana, Calif., 25 October 1987.

22. Marilyn Ferguson, *The Aquarian Conspiracy, Personal and Social Transformation in the 1980s* (Los Angeles: J. P. Tarcher, 1980), 385.

23. Cited in "Feedback: Politics, Education, Business, Science," *Aquarian Conspiracy Update* (newsletter) (October 1981), 2.

24. Marilyn Ferguson, interview with author, Los Angeles, Calif., 12 January 1988.

Chapter 7: Gifted Gurus

1. Laurence Zuckerman, "A Guru for Women Over 40," *TIME* 29 February 1988, 67.

2. Ronald Enroth, *Lure of the Cults & New Religions* (Downers Grove, Ill.: InterVarsity Press, 1987), 42.

3. Irving Hexham and Karla Poewe, *Understanding Cults and New Religions* (Grand Rapids: Eerdmans, 1986), 82–83.

4. Russell Chandler and Tyler Marshall, "Guru Brings His Ashram to Oregon," *Los Angeles Times*, 30 August 1981, pt. 1, 1.

5. James S. Gordon, *Golden Guru: The Strange Journey of Bhagwan Shree Rajneesh* (Lexington, Mass.: Stephen Greene Press, 1987), 191, 244; idem, interview with author, Los Angeles, Calif., 22 September 1987.

6. Rajneesh press release, Rajneeshdam, Poona, February 1988.

7. "Marin's Bhagwan Connection," *Marin Independent Journal*, 22 March 1987.

8. Marjorie Lee Chandler, "Churches Wary of 'New Age' Neighbors," *Moody Monthly Magazine* (September 1987): 95–97.

9. Russell Chandler and Norman B. Chandler, "Guru Ma— Leader of Multimillion-Dollar Church," *Los Angeles Times*, 11 February 1980, pt. 2, 1.

10. Peter H. King, "Montana's Wary of Church's Plans for Promised Land," *Los Angeles Times*, 25 January 1987, pt. 1, 3.

11. J. Gordon Melton, *Encyclopedia of American Religions*, 2d ed. (Detroit: Gale Research Co., 1987), 111.

12. Carol McGraw, "Seekers of Self Now Herald the New Age," *Los Angeles Times*, 17 February 1987, pt. 1, 3.

13. Carl A. Raschke, *Interruption of Eternity: Modern Gnosticism in the Origins of the New Religious Consciousness* (Chicago: Nelson-Hall, 1980), 232.

14. J. Gordon Melton, *Encyclopedic Handbook of Cults in America* (New York and London: Garland Publishing, 1986), 141–44; Enroth, *Lure of the Cults & New Religions*, 23.

15. Katy Butler, "New Age Flock of 'Zen Master' May Be Moving," *San Francisco Chronicle*, 14 January 1988.

16. "Swami Beyondananda, 'the Yogi from Muskogee,'" *Guide: A Calendar for the Whole Person* 1 (November 1987): 4, 8, 21.

Chapter 8: Communes and Groups

1. Quoted in Russell Chandler, "A Sampler's Directory to Meditation Groups," *Los Angeles Times*, 13 February 1977, pt. 2, 1.

2. 1987 Maharishi International University catalog, 3.

3. "Group Claims TM Movement Is a Cult," *Washington Post*, 2 July 1987.

4. J. Gordon Melton, *Encyclopedic Handbook of Cults in America* (New York and London: Garland Publishing, 1986), 159.

5. Russell Chandler and Evan Maxwell, "Krishnas—A Kingdom in Disarray," *Los Angeles Times*, 15 February 1981, pt. 1, 1.

6. Robert S. Ellwood and Harry B. Partin, *Religious and Spiritual Groups in Modern America* (Englewood Cliffs, N.J.: Prentice Hall, 1988), 141.

7. Brooks Alexander, "Scientology: Human Potential Bellwether," *Spiritual Counterfeits Project Journal* 4, no. 1 (Winter 1981–82): 27.

8. Jeremy Main, "Trying to Bend Managers' Minds," *Fortune Magazine*, 23 November 1987, 104.

9. Robert S. Greenberger, "East Meets Est: The Soviets Discover Werner Erhard," *Wall Street Journal*, 3 December 1986.

10. Ronald Enroth, *Lure of the Cults & New Religions* (Downers grove, Ill.: InterVarsity Press, 1986), 24.

11. Joh Leo et al., "A Holy Furor" (cover story), *TIME*, 15 August 1988, 36.

12. Quoted in Alice Lawhead and Stephen Lawhead, *Pilgrim's Guide to the New Age* (Batavia, Ill.: Lion Publishing Corp., 1986), 30.

13. Karen Hoyt, "The Use of Thought Reform in Large Group Awareness Trainings with Specific Focus on *est*," M.A. thesis, John F. Kennedy University, Orinda, California, 1985.

14. "Americans Get Religion in the New Age," *Christianity Today*, 16 May 1986, 21.

15. Main, "Trying to Bend Managers' Minds," 104.

16. J. Gordon Melton, *Encyclopedia of American Religions*, 2d ed. (Detroit: Gale Research Co., 1987), 740.

17. Melton, *Encyclopedic Handbook of Cults in America*, 146.

18. David Christopher Lane, "The Scientology Connection: Paul Twitchell and L. Ron Hubbard," in *Understanding Cults and Spiritual Movements* (Del Mar, Calif.: Del Mar Press, 1987), 14–15.

19. Ellwood and Partin, *Religious and Spiritual Groups in Modern America*, 220.

20. "Soul Travelers' Move," *San Jose Mercury News*, 24 August 1986.

21. Jerry Isamu Yamamoto, "Expanding Sufi Horizons," *Spiritual Counterfeits Project Tract*, Berkeley, Calif., 1983, 1–4.

22. Ellwood and Partin, *Religious and Spiritual Groups in Modern America*, 216–20.

23. Enroth, *Lure of the Cults & New Religions*, 32.

24. "Moon Believes a Follower Is Son Reincarnated," *Washington Post*, 30 March 1988.

25. Robert Peel, *Spiritual Healing in a Scientific Age* (San Francisco: Harper & Row, 1987), 34–35.

26. Irving Hexham and Karla Poewe, *Understanding Cults and New Religions* (Grand Rapids: Eerdmans, 1986), 82–83.

27. "Magic in Mormonism," *Salt Lake City Messenger* no. 65 (November 1987): 1–8.

Chapter 9: Choosing a Channel

1. Hilary Abramson, "Altered States," *Sacramento Bee Magazine*, 25 October 1987, 11.

2. Ibid., 18.

3. "Cosmic Chic: Channeling to Success," *New York Times*, 30 May 1987, 11.

4. Martin Gardner, *New Age: Notes of a Fringe-Watcher* (Buffalo, N.Y.: Prometheus Books, 1988), 202.

5. Brooks Alexander, "Theology from the Twilight Zone," *Christianity Today*, 18 September 1987, 22.

6. Caryline Waldron, "Bashar: An Extraterrestrial Among Us," *Life Times Magazine*, no. 3, 107.

7. Dick Roraback, "An Artist's Brush with Immortality," *Los Angeles Times*, 19 April 1988.

8. Jon Klimo, "The Psychology of Channeling," *New Age Journal* (November–December 1987): 35, 38.

9. Virginia Essene, "Secret Truths," *Life Times Magazine*, no. 3, 101.

10. William Lyman to Russell Chandler, 11 October 1987.

11. "Channeling," narrated by Stanley Ralph Ross (Los Angeles: Audio Renaissance Tapes, 1987).

12. *Channeling: A Resource Guide* (Los Angeles: Audio Renaissance Tapes, 1987), 30.

13. Colin Wilson, *Afterlife: An Investigation of the Evidence for Life after Death* (Garden City, N.Y.: Dolphin/Doubleday & Co., 1987), 127–31.

14. Ibid., 130.

15. H. Newton Malony, interview with author, Pasadena, Calif., 20 November 1987.

16. J. Gordon Melton, interview with author, Santa Barbara, Calif., 16 November 1987.

17. F. LaGard Smith, *Out on a Broken Limb* (Eugene, Oreg.: Harvest House Publishers, 1986), 102.

18. Robert Burrows, "At Issue,'" *Spiritual Counterfeits Project Journal* 7, no. 1 (1987): 5.

19. Katharine Lowry, "Channelers," *OMNI* (October 1987): 146.

20. Smith, *Out on a Broken Limb*, 103, 104.

21. Joseph Barber, interview with author, Fullerton, Calif., 9 March 1988.

22. Quoted in Beth Ann Krier, "Crystal Craze and Rock Mania," *Los Angeles Times*, 5 December 1987, pt. 5, 1.

23. Lowry, "Channelers," 148.

24. "Interview with Penny Torres," *Life Times Magazine*, no. 3, 93.

25. Quoted in Lowry, "Channelers," 146, 46.

26. Ross, "Channeling" (audiotape).

27. Lyssa Royal and staff, *Channeling and Mediumship—A Guideline* (Los Angeles: Bodhi Tree Bookstore, 1987), 2.

28. Klimo, "The Psychology of Channeling," 67.

Chapter 10: UFOs and ETIs

1. Robin Weston, *Channelers: A New Age Directory* (New York: Perigee/Putnam, 1988), 170.

2. "She's Having the Time of Her Lives," *People's Weekly*, 26 January 1987, 31.

3. Celebration of Innovation Workshop, San Francisco, 6 November 1987.

4. Shirley MacLaine, *It's All in the Playing* (New York: Bantam Books, 1987), 336.

5. Bill Lawren, "UFO Poll," *OMNI* (October 1987): 144.

6. Margaret Mead, "UFO's—Visitors from Outer Space," *Redbook Magazine*, September 1974, 57–58.

7. "Out of the Blue," *Philip Morris Magazine* (Summer 1987).

8. Robert S. Ellwood and Harry B. Partin, *Religious and Spiritual Groups in Modern America* (Englewood Cliffs, N.J.: Prentice Hall, 1988), 113.

9. Ibid., 111.

10. Aetherius Society materials, Hollywood, Calif., 1981.

11. Ibid.

12. "Out of the Blue."

13. Irving Hexham, "Yoga, UFOs, and Cult Membership," *Update: A Quarterly Journal of New Religious Movements* 10, no. 3 (September 1986): 11.

14. Martin Gardner, *New Age: Notes of a Fringe-Watcher* (Buffalo, N.Y.: Prometheus Books, 1988), 213.

15. Mark Albrecht and Brooks Alexander, "UFOs: Is Science Fiction Coming True?" *Spiritual Counterfeits Project Journal* 1, no. 2 (August 1977): 30.

Gardner, *New Age*, 213.

17. John Keel, *UFOs: Operation Trojan Horse* (New York: G. P. Putnam's Sons, 1970), 143.

18. Albrecht and Alexander, "UFOs: Is Science Fiction Coming True?" 17.

Chapter 11: Harmonic Convergence

1. Deirdre Donahue, "New Era for Earth or Just Moonshine?" *USA Today*, 12 August 1987.

2. Quoted in Jean Callahan, "Cosmic Expectations," *New Age Journal* (November–December 1987): 82.

3. Jack Friedman, "Hum If You Love the Mayans," *People's Weekly*, 31 August 1987, 26.

4. KABC-AM, Los Angeles, 12 August 1987.

5. Dick Roraback, "Resonating with Jose Arguelles, a New Age Scholar," *Los Angeles Times*, 12 August 1987, pt. 5, 1.

6. "The End of the World (Again)," *Newsweek*, 17 August 1987, 69.

7. Reprinted in Jose Arguelles, "Harmonic Convergence, Trigger Event: Implementation and Follow-Up," *Life Times Magazine*, no. 3, 65.

8. EP News Service, 21 August 1987.

9. Quoted in Roraback, "Resonating with Jose Arguelles."

10. Sy Fransky, "Editor's Note: A New World," *Sun* [Chapel Hill, N.C.], no. 143, October 1987, 5.

11. Ibid., 4.

12. Meg Sullivan, "New Age Will Dawn in August, Seers Say, and Malibu Is Ready," *Wall Street Journal*, 23 June 1987.

13. Callahan, "Cosmic Expectations," 82.

14. Arguelles, "Harmonic Convergence, Trigger Event," 63.

15. Cited in Ravi Dykema, "The Mythical Monkey Miracle," *Nexus* (Fall 1986): 4.

16. Quoted in Maureen O'Hara, "Of Myths and Monkeys: A Critical Look at Critical Mass," *Nexus* (Fall 1986), reprinted from *The Whole Earth Review* (Fall 1986).

17. Ibid., 4.

18. Tim Farrington, "The 101st Monkey," *Node* 2, no. 2 (Winter 1987): 2 [Performing Arts Social Society quarterly, San Francisco].

Chapter 12: Crystal Consciousness and Pyramid Power

1. Sivasiva Palani, "Let's Sue the New Age (editorial)," *Hinduism Today* 9, no. 6 (September 1987): 2.

2. Carol McGraw, "Seekers of Self Now Herald the New Age," *Los Angeles Times*, 17 February 1987, pt. 1, 3.

3. Advertisement in *India Journal* 8, no. 1 (February 1988): 2.

4. Martha Smilgis, "Rock Power for Health and Wealth," *TIME*, 19 January 1987, 66.

5. Lyssa Royal, "The Ultimate Crystal," *Conscious Connection* (October–November 1987): 23.

6. Cited in Wike Associates (Roanoke, Va.), *National & International Religion Report*, 23 January 1987.

7. Jack Page, "Supreme Quartz," *OMNI* (October 1987): 96.

8. Quoted in Beth Ann Krier, "Crystal Craze and Rock Mania," *Los Angeles Times*, 5 December 1987, pt. 5, 1.

9. Quoted in Shawn Hubler, "Crazy over Crystals: Quartz Rocks of Yore Revived as Talisman for '80s," *The Los Angeles Herald-Examiner*, 18 January 1987.

10. From personal conversation and literature at the Church of San Marga, Kauai, Hawaii, 14 May 1988.

11. Handout at Celebration of Innovation Workshop, San Francisco, 7 November 1987.

12. Page, "Supreme Quartz," 96.

13. Quoted in ibid., 100.

Chapter 13: Native Americans and Shamans

1. *Spiritual Counterfeits Project Special Collection Journal* 6, no. 1 (Winter 1984): 25.

2. Russell Chandler, "Foresters, Indians, Clash over Fate of Sacred Ground: Paved Logging Road on U.S. Land Called Threat to Freedom of Religion," *Los Angeles Times*, 25 August 1985, pt. 1, 3.

3. Cited in Alberto Villoldo and Stanley Krippner, *Healing States: A Journey into the World of Spiritual Healing and Shamanism* (New York: Simon & Schuster, 1987), 159.

4. Chandler, "Foresters, Indians, Clash over Fate of Sacred Ground."

5. Jon W. Magnuson, "Echoes of a Shaman's Song: Artifacts and Ethics in the Northwest," *Christian Century*, 29 April 1987, 407.

6. Jon W. Magnuson, "Affirming Native Spirituality: A Call to Justice," *Christian Century*, 9 December 1987, 1114.

7. Robert S. Ellwood and Harry B. Partin, *Religious and Spiritual Groups in Modern America* (Englewood Cliffs, N.J.: Prentice Hall, 1988), 13–14.

8. Brooks Alexander, "A Generation of Wizards: Shamanism & Contemporary Culture," *Spiritual Counterfeits Project Special Collection Journal* 6, no. 1 (Winter 1984): 28.

9. Michael Harner, *Way of the Shaman: A Guide to Power and Healing* (San Francisco: Harper & Row, 1980), 138.

10. Celebration of Innovation Workshop, San Francisco, 8 November 1987.

11. Ibid.

12. Ellwood and Partin, *Religious and Spiritual Groups in Modern America*, 168–70.

13. Cited in Beth Ann Krier, "The Medicine Woman of Beverly Hills," *Los Angeles Times*, 23 November 1987, pt. 5, 1.

14. Ibid.

15. Quoted in Rose Marie Staubs, "Andrews' Sisters," *OMNI* (October 1987): 28.

Chapter 14: Goddesses and Neopagans

1. Tamara Jones, "Fire Goddess Defended: Harnessing of Volcano Is Hot Hawaii Issue," *Los Angeles Times*, 9 February 1988, pt. 1, 1.

2. "New Age Movement and Anti-Semitism," 1987, a white paper prepared by Four Corners Associates, Denver, Colo., 5.

3. Regina Sara Ryan and John W. Travis, *Wellness Workbook* (Berkeley, Calif.: Ten Speed Press, 1981), 184.

4. Fritjof Capra, *Turning Point: Science, Society and the Rising Culture* (New York: Simon & Schuster, 1982), 292.

5. George A. Seielstad, *Cosmic Ecology: The View from the Outside In* (Berkeley and Los Angeles: University of California Press, 1983), 135.

6. Quoted in Kevin Kelly, "Deep Ecology as Religion," *Utne Reader* (October–November 1985): 68; excerpted from *Whole Earth Review* (May 1985).

7. Ken Wilber, *Up from Eden* (Garden City, N.Y.: Anchor Press/Doubleday, 1981), 188.

8. Charlene Spretnak, "Ecofeminism: Our Roots & Flowering," *Ecology Center Newsletter* 17 (November 1987): 1.

9. Robert Ellwood, interview with author, Los Angeles, Calif., 14 December 1987.

10. Spretnak, "Ecofeminism," 1–2.

11. Rosemary Curb and Nancy Manahan, eds., *Lesbian Nuns: Breaking Silence* (Tallahassee, Fla.: Naiad Press, 1985), xxx–xxxi.

12. Texe Marrs, *Dark Secrets of the New Age: Satan's Plan for a One World Religion* (Westchester, Ill.: Crossway Books/Good News Publishers, 1987), 76.

13. Quoted in Robert Burrows, "Americans Get Religion in the New Age," *Christianity Today*, 16 May 1986, 21–22.

14. Rose Marie Staubs, "Andrews's Sisters," *OMNI* (October 1987): 28.

15. Bear Tribe Medicine Society, *Bear Tribe Catalogue* (Spokane, Wash.: Bear Tribe Medicine Society, 1987), 33–37, 48.

16. Margot Adler, "A Modern Pagan Spiritual View," *World* (September–October 1987): 10.

17. Carol McGraw, "Bewitching: Covens of the '80s Don't Match Lore Stirred by Tales of Halloweens Past," *Los Angeles Times*, 31 October 1987, pt. 2, 1.

18. J. Gordon Melton, *Encyclopedic Handbook of Cults in America* (New York and London: Garland Publishing, 1986), 211.

19. "Specific Manifestations of the New Age Movement," lecture at Trinity United Presbyterian Church, Santa Ana, Calif., 24 October 1987.

20. McGraw, "Bewitching."

21. Robert S. Ellwood and Harry B. Partin, *Religious and Spiritual Groups in Modern America* (Englewood Cliffs, N.J.: Prentice Hall, 1988), 155.

22. "Channeling," narrated by Stanley Ralph Ross (Los Angeles: Audio Renaissance Tapes, 1987); *New Age Journal* (November–December 1987): 38.

Chapter 15: Commercial Appeal

1. Otto Friedrich et al., "New Age Harmonies" (cover story), *TIME*, 7 December 1987, 62.

2. Katharine Lowry, "Channelers," *OMNI* (October 1987): 48.

3. Friedrich, "New Age Harmonies," 64.

4. Nina Easton, "Shirley MacLaine's Mysticism for the Masses," *Los Angeles Times Magazine*, 6 September 1987, 7.

5. Rose Marie Staubs, "Andrews's Sisters," *OMNI* (October 1987): 28.

6. Carol McGraw, "Seekers of Self Now Herald the New Age," *Los Angeles Times*, 17 February 1987, pt. 1, 3.

7. David Tuller, "New Age," *Publishers Weekly*, 25 September 1987, 29.

8. According to an advertisement in *Life Times Magazine*, no. 3, 28.

9. Jeffrey A. Trachtenberg and Edward Giltenan, "Mainstream Metaphysics," *Forbes Magazine*, 1 June 1987, 156.

10. Martin Marty, "An Old New Age in Publishing (Editorial)," *Christian Century*, 18 November 1987, 1019.

11. "New Age on Tape," *Publishers Weekly*, 25 September 1987, 65.

12. "A User's Manual to the Brain, Mind and Spirit," *OMNI WholeMind Newsletter* (October 1987): 127.

13. Advertisement in *OMNI* (October 1987): 165.

14. Tom Spain, "New Media for a New Age," *Publishers Weekly*, 25 September 1987, 61.

15. Lowry, "Channelers," 50.

16. Karen Hoyt et al., *New Age Rage* (Old Tappan, N.J.: Revell, 1987), 44.

17. McGraw, "Seekers of Self Now Herald the New Age," pt. 1, 3.

18. Steve Chawkins, "Pyramids and Crystals Take Real Estate Firm into 'New Age," *Los Angeles Times*[Valley ed.], 21 June 1987, pt. 2, 6.

19. Friedrich, "New Age Harmonies," 69.

20. Laura Torbet, "Wall Street Psychics," *OMNI WholeMind Newsletter* (October 1987): 131.

21. According to an advertisement in *New Age Journal* (November–December 1987): 91.

22. *Mystic Trader* (catalog), Spring 1987, 19.

23. According to an advertisement in *Daybreak Magazine* (Autumn 1987).

24. Janie Gabbet, "Not Just a Vacation," *Life Times Magazine*, no. 3, 51.

25. Pat Linse and Al Seckel, "A Garden of Cosmic Delights—The New Age Marketplace," *LASER* [Los Angeles Skeptics Evaluative Report] (Summer 1988): 3.

26. Advertisement in *New Age Magazine* (April 1988): 43.

27. Christopher Lasch, "Soul of a New Age," *OMNI* (October 1987): 79.

28. Ravi Dykema, "Flying for Dollars," *New Age Journal* (November–December 1987): 14.

29. Ibid.; *Boston Globe*, 31 August 1987.

30. Marilyn Ferguson, *The Aquarian Conspiracy, Personal and Social Transformation in the 1980s* (Los Angeles: J. P. Tarcher, 1980), 324.

31. Ibid., 332.

32. Patricia King and Penelope Wang, "The Karma of Capitalism," *Newsweek*, 3 August 1987, 44.

33. Peggy Taylor, "Life at the Leading Edge: A New Age Interview with Marilyn Ferguson," *New Age Magazine* (August 1982): 34.

Chapter 16: Corporate Entities

1. Chris Majer, interview with author, Seattle, Wash., 21 December 1987.

2. Marilyn Ferguson, *The Aquarian Conspiracy, Personal and Social Transformation in the 1980s* (Los Angeles: J. P. Tarcher, 1980), 236–37.

3. Robert Lindsey, "New Age Invades American Way of Life," *International Herald Tribune*, 3 October 1986.

4. Karen Hoyt et al., *New Age Rage* (Old Tappan, N.J.: Revell, 1987), 99; Ferguson, *The Aquarian Conspiracy*, 347.

5. Mark Teich and Giselle Dodeles, "Mind Control: How to Get It, How to Use It, How to Keep It," *OMNI* (October 1987): 54.

6. Ibid., 53–60.

7. George Craig McMillan, "Laya Yoga and Enlightenment," *Life Times Magazine*, no. 3, 44–45.

8. "Personal Best: Mind over Muscle," *Women's Sports & Fitness Magazine* (May 1987): 60.

9. "Zen and the Art of Making Money," *Washington Post*, 9 January 1987.

10. Lindsey, "New Age Invades American Way of Life."

11. Richard L. Watring, "Transcendental Management" (1984), an abstract of "A Study of the Emergence of New Age Concepts in Human Resources Development," 4–5.

12. *New York Times*, 28 September 1986, pt. B.

13. Otto Friedrich et al., "New Age Harmonies" (cover story), *TIME*, 7 December 1987, 62–63.

14. "A User's Manual to the Brain, Mind and Spirit," *OMNI WholeMind Newsletter* (October 1987): 127.

15. Jeremy Main, "Trying to Bend Managers' Minds," *Fortune Magazine*, 23 November 1987, 96.

16. Ibid., 100.

17. Anetta Miller and Pamela Abramson, "Corporate Mind Control," *Newsweek*, 4 May 1987, 39.

18. "Management Training Gets Too Personal for Some at UC," *San Francisco Chronicle*, 23 March 1987.

19. John J. Reilly, "New Age, New Rage," *This World, A Journal of Religion and Public Life* (Winter 1988): 122.

20. Louis Tice, *New Age Training for Achieving Your Potential* (Seattle: Pacific Institute, 1980).

21. "CBS Evening News," 4 February 1988.

22. *Rockwell News* (Anaheim ed.), 12 October 1987.

23. Ron Zemke, "What's New in the New Age?" (cover story), *Training Magazine* (September 1987): 25–33.

Chapter 17: Education, Music, and Art

1. Suzanna Little, "Children in the New Age Bookstore," *Publishers Weekly*, 25 September 1987, 72.

2. Charles Olsen, "Please Turn Up the Lights" (sermon), 15 November 1987, Arcadia Presbyterian Church, Arcadia, Calif.

3. Cited in Frances Adeney, "Educators Look East," *Spiritual Counterfeits Project Journal* 4, no. 1 (Winter 1981–82): 29.

4. Lynn Smith, "Adult Type Education for School Children," *Los Angeles Times* [Orange Co. ed.], 24 June 1982, pt. 5, 1.

5. Marilyn Ferguson, *The Aquarian Conspiracy, Personal and Social Transformation in the 1980s* (Los Angeles: J. P. Tarcher, 1980), 281, 314.

6. Ibid., 284.

7. Pat Boerger, telephone interview with author, 19 January 1988.

8. 1988 Citrus Community College catalog, 69.

9. Fall 1987 calendar, California Institute of Integral Studies, San Francisco.

10. Celebration of Innovation Workshop, San Francisco, 7 November 1987.

11. John Dunphy, "A Religion for a New Age," *Humanist Magazine* (January-February 1983): 26.

12. Douglas R. Groothuis, *Unmasking the New Age* (Downers Grove, Ill.: InterVarsity Press, 1986): 26.

13. Otto Friedrich et al., "New Age Harmonies" (cover story), *TIME*, 7 December 1987, 69.

14. Jeffrey A. Trachtenberg and Edward Giltenan, "Mainstream Metaphysics," *Forbes Magazine*, 1 June 1987, 158; Carol McGraw, "Seekers of Self Now Herald the New Age," *Los Angeles Times*, 17 February 1987, pt. 1, 3.

15. "New Age Music and Video," *Guide to New Age Living* (Brighton, Mass.: Rising Star Associates, 1988), 85.

16. Peggy Taylor and Rick Ingrasci, "Synthesizing East and West," *New Age Journal* (September–October 1987): 70.

17. Mike Wyma, "Ancient Music for a New Age," *Los Angeles Times* [Valley ed.], 8 October 1987, pt. 5, 34.

18. Quoted in Marion Long, "In Search of a Definition," *OMNI* (October 1987): 162.

19. Pamela Bloom, "Soul Music," *New Age Journal* (March–April 1987): 58.

20. 1987 Iasos Inter-Dimensional Music catalog.

21. Bruce Schechter, "Fractal Fairy Tales," *OMNI* (October 1987): 91.

22. Karen Hoyt, interview with author, Berkeley, Calif., 24 November 1987.

23. Alice Lawhead and Stephen Lawhead, *Pilgrim's Guide to the New Age* (Batavia, Ill.: Lion Publishing Corp., 1986), 77.

24. Advent Design and Research Literature.

25. Doug Stewart, "Perfect Pitch," *New Age Journal* (February 1986): 40.

26. "The Artist: Sharon Skolnick," *Common Ground: Resources for Personal Transformation* 53 (Fall 1987): 2.

Chapter 18: Holistic Health and Healing

1. Jack Gordon, "Training Terms: What Does Wholistic Mean?" *Training Magazine* (September 1987): 66.

2. Marilyn Ferguson, *The Aquarian Conspiracy, Personal and Social Transformation in the 1980s* (Los Angeles: J. P. Tarcher, 1980), 242.

3. Elliot Miller, "Tracking the Aquarian Conspiracy," *Forward* (Fall 1986): 13.

4. Jeffrey A. Trachtenberg and Edward Giltenan, "Mainstream Metaphysics," *Forbes Magazine*, 1 June 1987, 157.

5. Patrick Mahony, "Humor for Health," *New Realities Magazine* (November–December 1984): 24.

6. Norman Cousins, "Healing and Belief," *Saturday Evening Post* (April 1982): 31.

7. Lewis M. Andrews, *To Thine Own Self Be True: The Rebirth of Values in the New Ethical Therapy* (New York: Doubleday & Co., 1987).

8. Michael Harner, *Way of the Shaman: A Guide to Power and Healing* (San Francisco: Harper & Row, 1980), 20.

9. Dana Ullman, "Holistic Health: Friend and Foe of Progressive Health Care," *International Journal of Holistic Health and Medicine* 2 (Winter 1984): 22.

10. Debbie Alexander, "New Medicine: A New Phase in Cultural Transformation," *Spiritual Counterfeits Project Report* (1975, rev. 1984), 2.

11. Advertisement for 21 November 1987 seminar at the American Red Cross Building in San Francisco.

12. James T. Carter, "What Is Iridology," *New Realities Magazine* (November–December 1984), 45.

13. Pamela Bloom, "Soul Music," *New Age Journal* (March–April 1987): 59.

14. John F. Miller III, "Healing in the New Age Groups," *Journal of Religion and Psychical Research* 7, no. 1 (1984): 44.

15. Trachtenberg and Giltenan, "Mainstream Metaphysics," 157.

16. Carol McGraw, "Seekers of Self Now Herald the New Age," *Los Angeles Times*, 17 February 1987, pt. 1, 3.

17. John F. DeVries with Dean A. Ohlman, *Spiritual Dangers in Holistic Medicine* (Grand Rapids: Bibles for India, n.d.), 17.

18. Jonathan Kirsch, "Can Your Mind Cure Cancer?" *New West Magazine*, 3 January 1977, 40.

19. Ibid., 43.

20. Alberto Villoldo and Stanley Krippner, *Healing States: A Journey into the World of Spiritual Healing and Shamanism* (New York: Simon & Schuster, 1987), 26–38.

21. Terry Clifford, "Healing or Hoping?" *American Health Magazine* (January–February 1987): 55.

22. Wayne Oates, "Some Functions of Belief in Illness and Health," *Thesis Theological Cassettes* (audiotape) 15, no. 7 (December 1984).

23. Ibid.

24. Ferguson, *The Aquarian Conspiracy*, 247, 253.

25. Karl Sabbagh, "The Psychopathology of Fringe Medicine," *Skeptical Inquirer* 10 (Winter 1985–86): 159.

26. Cited in Harner, *Way of the Shaman*, 135.

27. Villoldo and Krippner, *Healing States*, 198–99.

28. Paul C. Reisser, M.D., "Holistic Health Update: The Movement Comes of (New) Age," *Spiritual Counterfeits Project Newsletter* 9, no. 4 (September–October 1983): 4.

29. Roland Mick, interview with author, San Francisco, Calif., 8 November 1987.

30. J. Gordon Melton, interview with author, Santa Barbara, Calif., 16 November 1987.

Chapter 19: Psychology: Outside In

1. Chris Majer, interview with author, Seattle, Wash., 21 December 1987.

2. Alice Kahn, "Esalen at 25," *Los Angeles Times Magazine*, 6 December 1987.

3. Douglas R. Groothuis, *Unmasking the New Age* (Downers Grove, Ill.: InterVarsity Press, 1986), 74.

4. Cited in Jon Klimo, "The Psychology of Channeling," *New Age Journal* (November–December 1987): 62.

5. M. Scott Peck, *Road Less Traveled: A New Psychology of Love, Traditional Values and Spiritual Growth* (New York: Simon & Schuster, 1978), 252.

6. Carl A. Raschke, *Interruption of Eternity: Modern Gnosticism in the Origins of the New Religious Consciousness* (Chicago: Nelson-Hall, 1980), 145–46.

7. Abraham H. Maslow, *Toward a Psychology of Being* (New York: Van Nostrand Reinhold, 1968), 5.

8. Jeannette DeWyze, "An Encounter with Bill Coulson," *Reader* [San Diego], 20 August 1987, 19.

9. Karen Hoyt et al., *New Age Rage* (Old Tappan, N.J.: Revell, 1987), 121–22.

10. "Psychiatrist Scott Peck's Best-seller Came by 'The Road Less Traveled'," *Brain/Mind Bulletin*, 26 May 1986, 1.

11. Peck, *The Road Less Traveled*, 169–70.

12. "Elysium Institute Seminar Schedule," *JOTS: Journal of the Senses* 81 (October–November–December 1987): 26.

13. Shakti Gawain and Laurel King, "Trusting Your Intuition," *New Age Journal* (July–August 1987): 50.

14. Neal Vahle, "Robert Fritz and Technologies for Creating," *New Realities Magazine* (January–February 1987): 27.

15. According to material assimilated at Celebration of Innovation Workshop, San Francisco, 7 November 1987.

16. Ibid.

17. James S. Gordon, *Golden Guru: The Strange Journey of Bhagwan Shree Rajneesh* (Lexington, Mass.: Stephen Greene Press, 1987), 66.

18. Cited in Hoyt et al., *New Age Rage*, 213.

19. Ibid., 148.

20. Groothuis, *Unmasking the New Age*, 79; Frances Adeney, "The Flowering of the Human Potential Movement," *Spiritual Counterfeits Project Journal* 4, no. 1 (Winter 1981–82): 15.

21. Adeney, "The Flowering of the Human Potential Movement," 15.

22. Russell Chandler, "A Sampler's Directory to Meditation Groups," *Los Angeles Times*, 13 February 1977, pt. 2, 1.

Chapter 20: Science: Universal Mind Over Matter

1. Jack Houck, interview with author, San Francisco, Calif., 7 November 1987.

2. Cited in Marilyn Ferguson, *The Aquarian Conspiracy, Personal and Social Transformation in the 1980s* (Los Angeles: J. P. Tarcher, 1980), 262n.

3. Ibid., 152.

4. Robert Ellwood, interview with author, Los Angeles, Calif., 14 December 1987.

5. Beth Ann Krier, "The Curious Hot Foot It to a New Fad," *Los Angeles Times*, 11 April 1984, pt. 1, 1.

6. Al Seckel's lecture was delivered 4 November 1987 at California State University at Fullerton.

7. Edgar D. Mitchell to readers of his bimonthly *Noetics Bulletin* (n.d.).

8. William Kautz related this information to the author, 8 November 1987, during the Celebration of Innovation workshop in San Francisco.

9. *Los Angeles Times*, 13 January 1980, pt. 1, 2, and 20 January 1980, pt. 1, 2; Paul Dean, "Psychic Discovery of a Queen's Palace?" *Los Angeles Times*, 25 January 1980, pt. 4, 1; Robert J. Mandell, "Some Insights into Psychic Abilities," *Los Angeles Times*, 5 June 1981, pt. 5, 3.

10. Doug Stewart, "The Chaos Connection," *New Age Journal* (April 1986): 17.

11. Alice Lawhead and Stephen Lawhead, *Pilgrim's Guide to the New Age* (Batavia, Ill.: Lion Publishing Corp., 1986), 8.

12. Quoted in Fred Alan Wolf, *Taking the Quantum Leap* (San Francisco: Harper & Row, 1981), 151.

13. K. C. Cole, "Why Einstein May Have Been Wrong," *Discover Magazine* (December 1984): 36.

14. Wolf, *Taking the Quantum Leap*, 63.

15. Douglas R. Hofstadter, *Metamagical Themas: Questing for the Essence of Mind and Pattern* (New York: Basic Books, 1985), 465.

16. Cited in Stewart, "The Chaos Connection," 17.

17. David Bohm, *Wholeness and the Implicate Order* (London: Routledge & Kegan Paul, 1980), 134.

18. Ferguson, *The Aquarian Conspiracy*, 420.

19. Clarice Lolich, "An Explication of the Theory of Simultaneous Interior Combustion in Its Study of the Relationship between Matter and Spirit," Ph.D. diss., University of Humanistic Studies, Del Mar, Calif., 1986.

20. Fritjof Capra, *Tao of Physics* (Berkeley, Calif.: Shambhala, 1975), 25.

21. Ibid., 11.

22. Fritjof Capra, *Turning Point: Science, Society and the Rising Culture* (New York: Simon & Schuster, 1982), 87.

23. Dean C. Halverson, interview with author, Denver, Colo., 1 December 1987.

24. Douglas R. Groothuis, *Unmasking the New Age* (Downers Grove, Ill.: InterVarsity Press, 1986), 98.

25. Michael Talbot, *Mysticism and the New Physics* (New York: Bantam Books, 1981), 54, 152.

26. K. C. Cole, "A Theory of Everything," *New York Times Magazine*, 18 October 1987, 22, 24.

27. Ibid., 25.

28. Judith Hooper and Dick Teresi, *Three-Pound Universe: Revolutionary Discoveries about the Brain from the Chemistry of the Mind to the New Frontiers of the Soul* (New York: Macmillan, 1986), 346.

29. Ibid., 348.

30. Groothuis, *Unmasking the New Age*, 99.

31. Hooper and Teresi, *Three-Pound Universe*, 351.

32. Ferguson, *The Aquarian Conspiracy*, 182.

33. Ken Wilber, ed., *Quantum Questions: Mystical Writings of the World's Great Physicists* (Boulder, Colo.: Shambhala Publications, 1984), preface, 5, 27.

Chapter 21: The Politics of Mysticism

1. Marilyn Ferguson, *The Aquarian Conspiracy, Personal and Social Transformation in the 1980s* (Los Angeles: J. P. Tarcher, 1980), 212.

2. David Horner, "New Age Politics and the Influence of Pierre Teilhard de Chardin" (pt. 2), *Apologia, Newsletter of Christian Research Associates*, 7, no. 11 (November 1987): 5.

3. Robert Burrows, "Americans Get Religion in the New Age," *Christianity Today*, 16 May 1986, 19.

4. Beverly Rubik, "Healing the Rift between Science and Spirituality" (audiotape), (Oakland, Calif.: Internode Productions, n.d.).

5. Ferguson, *The Aquarian Conspiracy*, 197.

6. Carl A. Raschke, interview with author, Denver, Colo., 2 December 1987.

7. Robert Muller, *New Genesis: Shaping a Global Spirituality* (Garden City, N.Y.: Doubleday & Co., 1982), 183, 191.

8. Fritjof Capra, *Turning Point: Science, Society and the Rising Culture* (New York: Simon & Schuster, 1982), 412.

9. Bob Hunter, "Environmentalism in the 1980s," *Greenpeace Chronicles* no. 18 (August 1979): 3.

10. Harold Gilliam, "Deep Ecology vs. Environmentalism," *Utne Reader* (October-November 1985): 66ff.; excerpted from *This World* (*San Francisco Chronicle*), 10 March 1985.

11. Petra K. Kelly, "Growing Up Green," *New Age Journal* (November–December 1987): 73.

12. Alice Bailey, *Reappearance of the Christ* (New York: Lucis Publishing Co., 1969), 111.

13. Earl D. Brewer, "A Religious Vision for the 21st Century," *Futurist* (July–August 1986): 15.

14. Mark Satin, *New Age Politics: Healing Self and Society* (New York: Dell Publishing Co., 1978), 22.

15. New Options, P.O. Box 19324, Washington, D.C. 20036.

16. New Options newsletter promotional letter (n.d.).

17. Karen Hoyt et al., *New Age Rage* (Old Tappan, N.J.: Revell, 1987), 94.

18. Muller, *New Genesis*, 184.

19. Sri Chinmoy, "The United Nations—An Instrument of Unification," *Share International Magazine* 4, no. 3 (March 1985): 15–16.

20. Advertisement appearing in *Los Angeles Times*, 25 April 1982.

21. Cited in John Dart, "Spiritual Growth Evangelism: Path to World Peace?" *Los Angeles Times*, 17 June 1987, pt. 5, 1.

22. Douglas R. Groothuis, *Unmasking the New Age* (Downers Grove, Ill.: InterVarsity Press, 1986), 122.

23. Beth Ann Krier, "Self-Esteem: Task Force Gets Down to Grass Roots," *Los Angeles Times*, 18 September 1987, pt. 5, 1.

24. John Naisbitt, *Megatrends* (New York: Warner Books, 1982), 192–93.

25. Ferguson, *The Aquarian Conspiracy*, 213, 217, 35.

26. Marilyn Ferguson, interview with author, Los Angeles, Calif., 12 January 1988.

27. J. Gordon Melton, interview with author, Santa Barbara, Calif., 16 November 1987.

28. Carl A. Raschke, interview with author, Denver, Colo., 2 December 1987.

29. Ibid.

30. Robert Burrows, "The New Age Movement: Conspiracy or Chameleon?" *Evangelical Newsletter*, 11 May 1984, 4.

Chapter 22: Religion and Churches

1. Jeffrey A. Trachtenberg and Edward Giltenan, "Mainstream Metaphysics," *Forbes Magazine*, 1 June 1987, 156.

2. Ibid.

3. Carl A. Raschke, *Interruption of Eternity: Modern Gnosticism in the Origins of the New Religious Consciousness* (Chicago: Nelson-Hall, 1980), 175.

4. J. Gordon Melton, *Encyclopedic Handbook of Cults in America* (New York and London: Garland Publishing, 1986), 108.

5. Raschke, *Interruption of Eternity*, 178.

6. Cited in ibid., 197.

7. Carl A. Raschke, interview with author, Denver, Colo., 2 December 1987.

8. November 1987 news release, Institute of Metaphysics, Los Angeles, Calif.

9. Armando Acuna, "Cole-Whittaker Returns to Conduct 'Spiritual Tours,'" *Los Angeles Times* [San Diego ed.], 28 February 1986, pt. 2, 1.

10. Baha'i International Community, Office of Public Information, New York, 9 October 1987 news release.

11. William F. Schulz, interview with author, Pasadena, Calif., 14 February 1986.

12. Dialogue House/National Intensive Journal Workshop, Los Angeles, Calif., 15 May 1981.

13. Ira Progoff, telephone interview with author, 17 May 1981.

14. Bear Tribe Medicine Society Workshop, Medicine Wheel Gathering, Santa Monica Mountains, Calif., 31 October 1987.

15. Russell Chandler, "Oakland Priest May Be Next in Line for Vatican Censure," *Los Angeles Times*, 20 December 1986, pt. 8, 1.

16. Ibid.

17. Gerald G. Jampolsky, *Teach Only Love* (New York: Bantam Books, 1983), 25, 40.

18. Tara Singh, *How to Learn from a Course in Miracles* (Los Angeles: Life Action Press, 1988), 17.

19. Robert Skutch, *Journey with Distance: The Story behind a Course in Miracles* (Berkeley, Calif.: Celestial Arts, 1984), 54.

20. Dean Halverson, "A Matter of Course: Conversation with Kenneth Wapnick," *Spiritual Counterfeits Project Journal* 7, no. 1 (1987): 16.

21. Ibid., 11–17.

22. Dean Halverson, "A Course in Miracles: Seeing yourself as Sinless," *Spiritual Counterfeits Project Journal* 7, no. 1 (1987): 23.

Chapter 23: Positive Images

1. Beth Ann Krier, "Breakfast Club for New Age Thinkers," *Los Angeles Times*, 5 November 1987, pt. 5, 1.

2. Quoted in Martin Marty, "An Old New Age in Publishing (Editorial)," *Christian Century*, 18 November 1987, 1019.

3. Ibid.

4. Richard Spencer, interview with author, Arcadia, Calif., 20 November 1987.

5. Chris Majer, interview with author, Seattle, Wash., 21 December 1987.

6. J. Gordon Melton, *Encyclopedic Handbook of Cults in America* (New York and London: Garland Publishing, 1986), 107.

7. Otto Friedrich et al., "New Age Harmonies" (cover story), *TIME*, 7 December 1987, 72.

8. Isaac Asimov, "The Perennial Fringe," *Skeptical Inquirer* 10 (Spring 1986): 212.

9. Karen Hoyt, interview with author, Berkeley, Calif., 24 November 1987.

10. Dave Hunt and T. A. McMahon, *Seduction of Christianity: Spiritual Discernment in the Last Days* (Eugene, Oreg.: Harvest House Publishers, 1985), 221.

11. Ivan Illich, *Medical Nemesis* (New York: Pantheon Press, 1982), 3.

12. J. Ronald Engel, "Teaching the Eco-Justice Ethic: The Parable of the Billerica Dam," *Christian Century*, 13 May 1987, 466.

13. Blaise Pascal, *Pensees* 2.72.

14. Fritjof Capra, *Turning Point: Science, Society and the Rising Culture* (New York: Simon & Schuster, 1982), 31.

15. Ronald J. Sider, "Green Politics: Biblical or Buddhist?" *Spiritual Counterfeits Project Newsletter* 11, no. 3 (Fall 1985): 11.

16. Robert N. Bellah, interview with author, Berkeley, Calif., 25 November 1987.

17. Robert Ellwood, interview with author, Los Angeles, Calif., 14 December 1987.

18. J. Gordon Melton, interview with author, Los Angeles, Calif., 16 November 1987.

19. Carl F. H. Henry, interview with author, Monrovia, Calif., 2 November 1987.

Chapter 24: Conspiracy Theories

1. Conference on the Cults, El Toro, Calif., 18 November 1983.

2. Karen Hoyt et al., *New Age Rage* (Old Tappan, N.J.: Revell, 1987), 188.

3. Texe Marrs, *Dark Secrets of the New Age: Satan's Plan for a One World Religion* (Westchester, Ill.: Crossway Books/Good News Publishers, 1987), 262.

4. Elissa Lindsey McClain, *Rest from the Quest* (Shreveport, La.: Huntington House, 1984), preface.

5. Marilyn Ferguson, *The Aquarian Conspiracy, Personal and Social Transformation in the 1980s* (Los Angeles: J. P. Tarcher, 1980), 23.

6. Ibid., 63.

7. Constance Cumbey, *Hidden Dangers of the Rainbow* (Shreveport, La.: Huntington House, 1983), 115, 90.

8. Elliot Miller, "A Summary Critique," *Christian Research Journal* (Summer 1987): 26.

9. Cited in ibid., 28.

10. Advertisement for School of Esoteric Studies, *New Age Journal* (November–December 1987): 59; Alice Bailey, *Reappearance of the Christ* (New York: Lucis Publishing Co., 1969), 77, 111.

11. Dave Hunt and T. A. McMahon, *Seduction of Christianity: Spiritual Discernment in the Last Days* (Eugene, Oreg.: Harvest House Publishers, 1985), 12, 143.

12. H. Newton Malony, interview with author, Pasadena, Calif., 20 November 1987.

13. Otto Friedrich et al., "New Age Harmonies" (cover story), *TIME*, 7 December 1987, 72.

14. Douglas R. Groothuis, *Unmasking the New Age* (Downers Grove, Ill.: InterVarsity Press, 1986), 35.

15. Douglas R. Groothuis, interview with author, Seattle, Wash., 21 December 1987.

16. Robert Burrows, "Buzz Words and Worldview," *Spiritual Counterfeits Project Newsletter* (Winter 1984–85): 5.

17. Maurice Smith, "Understanding and Responding to the New Age Movements," Interfaith Witness Department, Home Mission Board, Southern Baptist Convention, 1985, 8.

18. Carl A. Raschke, interview with author, Denver, Colo., 2 December 1987.

19. Robert Ellwood, interview with author, Los Angeles, Calif., 14 December 1987.

Chapter 25: Fakes, Frauds, and Placebos

1. Cited by Martin Marty from *Theology Today* in "Taken out of Context," *Context Newsletter*, 1 October 1987.

2. Paul C. Reisser, M.D., "Holistic Health Update: The Movement Comes of (New) Age," *Spiritual Counterfeits Project Newsletter* 9, no. 4 (September–October 1983): 4.

3. 6 November 1987.

4. Theodore Roszak, *Making of a Counter Culture* (London: Faber and Faber, 1970), 215.

5. Marilyn Ferguson, *The Aquarian Conspiracy, Personal and Social Transformation in the 1980s* (Los Angeles: J. P. Tarcher, 1980), 262n.

6. Cited in Stephen H. Allison and Newton Malony, "Filipino Psychic Surgery: Myth, Magic, or Miracle," *Journal of Religion and Health* 20 (Spring 1981): 57.

7. Bela Scheiber, "Psychic Surgery Comes to Denver," *Rocky Mountain Skeptic* 4, no. 3 (September–October 1986): 1, 3.

8. Peter Glick, "Crosstalk: Stars in Our Eyes," *Psychology Today* (August 1987): 7.

9. Reuter's News Service, 5 May 1988.

10. Cited by Associated Press, 3 May 1988.

11. Quoted in ibid.

12. Ibid.

13. Karl Sabbagh, "The Psychopathology of Fringe Medicine," *Skeptical Inquirer* 10 (Winter 1985–86): 162.

14. Patricia-Rochelle Diegel, conversation with author, San Francisco, Calif., 6 November 1987.

15. Danny Korem and Paul Meier, *Fakers: Exploding the Myths of the Supernatural* (Grand Rapids: Revell/Baker Book House, 1980), 22–29.

16. Quoted in Ben Fong-Torres, "A Cynic in the Midst of the Believers," *San Francisco Chronicle*, 28 April 1988.

17. Robert Gillette, "Exotic Ways to Learn Doubted by U.S. Study," *Los Angeles Times*, 4 December 1987, pt. 1, 1.

18. Ibid.

19. Irving Hexham, "Yoga, UFOs, and Cult Membership," *Update: A Quarterly Journal of New Religious Movements* 10, no. 3 (September 1986): 14.

20. Cited in Robert Burrows, "Corporate Management Cautioned on New Age," *Eternity Magazine* (February 1988): 33.

21. Timothy Philibosian, interview with author, Denver, Colo., 1 December 1987.

22. Isaac Asimov, "The Perennial Fringe," *Skeptical Inquirer* 10 (Spring 1986): 213.

23. Daniel Davis, interview with author, Denver, Colo., 1 December 1987.

24. Karen Hoyt, interview with author, Berkeley, Calif., 24 November 1987.

25. Al Seckel, telephone interview with author, 10 November 1987.

26. Robert Gordis, "The Book of Job," *Thesis Theological Cassettes* (audiotape) 15, no. 7 (December 1984).

Chapter 26: Unproven Hypotheses and Non Sequiturs

1. Fritjof Capra, *Tao of Physics* (Berkeley, Calif.: Shambhala, 1975), 57.

2. Michael Wiebe, "Science and the New Age," *Rivendell Times*, 1 September 1987.

3. Mark Albrecht and Brooks Alexander, "The Sellout of Science," *Spiritual Counterfeits Project Journal* (August 1978): 26.

4. Wiebe, "Science and the New Age."

5. Capra, *Tao of Physics*, 11.

6. Albrecht and Alexander, "The Sellout of Science," 26.

7. Cited in Marilyn Ferguson, *The Aquarian Conspiracy, Personal and Social Transformation in the 1980s* (Los Angeles: J. P. Tarcher, 1980), 171.

8. Wiebe, "Science and the New Age."

9. Tim Stafford, "Cease-fire in the Laboratory," *Christianity Today*, 3 April 1987, 19.

10. Regina Sara Ryan and John W. Travis, *Wellness Workbook* (Berkeley, Calif.: Ten Speed Press, 1981), 209–10.

11. Quoted in Robert G. Cowen, "Debunking, Again, the Belief in ESP and the Occult," *Christian Science Monitor*, 7 July 1987.

12. Ferguson, *The Aquarian Conspiracy*, 163.

13. Ibid., 164–65.

14. M. Scott Peck, *Road Less Traveled: A New Psychology of Love, Traditional Values and Spiritual Growth* (New York: Simon & Schuster, 1978), 263–67.

15. Ferguson, *The Aquarian Conspiracy*, 169.

16. Ibid., 156.

17. Ryan and Travis, *Wellness Workbook*, 150.

18. Maureen O'Hara, "Of Myths and Monkeys: A Critical Look at Critical Mass," *Nexus* (Fall 1986): 4; reprinted from *The Whole Earth Review* (Fall 1986).

19. Karen Hoyt et al., *New Age Rage* (Old Tappan, N.J.: Revell, 1987), 35.

Chapter 27: Cautions and Dangers

1. Jeremy P. Tarcher, "New Age as Perennial Philosophy," *Los Angeles Times Book Review*, 7 February 1988, 15.

2. Regina Sara Ryan and John W. Travis, *Wellness Workbook* (Berkeley, Calif.: Ten Speed Press, 1981), 69.

3. Ibid., 211–12.

4. Gregg Piburn, telephone interview with author, 12 March 1988.

5. Ron Zemke, "What's New in the New Age?" (cover story), *Training Magazine* (September 1987): 30.

6. Richard L. Watring, "New Age Training in Business: Mind Control in Upper Management?" *Eternity Magazine* (February 1988): 32.

7. Cited in Elliot Miller, "Tracking the Aquarian Conspiracy," *Forward* (Fall 1986): 27.

8. Robert Gillette, "Exotic Ways to Learn Doubted by U.S. Study," *Los Angeles Times*, 4 December 1987, pt. 1, 1.

9. Dave Hunt and T. A. McMahon, *Seduction of Christianity: Spiritual Discernment in the Last Days* (Eugene, Oreg.: Harvest House Publishers, 1985), 173.

10. "Under Fire: Two Christian Leaders Respond to Accusations of New Age Mysticism," *Christianity Today*, 18 September 1987, 17.

11. Hunt and McMahon, *Seduction of Christianity*, 148.

12. Irving Hexham, "Yoga, UFOs, and Cult Membership," *Update: A quarterly journal of New Religious Movements* 10, no. 3 (September 1986): 6.

13. Marilyn Ferguson, *The Aquarian Conspiracy, Personal and Social Transformation in the 1980s* (Los Angeles: J. P. Tarcher, 1980), 89.

14. Judith Hooper, "A User's Manual to the Brain, Mind and Spirit," *OMNI WholeMind Newsletter* (October 1987): 125, 132.

15. Stanley Dokupil, "Dungeons and Dragons: Fantasy Role-Playing and the Occult," Spiritual Counterfeits Project, 1928, 4.

16. See Peter Leithard and George Grant, *A Christian Response to Dungeons & Dragons* (Fort Worth, Tex.: Dominion Press, 1987).

17. Cited in Hilary Abramson, "Altered States," *Sacramento Bee Magazine*, 25 October 1987.

18. Quoted in ibid.

19. M. Scott Peck, *Road Less Traveled: A New Psychology of Love, Traditional Values and Spiritual Growth* (New York: Simon & Schuster, 1978), 283.

20. "The Scribe," *A Course in Miracles*, 3 vols. (Tiburon, Calif.: Foundation for Inner Peace, 1976), 1:81.

Chapter 28: Reincarnation or Resurrection?

1. Princeton Religion Research Center Fact Sheet, vol. 4, no. 7, 1982.

2. Statistics provided by the Roper Center, University of Connecticut, Storrs, Conn., 15 February 1988.

3. F. LaGard Smith, *Out on a Broken Limb* (Eugene, Oreg.: Harvest House Publishers, 1986), 14.

4. Cited in Ray Nelson, "New Age, Old Lie," *Passport Magazine* (October–November 1987): 4.

5. Mark C. Albrecht, *Reincarnation: A Christian Critique of New Age Doctrine* (Downers Grove, Ill.: InterVarsity Press, 1982), 31–32.

6. See Norman L. Geisler and J. Yutaka Amano, *Reincarnation Sensation* (Wheaton, Ill.: Tyndale House Publishers, 1986).

7. Helena Petrovna Blavatsky, *Secret Doctrines*, 2 vols. (1888; reprint, Pasadena, Calif.: Theosophical University Press, 1977), 2:420.

8. John Snyder, *Reincarnation vs. Resurrection* (Chicago: Moody Press, 1984), 73.

9. Colin Wilson, *Afterlife: An Investigation of the Evidence for Life after Death* (Garden City, N.Y.: Dolphin/Doubleday & Co., 1987), 198–202.

10. Lanny Steven Buettner, "Ethics in Contemporary Psychic Experience: A Descriptive Analysis," M.A. thesis, University of Southern California, 1984, 19.

11. Ibid., 20.

12. Trance Medium Workshop, San Francisco, Calif., 6 November 1987.

13. Albrecht, *Reincarnation*, 96.

14. Cited in Dave Hunt and T. A. McMahon, *Seduction of Christianity: Spiritual Discernment in the Last Days* (Eugene, Oreg.: Harvest House Publishers, 1985), 43.

15. Wilson, *Afterlife*, 214–15.

16. Snyder, *Reincarnation vs. Resurrection*, 75.

17. Albrecht, *Reincarnation*, 36–41.

18. Ibid., 36, 40.

19. James W. Sire, *Scripture Twisting* (Downers Grove, Ill.: InterVarsity Press, 1980), 92.

20. Gordon Lewis, interview with author, Denver, Colo., 1 December 1987.

21. Joseph P. Gudel, Robert M. Bowman, Jr., and Dan R. Schlesinger, "Reincarnation—Did the Church Suppress It?" *Christian Research Journal* (Summer 1987): 12.

22. Origen, *De Principiis* ("On First Principles") 3.5; cited in ibid.

23. Snyder, *Reincarnation vs. Resurrection*, 76.

Chapter 29: Satan and the Problem of Evil

1. Russell Chandler, "Exorcism Issue Putting Satan in the Spotlight," *Los Angeles Times*, 19 January 1974, pt. 1, 1.

2. Cited in George A. Mather and Larry Nichols, "Doorways to the Demonic," *Lutheran Witness Magazine* (October 1987): 3.

3. Robert S. Ellwood and Harry B. Partin, *Religious and Spiritual Groups in Modern America* (Englewood Cliffs, N.J.: Prentice Hall, 1988), 176.

4. Marilyn Ferguson, interview with author, Los Angeles, Calif., 12 January 1987.

5. See Mary Baker Eddy, *Science and Health with Key to the Scriptures*, authorized ed. (1875); (Boston: First Church of Christ, Scientist, 1971), 496–97.

6. Karen Hoyt et al., *New Age Rage* (Old Tappan, N.J.: Revell, 1987), 234.

7. Quoted in Debbie Alexander, "The New Medicine: A New Phase in Cultural Transformation," *Spiritual Counterfeits Project Report* (1975, rev. 1984), 4.

8. Cited in Lanny Steven Buettner, "Ethics in Contemporary Psychic Experience: A Descriptive Analysis," M.A. thesis, University of Southern California, 1984, 65–67.

9. Ibid.

10. Carl A. Raschke, *Interruption of Eternity: Modern Gnosticism in the Origins of the New Religious Consciousness* (Chicago: Nelson-Hall, 1980), 147.

11. Buettner, "Ethics in Contemporary Psychic Experience," 95.

12. Ferguson, interview with author, Los Angeles, Calif., 12 January 1987.

13. Ken Wilber, *Up from Eden* (Garden City, N.Y.: Anchor Press/Doubleday, 1981), 297.

14. Ibid., 298.

15. Ibid., 1.

16. Hoyt et al., *New Age Rage*, 234.

17. Brooks Alexander, "The Disappearance of the Devil," *Spiritual Counterfeits Project Newsletter* (July–August 1984): 6.

18. Robert Gordis, "The Book of Job," *Thesis Theological Cassettes* (audiotape) 15, no. 7 (December 1984).

19. Ibid.

20. Denis de Rougemont, *Devil's Snare* (New York: Meridian Books, 1956), 20–21.

21. C. S. Lewis, *Screwtape Letters* (New York: Macmillan, 1961), preface.

Chapter 30: Absolute Relativity

1. John Paul II, 18 September 1987, San Francisco, Calif.; text of address provided by the Vatican via the U.S. Catholic Conference, Washington, D.C.

2. Quoted in George W. Cornell, "Paganism Seen Ruin of Western Civilization," *Los Angeles Times*, 11 July 1987, pt. 2, 6.

3. Quoted in George W. Cornell, "U.S. Is Undergoing 'Spiritual Malaise,' Pollster Finds," *Los Angeles Times*, 18 July 1987.

4. Ezra Bowen, "Ethics: Looking to Its Roots," *TIME*, 25 May 1987, 26.

5. Michael Gelven, "Book World Review: Why Johnny Can't Think," *World & I* (July 1987): 410.

6. Allan Bloom, *Closing of the American Mind* (New York: Simon & Schuster, 1987), 25–26.

7. Ibid., 38, 40, 34.

8. Bowen, "Ethics," 26.

9. Quoted in Carl F. H. Henry, "Uneasy Conscience Revisited" (speech), 3 November 1987, fortieth anniversary of Fuller Theological Seminary, Pasadena, Calif., 9.

10. Evangelical Press News Service, 28 August 1987 (reprinted from *Christianity Today*, by permission of Prison Fellowship).

11. Bloom, *Closing of the American Mind*, 32.

12. Gelven, "Why Johnny Can't Think," 415.

13. Carl F. H. Henry, interview with author, Monrovia, Calif., 2 November 1987.

14. Charles Colson, with Ellen Santilli Vaughn, *Kingdoms in Conflict* (New York: William Morrow; Grand Rapids: Zondervan Publishing House, 1987), 212.

15. Quoted in ibid., 185.

16. Gelven, "Why Johnny Can't Think," 417.

17. Henry, "Uneasy Conscience Revisited," 20.

18. Margot Adler, "A Modern Pagan Spiritual View," *World* (September–October 1987): 10.

19. Quoted in Cornell, "Paganism Seen Ruin of Western Civilization."

20. Douglas R. Groothuis, interview with author, Seattle, Wash., 21 December 1987.

21. Colson, *Kingdoms in Conflict*, 231.

22. F. LaGard Smith, *Out on a Broken Limb* (Eugene, Oreg.: Harvest House Publishers, 1986), 34.

23. David Spangler, *Relationship & Identity* (Forres, Scotland: Findhorn Publications, 1978), 89, 91, 93.

24. Douglas R. Groothuis, *Unmasking the New Age* (Downers Grove, Ill.: InterVarsity Press, 1986), 126.

25. John F. DeVries, "Spiritual Danger in Holistic Medicine," *India Journal* (September 1984): 7.

26. Kevin Kelly, "Deep Ecology as Religion," *Utne Reader* (October–November 1985): 69; excerpted from *Whole Earth Review* (May 1985).

27. Cited in Smith, *Out on a Broken Limb*, 191.

28. Segment from "20/20" presented at Trinity United Presbyterian Church, Santa Ana, Calif., 25 October 1987.

29. See R. C. Zaehner, *Our Savage God: The Perverse Use of Eastern Thought* (New York: Sheed and Ward, 1974), 69–71.

30. James S. Gordon, *Golden Guru: The Strange Journey of Bhagwan Shree Rajneesh* (Lexington, Mass.: Stephen Greene Press, 1987), 245.

31. Marilyn Ferguson, *The Aquarian Conspiracy, Personal and Social Transformation in the 1980s* (Los Angeles: J. P. Tarcher, 1980), 397, 398n.

32. Regina Sara Ryan and John W. Travis, *Wellness Workbook* (Berkeley, Calif.: Ten Speed Press, 1981), 192.

33. Henry, "Uneasy Conscience Revisited," 15.

34. David Spangler, *Emergence: Rebirth of the Sacred* (Forres, Scotland: Findhorn Publications, n.d.), 144; cited in *Passport Magazine* (October–November 1987): 6.

35. George Craig McMillan, "Laya Yoga and Enlightenment," *Life Times* vol. 1, no. 3, 43.

36. Colson, *Kingdoms in Conflict*, 183.

37. Steve Berta, "Getting in Touch with the 'All-knowing Self,'" *Montecito Life*, 12 November 1987, 17.

38. Gordon R. Lewis and Bruce A. Demarest, *Integrative Theology* (Grand Rapids: Zondervan, 1987), 1:204.

39. Emil Brunner, *The Christian Doctrine of God* (Philadelphia: Westminster Press, 1950), 269.

40. Ferguson, *The Aquarian Conspiracy*, 316.

41. Jeannette DeWyze, "An Encounter with Bill Coulson," *Reader* [San Diego], 20 August 1987.

42. Ibid.

43. Ibid.

44. Gelven, "Why Johnny Can't Think," 412.

45. Elliot Miller, "The New Myth," *Forward* (Winter 1986): 11.

Chapter 31: Beyond the Self

1. J. D. Douglas, ed., *New Bible Dictionary* (London: InterVarsity Fellowship, 1967), 116–17.

2. William H. Willimon, "Community & Computers: Babel, Bytes & Bits" (editorial), *Christian Century*, 9–16 September 1987, 741.

3. Richard John Neuhaus, *Naked Public Square* (Grand Rapids: Eerdmans, 1984), 153.

4. Charles Colson, with Ellen Santilli Vaughn, *Kingdoms in Conflict* (New York: William Morrow; Grand Rapids: Zondervan Publishing House, 1987), 78.

5. John Stott, lecture given at All Saints by the Sea Episcopal Church, Santa Barbara, Calif., 14 November 1987.

6. Sri Chinmoy, "The United Nations—An Instrument of Unification," *Share International Magazine* 4, no. 3 (March 1985): 16.

7. M. Scott Peck, *Road Less Traveled: A New Psychology of Love, Traditional Values and Spiritual Growth* (New York: Simon & Schuster, 1978), 281, 283.

8. Marilyn Ferguson, *The Aquarian Conspiracy, Personal and Social Transformation in the 1980s* (Los Angeles: J. P. Tarcher, 1980), 382.

9. Ibid., 378–79.

10. Marilyn Ferguson and Ray Gottlieb, "New Common Sense: Secrets of the Visionary Life" (manuscript draft), 80–81.

11. Quoted in Russell Chandler, "An Ascetic Way to Transcend the Tangible," review of Deng Ming Dao, *The Wandering Taoist* (San Francisco: Harper & Row, 1983), *Los Angeles Times Book Review*, 24 July 1983.

12. Brooks Alexander, "A Generation of Wizards: Shamanism & Contemporary Culture," *Spiritual Counterfeits Project Special Collection Journal* 6, no. 1 (Winter 1984): 18.

13. Robert S. Ellwood and Harry B. Partin, *Religious and Spiritual Groups in Modern America* (Englewood Cliffs, N.J.: Prentice Hall, 1988), 31.

14. Carl A. Raschke, *Interruption of Eternity: Modern Gnosticism in the Origins of the New Religious Consciousness* (Chicago: Nelson-Hall, 1980), 238.

15. Ibid., 238–39.

16. J. Gordon Melton, "Toward a Christian Response to the New Age Movement," 1985, 1.

17. James W. Sire, *Scripture Twisting* (Downers Grove, Ill.: InterVarsity Press, 1980), 29–30.

18. Carl F. H. Henry, interview with author, Monrovia, Calif., 2 November 1987.

19. Mark C. Albrecht, *Reincarnation: A Christian Critique of New Age Doctrine* (Downers Grove, Ill.: InterVarsity Press, 1982), 89.

20. F. LaGard Smith, *Out on a Broken Limb* (Eugene, Oreg.: Harvest House Publishers, 1986), 177.

21. Karen Hoyt et al., *New Age Rage* (Old Tappan, N.J.: Revell, 1987), 42.

22. Alexander, "A Generation of Wizards," 19.

23. Douglas R. Groothuis, *Unmasking the New Age* (Downers Grove, Ill.: InterVarsity Press, 1986), 167.

24. Alice Lawhead and Stephen Lawhead, *Pilgrim's Guide to the New Age* (Batavia, Ill.: Lion Publishing Corp., 1986), 33.

25. Hoyt et al., *New Age Rage*, 214.

26. Gordon R. Lewis and Bruce A. Demarest, *Integrative Theology* (Grand Rapids: Zondervan, 1987), 1:203.

27. Ibid., 1:209.

28. Hoyt et al., *New Age Rage*, 88.

29. Mark Albrecht and Brooks Alexander, "The Sellout of Science," *Spiritual Counterfeits Project Journal* (August 1978): 28.

30. John Stott, lecture given at All Saints by the Sea Episcopal Church, Santa Barbara, Calif., 14 November 1987.

31. Chuck Colson, Christian Booksellers' Association Convention, Anaheim, Calif., 12 July 1987; idem, El Montecito Presbyterian Church, Santa Barbara, Calif., 18 October 1987.

32. Blaise Pascal, *Pensees* 7.430.

33. Groothuis, *Unmasking the New Age*, 87.

34. John Stott, lecture given at All Saints by the Sea Episcopal Church, Santa Barbara, Calif., 14 November 1987.

35. Ibid.

Chapter 32: The Broad Way and the Narrow Way

1. Carl Michalson, *Faith for Personal Crises* (New York: Scribner's, 1958), 67.

2. Quoted in ibid., 70.

3. Peter L. Berger, *A Rumor of Angels* (Garden City, N.Y.: Doubleday & Co., 1969), 120, 26.

4. Halverson, Dean. "A Matter of Course: Conversation with Kenneth Wapnick," *Spiritual Counterfeits Project Journal* 7, no. 1 (1987): 16–17.

5. Irving Hexham and Karla Poewe, *Understanding Cults and New Religions* (Grand Rapids: Eerdmans, 1986), 85–86.

6. Chris Majer, interview with author, Seattle, Wash., 21 December 1987.

7. Douglas R. Groothuis, *Unmasking the New Age* (Downers Grove, Ill.: InterVarsity Press, 1986), 90.

8. Karen Hoyt et al., *New Age Rage* (Old Tappan, N.J.: Revell, 1987), 252.

9. Elliot Miller, "Sufis, the Mystical Muslims," *Forward* (Spring–Summer 1986): 22.

10. John Stott, lecture given at All Saints by the Sea Episcopal Church, Santa Barbara, Calif., 14 November 1987.

11. Hexham and Poewe, *Understanding Cults and New Religions*, 87.

12. "Out on a Limb," ABC miniseries, 18–19 January 1987.

13. Craig V. Anderson, "Pruning Time for Shirley MacLaine?" *Christian Century*, 15 February 1987, 182.

14. Hexham and Poewe, *Understanding Cults and New Religions*, 86.

15. Lev. 19:26, 31; 20:6; Deut. 18:9–13; 1 Sam. 28; 1 Chron. 10:13–14; Isa. 8:19–22; 19:3–4; 47:9–14; Jer. 29:8–9; Matt. 7:22–

23; Acts 13:6–12; 16:16–18; Gal. 5:19–21; Rev. 9:21; 18:23; 21:8; 22:15.

16. Flavius Josephus, *Life and Times of Flavius Josephus; The Learned and Authentic Jewish Historian and Celebrated Warrior*, trans. William Whiston (Philadelphia: John C. Winston Col, 1957), 535.

17. Mark C. Albrecht, *Reincarnation: A Christian Critique of New Age Doctrine* (Downers Grove, Ill.: InterVarsity Press, 1982), 70.

18. John Snyder, *Reincarnation vs. Resurrection* (Chicago: Moody Press, 1984), 71; see also F. F. Bruce, *New Testament Documents: Are They Reliable?* (Grand Rapids: Eerdmans, 1968), 16ff., cited in this text.

19. Quoted in *Context Newsletter*, 1 April 1987, 3.

20. I. Howard Marshall, *Biblical Inspiration* (Grand Rapids: Eerdmans, 1983), 119–20.

Chapter 33: The Man for All Ages

1. Matt. 8:23–27; Mark 4:35–41; Luke 8:22–25.

2. James W. Sire, *Scripture Twisting* (Downers Grove, Ill.: InterVarsity Press, 1980), 24.

3. Douglas R. Groothuis, *The New Age Movement* (Downers Grove, Ill.: InterVarsity Press, (1986), 22.

4. J. Gordon Melton, "Toward a Christian Response to the New Age Movement," 1985, 2–3.

5. John Snyder, *Reincarnation vs. Resurrection* (Chicago: Moody Press, 1984), 67.

6. Ray Bradbury, in a telephone conversation with author, 18 August 1988, said that he could not immediately determine the source of this quote but that he believed it was probably from an article he wrote for *Life* magazine in the early 1960s.

7. Otto Friedrich et al., "New Age Harmonies" (cover story), *Time*, 7 December 1987, 72.

8. Carl F. H. Henry, "Uneasy Conscience Revisited" (speech), 3 November 1987, fortieth anniversary of Fuller Theological Seminary, Pasadena, Calif., 21.

9. Melton, "Toward A Christian Response to the New Age Movement," 2.

10. Ronald Goetz, "Cosmic Groanings," *Christian Century*, 2 December 1987, 1086–87.

11. Matt. 27:51; Mark 15:38; Luke 23:46.

12. Snyder, *Reincarnation vs. Resurrection*, 67.

13. Brooke Foss Westcott, *Gospel of the Resurrection* (New York: Macmillan, 1902), 97.

14. Alice Lawhead and Stephen Lawhead, *Pilgrim's Guide to the New Age* (Batavia, Ill.: Lion Publishing Corp., 1986), 198, 105.

15. John Stott, lecture given at All Saints by the Sea Episcopal Church, Santa Barbara, Calif., 14 November 1987.

16. Charles Colson, with Ellen Santilli Vaughn, *Kingdoms in Conflict* (New York: William Morrow; Grand Rapids: Zondervan Publishing House, 1987), 84–85.

Glossary

Words set in SMALL CAPS are defined elsewhere in the Glossary.

ACUPUNCTURE. Holistic health technique defining disease as an imbalance in "energy flow"; seeks to restore and redirect the flow and balance by inserting needles at key points on the body. Acupuncture, acupressure, and allied therapies are derived from ancient Chinese medicine and philosophy. (See also HOLISTIC.)

AKASHIC RECORDS. Assumed vast reservoir of omniscient knowledge. Some New Agers believe the events of all human lives have been recorded in the "Universal Mind," or "Memory of Nature," in a region in space known as "the ether."

ALCHEMY. Often associated with medieval folklore, this is a chemical science and speculative philosophy designed to transform base metals into gold. Figuratively used regarding the change of base human nature into the divine.

ALTERED STATES. States other than normal waking consciousness, such as daydreaming, sleep-dreaming, hypnotic TRANCE; meditative, mystical, or drug-induced states. Also includes unconscious states.

ASCENDED MASTER. A "highly evolved" individual no longer required to undergo lifetimes on the physical plane in order to achieve spiritual growth.

ASTRAL. Nonphysical level characterized primarily by emotion. Said to be the place where most humans go after they die and where they exist between earthly incarnations. An astral projection, or Out-of-Body Experience (OBE), is an experience where one seems to be in a place separate from one's physical body while fully and normally conscious. The experience, which may be hallucinatory

337

in nature, can be spontaneous or induced. The astral and physical bodies generally remain connected by a distended "cord" during the projection.

ASTROLOGY. Art or pseudoscience of deciphering the influence that cosmic forces radiating from celestial bodies supposedly have on any part of the universe, particularly humans. Astrology originated at least 5000 years ago, probably in Babylon. It is based on the erroneous belief that the Earth is the center of the universe and is circled by the ZODIAC.

AURA. An apparent envelope or field of colored radiation said to surround the human body and other animate objects, with the color or colors indicating different aspects of the person's physical, psychological, and spiritual condition. (See also KIRILIAN.)

BHAGAVAD GITA. Sanskrit poem relating a dialogue between Lord Krishna and Arjuna consisting of 700 2-line stanzas in 18 chapters; part of Krishna's revelation called an UPANISHAD, which is a succinct summary of dominant themes in Hindu theology.

BIOFEEDBACK. Technique using instruments to self-monitor normally unconscious, involuntary body processes such as brain waves, heartbeat, and muscle tension. As this information is fed back to the person, he or she can then consciously and voluntarily control internal biological functions.

CHANNELING. Process of receiving information from some level of reality other than the ordinary physical one and from beyond the "self" as it is generally understood. A "channeler," or medium, usually goes into a TRANCE to establish contact with a spirit, ASCENDED MASTER, higher consciousness, or some other entity, and then receives and repeats messages from "the other side" of the physical world.

CHAKRAS. The seven energy points on the human body, according to New Agers and YOGI(s) "Raising" the KUNDALINI up through the chakras is the aim of YOGA meditation. Enlightenment (SAMADHI) is achieved when kundalini reaches the "crown chakra" at the top of the head.

CLAIRAUDIENCE. Extrasensory data perceived as sound; generally considered a facet of CLAIRVOYANCE.

CLAIRVOYANCE. Mental "seeing" of physical objects or events at a distance by PSYCHIC means. Distinguished from TELEPATHY, which involves ESP.

CONSCIOUSNESS. Mental awareness or present "knowing." New Agers usually refer to consciousness as the awareness or perception of one's "inner self," or of inward awareness of external objects or facts.

CULT. A religious organization founded by and built upon the teachings of a central charismatic figure whose authority is viewed as being equal to or greater than the established scriptures of the major religions. In Christian understanding, the teachings of a cult oppose or differ from historic biblical theology.

DHARMA. Law, truth, or teaching; used to express the central teachings of Hindu and Buddhist religion. Dharma implies that essential truth can be stated about the way things are, and that people should comply with that norm.

DIVINATION. Methods of discovering the personal, human significance of present or future events. Means to obtain insights may include dreams, hunches, involuntary body actions, mediumistic possession, consulting the dead, observing the behavior of animals and birds, tossing coins, casting lots, and "reading" natural phenomena.

ENTROPY. Degradation of the matter and energy in the universe to an ultimate state of inert uniformity. (See also SYNTROPY, entropy's opposite.)

ESP. Extrasensory perception; the experience of, or response to, an external event, object, state, or influence without apparent contact through the known sense. ESP may occur without those involved being aware of it.

GNOSTICISM. Refers to the secret doctrines and practices of MYSTICISM whereby a person may come to enlightenment or realization that he or she is of the same essence as God or the Absolute. The Greek word *gnosis* means knowledge, and at the heart of Gnostic thought is the idea that revelation of the hidden gnosis frees one from the fragmentary and illusory material world and teaches him or her about the origins of the spiritual world, to which the gnostic belongs by nature.

GURU. Spiritual teacher who instructs disciples in the "way" of enlightenment. The guru's authority is to be implicitly accepted.

HIGHER SELF. The most "spiritual" and "knowing" part of oneself, said to lie beyond the ego, the day-to-day personality, and the personal unconscious. The Higher Self can be channeled for wisdom and guidance. Variations include the Oversoul, the Superconsciousness, the Atman, the Christ (or Krishna or Buddha) Consciousness, and the God Within.

HOLISTIC. Alternatively, but less frequently, spelled "wholistic"; derived from the Greek *holos*, meaning "whole" in the sense of "entire" or "unified." Holistic health practices emphasize the whole person, the impact of the environment, and the interdependence of all parts of the body, mind, and spirit in the prevention and treatment of ailments.

HYPNOSIS. State resembling deep sleep or TRANCE, but more active in that the person has some will and feeling but acts according to suggestions presented; a heightened sense of suggestibility to the imagination.

HUMANISM. System of philosophy that upholds the primacy of human beings rather than God or any abstract or META-PHYSICAL system. Humanism holds that man is the measure of all things.

I CHING. Chinese book of DIVINATION associated with TAOISM; the ancient system of telling fortunes by throwing sticks into six-sided figures.

INTUITION. Ability of knowing, or the knowledge obtained, without conscious recourse to inference or reasoning.

KABALA. System of Jewish OCCULT MYSTICISM developed by certain rabbis, especially during the Middle Ages, relying heavily on mathematical interpretation of Scripture; also spelled "Cabala."

KARMA. Hindu term for the "law" of justice, or cause and effect, requiring that the accumulated effect of one's actions in this life determine the type of existence the soul will have in the next life; you reap what you sow. (See also REINCARNATION.)

KIRILIAN. A type of high-voltage photography that uses a pulsed, high-frequency electrical field and two electrodes, between which are placed the object to be photographed and an unexposed film plate. The image captured is purported to be an AURA of energy that emanates from plants, animals, and humans and changes in accordance with physiological or emotional shifts.

KINESIOLOGY. Study of the principles of mechanics and anatomy in relation to human movement.

KUNDALINI. Psycho-spiritual power thought by YOGI(S) to lie dormant at the base of the spine. Believed to be a goddess, kundalini is referred to as "the serpent power."

MANTRA. A "holy" word, phrase, or verse in Hindu or Buddhist meditation techniques. A mantra is usually provided to an initiate by a GURU who is supposed to hold specific insights regarding the needs of his pupils. The vibrations of the mantra are said to lead the meditator into union with the divine source within.

METAPHYSICS. System of principles relating to the transcendent or supernatural.

MONISM. Literally means "one." In a spiritual framework, it refers to the classical OCCULT philosophy that "All Is One"; all reality may be reduced to a single, unifying principle partaking of the same essence and reality. Monism also relates to the belief in PANTHEISM that there is no ultimate distinction between the Creator and the creation.

MYSTICISM. Belief that God is totally different than anything the human mind can think and must be approached by a mind without content. Spiritual union or direct communion with Ultimate Reality can be obtained through subjective experience such as INTUITION or a unifying vision.

NATURALISM. View that asserts that nothing beyond nature is real. Human beings are therefore to be understood strictly in terms of heredity and environment.

NEOPAGAN. Follower of some Western religious tradition other than Judaism or Christianity. Neopagan groups have a close affinity for nature, OCCULT, and initiatory traditions, and may be patrons of ancient Greek or Egyptian religions, Druidism, WITCHCRAFT, ceremonial MAGIC, or even satanism.

NIRVANA. Literally, a "blowing out" or a "cooling" of the fires of existence; the main word used in Buddhism for final release from the cycle of birth and death into bliss.

NUMEROLOGY. Study of the OCCULT, or secret, significance of numbers, especially in regard to DIVINATION.

OCCULT. Often spoken of as "the occult"; that which is not easily understood, revealed, or apprehended. Matters regarded as involving the action or influence of supernatural agencies or some secret knowledge of them.

PANTHEISM. Belief that God and the world are ultimately identical; "All is God." Everything that exists constitutes a unity, and this all-inclusive unity is divine. God is the forces and laws of the universe but is not a Being with personality.

PARANORMAL. Faculties and phenomena in psychical research that are beyond the "normal" in terms of cause and effect as presently understood.

PSI. The twenty-third letter of the Greek alphabet; a general Christian term for ESP, PSYCHOKINESIS, TELEPATHY, CLAIRVOYANCE, CLAIRAUDIENCE, precognition, and other PARANORMAL phenomena that are nonphysical in nature.

PSYCHIC. A medium, "sensitive," or channeler. Also means PARANORMAL events that can't be explained by established physical principles.

PSYCHOKINESIS. Power of the mind to influence matter or move objects. Popularly known as PK. (See also TELEKINESIS.)

REINCARNATION. Belief that the soul moves from one bodily existence to another until, usually following many particular existences, it is released from historical existence and absorbed into the Absolute. (See also KARMA.)

SAMADHI. Ultimate or highest state of God-consciousness or enlightenment in classical Hindu YOGA. SATORI is the equivalent in Zen Buddhism: a state of existential intuitive enlightenment.

SORCERY. Assumed power to manipulate and alter natural and supernatural events or states with proper knowledge of MAGIC and performance of ritual; typically understood as being available for good or evil use. (See also WITCHCRAFT.)

SYNCRETISM. Fusion of different forms of belief or practice; the claim that all religions are one and share the same core teachings.

SYNCHRONICITY. Meaningful coincidences interpreted as having some higher, connecting purpose that could be accounted for by PSI phenomena.

SYNERGY. Quality of "whole making"; the New Age belief in the cooperation of natural systems to put things together in ever more meaningful patterns.

SYNTROPY. Belief that living matter has an inherent drive to perfect itself in increasingly complex patterns of association, communication, cooperation, and awareness. The opposite of ENTROPY.

TANTRA. Series of Hindu and Buddhist scriptures concerned with special yogic practices for swift attainment of enlightenment; also, the practices, techniques, and traditions of these teachings.

TAO. Pronounced "dow"; a Chinese concept of the Way, which is both a path of conduct and the principle governing the operations of the entire universe.

TAROT. Deck of picture cards used for DIVINATION or fortune-telling. Developed in its present form in the last century, it now includes twenty-two characters, among them the magician, death, the pope, the popess, the Devil, and the fool, who represents any human on the path of life—which is seen as all foolishness. Similar to the I CHING.

TELEKINESIS. Form of PSYCHOKINESIS, or PK; the apparent movement of stationary objects without the use of any known physical force.

TELEPATHY. Silent transfer of thoughts from one mind to another; ESP of another person's mental state or thoughts.

THEISM. Belief in one Personal Creator who is independent from, and sovereign over, his creation.

TRANCE. An ALTERED STATE of CONSCIOUSNESS, induced or spontaneous, that gives access to many ordinarily inhibited capacities of the mind-body system. Trance states are generally self-induced.

UPANISHADS. Philosophical literature by Indo-Aryans regarding the nature of ultimate truth and reality. The final section of the VEDAS.

VEDAS. The oldest Hindu scriptures, including a collection of hymns, prose texts on sacrificial rites and ceremonies, advice for the elderly retired, and the MONISTIC philosophical speculations of the UPANISHADS. The main ideas are called Vedanta Hinduism.

WITCHCRAFT. Believed to be possessed as an inherited mystical power, traditionally used by witches for evil ends. Wicca (Old English for "male magician") groups practice ritual MAGIC and/or nature-oriented NEOPAGAN(ism). Contemporary witchcraft was founded by Gerald B. Gardner (1884–1964), a British civil servant and amateur archaeologist.

WORLDVIEW. A common consensus about the nature of reality; a set of presuppositions or premises held consciously or unconsciously about the makeup of the cosmos.

YOGA. Literally, "yoking" or "joining"; any system or spiritual discipline by which the practitioner or YOGI seeks to condition the self at all levels—physical, psychical, and spiritual. The goal of the Indian religious tradition is a state of well-being, the loss of self-identity, and absorption into union with the Absolute, or Ultimate Being.

YOGI. Master of one or more methods of YOGA who teaches it to others.

ZEN. Two-branched type of Buddhist thought best known for its emphasis on an experience of enlightenment that occurs from breaking down the commitment and attachment to the logical and rational ordering of experience.

ZODIAC. Imaginary belt in the heavens that encompasses the apparent paths of the principal planets except Pluto. Divided into twelve constellations or signs based on the assumed dates that the sun enters each of these "houses" or symbols, the Zodiac is used for predictions in ASTROLOGY.

Compiled from a variety of sources.

Discussion Guide

The New Age Movement is a complex and multifaceted phenomenon. Although its philosophy and underlying assumptions are not new, particular aspects and manifestations of the movement are constantly shifting and changing, like the images and designs you see when you peer into a rotating kaleidoscope. This discussion guide is designed to help you better understand where the New Age is coming from, where it is headed, and how it is affecting you, your family, your church, and your culture. The questions can be used for a self-study guide, but their greatest value is in a discussion with a spouse, a friend—or best of all—in the context of a small group that has been reading the book together.

The guide is divided into twelve units. This makes for easy assignments, integrating a weekly class or study period that covers one quarter of the year. I have tried to follow a natural division of topics flowing out of the context of the chapters in the book. Some chapters are longer than others, of course, and some may provoke more questions and study.

Here are a few tips for leaders—and for individuals—as you use the guide:

- Read and become familiar with the chapters that the questions relate to before you try to discuss the material. That way, the discussion will be more fruitful.

- Don't feel that you must answer every question. Some will spark animated and intense discussion; others may elicit little comment. Follow the leading of the Holy Spirit. And don't be afraid to explore other avenues of discussion or to raise questions that aren't listed here, as long as they are "on target" for the goals of your study.

- If you have a designated leader, choose him or her in advance. It may be that the same person will be the "teacher" or leader throughout the twelve weeks. Or you may rotate the leadership from week to week. But make sure the leader doesn't hit the discussion time "cold." Assign the task at least a week ahead. The leader should take responsibility for guiding the discussion, determining relevance, and making sure that everyone who feels comfortable in taking part does so.

- Don't be afraid to challenge assumptions. Just because the book or someone in the group says something is true, don't accept it if there is good reason to differ or at least raise alternative points of view. And remember, no question is too "dumb" or "unspiritual" if it needs to be dealt with.

- Move in the discussion from analyzing "facts" and "information" to considering "causes and effects," and, finally, to making personal applications. The goal is to explore how the New Age has touched *you* and how the Bible and Jesus Christ—the "Man for All Ages"—provide an alternative to the New Age version of spirituality.

- In addition to several "field trips" or "projects" suggested in this guide, the leader might consider assigning each person a "partner." The partners would continue discussion, make investigations, and report back to the entire group the next session. Also, the leader should encourage each participant to look for items in newspapers, magazines, and other sources that present current evidence of New Age influences. Share these with the group.

- If the group is ready for it by the concluding session, you might try role playing. One member of the class could volunteer to take the position of a New Age believer or practitioner, and another could role-play a Christian's attempting to dialogue and witness to the New Ager. Have the rest of the group critique the episode afterward.

SESSION 1

Chapter 1: Preview of the New Age

1. When was the first time you heard the phrase "New Age"? What did it mean to you then? Has your perception changed? How?
2. The author says there are few, if any, "card-carrying" New Agers. Why is that? How do you know if someone is into New Age?

Chapter 2: Prevalence of the New Age

3. How has the New Age "touched" you or someone close to you?
4. Are there New Agers in your family or among your circle of close friends? Share with the group how they got involved with the New Age Movement if you know and feel comfortable talking about it.
5. Review recent motion pictures, television programs, or books that express an underlying New Age worldview or philosophy.

SESSION 2

Chapter 3: Premises of the New Age

1. How would you define the New Age Movement? If you are in a group, start with one facet or aspect of New Age and have each person add one new part to the definition until you reach a consensus that you have formulated a good, concise but inclusive description. (You may want to use a blackboard, overhead projector, or turnover chart to do this.)
2. Construct a "Worldview Chart" comparing the New Age and the biblical worldviews. On the left of the chart write "New Age," and on the right, "Bible." Then, compose short descriptions for the two worldviews under these headings:

NEW AGE		BIBLE
	God	
	Creation	
	Humans	
	The Problem	
	The Solution	
	Goals	

3. At the end of this chapter, the author describes the New Age agenda. Do you agree? Would you add to it, or modify it, based on your perceptions? What evidences of this agenda do you see in your community?

Chapter 4: The Mind of the New Age

4. Why does the author say that the mind "is the heart of the New Age"? How does the New Age Movement's "use" or "structuring" of the mind differ from the biblical concept of the mind and of God?

5. When Paul writes in Philippians 2:5, "Let this mind be in you, which was also in Christ Jesus" (King James Version), do you think he means that we can know the mind of the Lord? How capable are human beings of understanding God's mind? Can we understand enough to be sure of his will for our lives?

SESSION 3

Chapter 5: Historical Roots

1. If the "New Age" really isn't new, why is it called that? Review the historical roots of the movement traced in this chapter.

Chapter 6: Headliners and Honchos

2. J. Z. Knight, among other New Age celebrities, has said that murder may not be wrong, given the reality of reincarnation. Where does this argument finally lead?

Chapter 7: Gifted Gurus

3. What common thread seems to be present among the "gifted gurus" described in this chapter? Why do you think so many people follow them? Has anyone in your group been a follower of a "guru"? Could a church pastor or evangelist be a "guru"?

Chapter 8: Communes and Groups

4. Although there are many New Age groups and communities, few identify themselves as a "church." Why do you think that is true?

5. Discuss the degree to which the Unification Church, the Christian Science Church, and the Church of Jesus Christ of Latter-day Saints (Mormons) incorporate New Age thinking or practice. Is it misleading or unfair to label them "New Age"? Why or why not?

SESSION 4

Chapter 9: Choosing a Channel

1. The author lists six alternatives regarding the source of "channeled" messages. Which explanation seems the most likely to you? Why?

Chapter 10: UFOs and ETIs

2. Despite a lack of concrete evidence, stories of UFOs and alien abductions keep popping up. Do you think information has been suppressed? Evaluate the claim that UFOs and ET contacts are caused by demonic activity. What do you make of the fact that much of the message content from ETIs seems to mirror "channeled" information?

Chapter 11: Harmonic Convergence

3. Should we make fun of harmonic convergence theories? How does such a gathering differ from a mass-prayer rally?
4. What is the "hundredth monkey" theory, and is it dangerous?

Chapter 12: Crystal Consciousness and Pyramid Power

5. Should Christians wear crystals or hang or display them in their cars, homes, or offices? What would you say to your young teenage daughter who wants to wear a crystal unicorn pendant?

SESSION 5

Chapter 13: Native Americans and Shamans

1. Are there aspects of Native American religion that you admire or respect? What is the departure of Native American religion from Christianity if any?
2. What is "New Age" about Native American religion? Do you think the New Age Movement has co-opted Native American customs, beliefs, and rituals for its own ends?

Chapter 14: Goddesses and Neopagans

3. Has the New Age Movement caused the church and Christians to look more carefully at the "stewardship of the Earth" and ecology issues? What ones need further exploration/effort?
4. Because women have been denied places of leadership and authority in traditional churches and synagogues, do you think that they find the goddess and empowerment aspects of New Age appealing? Should something be done about this?
5. The so-called Men's Movement has been growing rapidly. Is it perhaps an even more potent spin-off from New Age spirituality than radical feminism and the goddess/witches movement?

SESSION 6

Chapter 15: Commercial Appeal

1. Visit a psychic fair or New Age expo if there is one in your area. What products and emphases are prominent? What kind of people are there? What do they seem to be seeking?
2. Have several teams from your group visit the major secular bookstores in your area. Look in the self-help and psychology sections. Are books that are overtly New Age represented? Or books that do not directly tie in with New Age but have a distinct Christian flavor or worldview? Is there a separate section for New Age books, or have they been blended into the other categories? Where are the Christian books? Is there a representative selection? Speak to the bookstore manager or owner if you are not satisfied that the selection or labeling is clear and fair.
3. Have several teams from your group visit major secular music and video stores. Is there a New Age category? How does it compare to the Christian section in the store if there is one?
4. Visit organic- or health-food stores in your area. Are New Age products or influences present? Would a shopper be innocently drawn into the New Age Movement by shopping there, or is that unlikely and an exaggeration?

After each of the above "field trips," report and discuss your findings with the rest of the group.

Chapter 16: Corporate Entities

5. Have you heard of any management training programs in your area that incorporate New Age teaching or practices? Are these exercises or programs voluntary, or mandatory? As a group, try to determine some standards for such courses—what kinds of psychological and training techniques do you consider beneficial or at least value-neutral? And where should the line be drawn for those that a Christian should refuse to engage in? What alternatives could an employee appeal to in order to keep a job if he or she is caught in such a dilemma?

SESSION 7

Chapter 17: Education, Music, and Art

1. Find course catalogs for your local community colleges. Look for examples of courses that teach Eastern philosophy, meditation, martial arts, yoga, and the like. Perhaps someone in the class could visit or audit a class or two. Is a religious philosophy being presented or endorsed? Now, examine the course catalog again to see if any courses on Judaism or Christianity are listed. Are there any that teach the Bible or church history? Does it appear that there is a bias against Judeo-Christian content? Do you think the school administrators are aware that New Age philosophy and worldviews spring from a spiritual, religious base?

2. Read Psalms 8 and 19 aloud. Consider meditating on these passages and sharing your insights. How does this differ from the New Age style of meditation or "centering"?

3. Douglas Groothuis, in his book *Confronting the New Age*, draws a distinction between two kinds of New Age music. "Progressive" New Age music is instrumental, relaxing, and no worldview is expressed. This kind may indeed be safe and soothing. "Mystical" New Age music integrates Eastern mystical practices with the music (for example, you are told to focus on the *chakras* and "welcome the energy of divine consciousness"); it induces "altered states" of consciousness and encourages meditation practices while listening to the music.[1]

   Listen to some samples of New Age music as a group and identify which kind you are hearing. Can you come up with some workable guidelines for discerning New Age music that you would be comfortable listening to repeatedly?

Chapter 18: Holistic Health and Healing

4. How would you define "holistic health" or healing? Is the basic concept biblical? Has anyone in your group been treated by acupuncture or reflexology? Hypnosis? What were the results?

5. If there is a physician or nurse in your group or church who could speak to you about holistic health issues from a

Christian perspective, invite him or her to give you an overview, particularly regarding the controversial practice of "therapeutic touch." When should you definitely NOT rely on the advice of a New Age health practitioner?

SESSION 8

Chapter 19: Psychology: Outside In

1. Examine some of the latest self-help and psychology books in local bookstores. Can you identify what worldview is implicit or assumed? Would an unsophisticated Christian be misled?
2. Critique the idea that "personal growth is the highest good." What would you say is the highest good?

Chapter 20: Science: Universal Mind Over Matter

3. Has anyone in the group had an "ESP" experience? How do you explain it?
4. If paranormal experiences should receive wholehearted support and endorsement from the mainstream scientific community sometime in the future, would this affect your faith? Is the "supernatural" simply a part of nature that we haven't discovered yet? What is the problem with "hitching a religious philosophy to a contemporary science," as one author-scientist talks about in this chapter?

Chapter 21: The Politics of Mysticism

5. To promote New Age thinking and acceptance in this country, do you think New Agers need to run for political office? Why or why not? Do you know of any who hold important leadership positions? Do they violate the separation of church and state by using their office to inject the New Age worldview into public affairs?

SESSION 9

Chapter 22: Religion and Churches

1. Through which "doorways" is the New Age philosophy most apt to enter our churches and synagogues?

2. Are you or others in the group aware of such inroads? Talk about how and why they are happening.
3. Do you see any similarity between the New Age concept of "creating your own reality," and the "prosperity—name it and claim it—gospel," where preachers tell people to visualize whatever material things they want and "command" them into appearing "in Jesus' name"?

Chapter 23: Positive Images

4. What areas of agreement are there between the New Age Movement and Christianity? In what issues, if any, can there be cooperation between the two?

Chapter 24: Conspiracy Theories

5. In chapter 3, the author describes the New Age agenda. In light of chapter 24, who do you think is behind that agenda? What do you think of the statement that the conspiracy is one of "consensus" rather than a deliberate worldwide-takeover plot masterminded by a corps of New Age strategists?

SESSION 10

Chapter 25: Fakes, Frauds, and Placebos

1. Discuss the appeal of astrology. One-third of Americans believe there is a scientific basis for astrology. What do you think? What are the arguments in favor of this scientific basis? Why then do people follow their astrological "signs"?
2. Which of the following would you feel all right about doing or having your children engage in? Which would you disapprove of? Why?
   - Lying on the floor, imagining you are one with the sun.
   - Talking with animals.
   - Mentally reviewing the cross-country run, or the debate that you will be engaging in later that day.
   - Listening to audiotapes that have subliminal messages on them.
   - Sitting in a lotus position and chanting or meditating to merge your consciousness with the divine "One."

- Sitting on the floor, relaxing and watching tropical fish in an aquarium.

Chapter 26: Unproven Hypotheses and Non Sequiturs

3. Look up the definition of *synchronicity* in the glossary of this book. Does this seem at all like "Providence" that a Christian or Jew might speak about? Could you call synchronicity "answered prayer"? Why?

Chapter 27: Cautions and Dangers

4. Have you or someone in your group ever experimented with a Ouija board? With what results? What feelings do you have about it now? Would you let your kids play with one?
5. New Age publisher Jeremy P. Tarcher said in 1989 that "the glowing future of New Age publishing will be in its becoming so visible that it is invisible, in being taken for granted as part of an accepted truth—in other words, in simply being the culture."[2] What do you think Tarcher meant by this? How successful do you think this campaign has been? (Recall your group's trip to secular bookstores in Session 6.)

SESSION 11

Chapter 28: Reincarnation or Resurrection?

1. Review the arguments, pro and con, for reincarnation. Which seem most convincing?
2. The reincarnation theme repeatedly shows up in contemporary literature, films, and music. Can you think of several examples? Some of this may be lighthearted and innocuous, but what would happen to the biblical worldview if reincarnation should become a generally accepted belief? What implications would it have for society and the legal system, for example?

Chapter 29: Satan and the Problem of Evil

3. In light of this chapter about Satan and evil, what do you think about one possible explanation the author gives in

chapter 9, that channeled entities are demonic or demon-influenced?

4. The author cautions about believing in "too many evils." Do you agree this is a problem? Why?

Chapter 30: Absolute Relativity

5. The author calls moral relativity both the "appeal" and "the Achilles' heel" of the New Age Movement. Why? Could this be a starting point for dialogue with a New Ager?

SESSION 12

Chapter 31: Beyond the Self

1. New Age philosophy seeks to "look within" to find answers to life's problems, but at the same time many New Agers seek and obey the advice of gurus and channelers. Why both? Is this an inconsistency? Could this be a point for dialogue with a New Ager? Where would you point them for answers?

2. Discuss the meaning of Luke 17:21 regarding the kingdom of God being "within" or "in the midst." Compare several versions and consult a reliable commentary. New Agers often construe this verse to mean that God and the self are one, or "I am God."

Chapter 32: The Broad Way and the Narrow Way

3. Review Scripture verses that prohibit necromancy, occult involvement, astrology, fortune-telling, and the like. (See endnote #15 in this chapter for some references.) Can you add others?

4. Role play a conversation between a New Age follower and a Christian. Have one person take the New Age position and another the perspective of a Christian attempting to dialogue and witness to the New Ager. Ask the rest of the group to critique the episode afterward.

Chapter 33: The Man for All Ages

5. The New Age movement may succeed in changing our society. But there is only one way society can be *transformed*. How is that? Would you like to make a commitment now, through the power of the Holy Spirit, to be a part of that transformation process for the glory of God?

SOURCES

1. Douglas Groothuis, *Confronting the New Age* (Downers Grove: InterVarsity Press, 1988), 191–95.
2. Jeremy P. Tarcher, "Here's to the End of 'New Age' Publishing," *Publishers Weekly*, 5 November 1989, 36.

INDEX

128733